D1242866

AESTHETIC RECONSTRUCTIONS:
THE SEMINAL WRITINGS OF LESSING, KANT AND SCHILLER

Aristotelian Society Series

Anthony Savile

Aesthetic Reconstructions: The Seminal Writings of Lessing, Kant and Schiller

Aristotelian Society Series

Volume 8

Basil Blackwell · Oxford

First published 1987
in cooperation with The Aristotelian Society
Birkbeck College, Malet Street, London WC1E 7HX

Basil Blackwell Ltd
108 Cowley Road, Oxford OX4 1JF, England

Basil Blackwell Inc.
432 Park Avenue South, Suite 1503
New York, NY 10016, USA

British Library Cataloguing in Publication Data

Savile, Anthony
Aesthetic reconstructions: the seminal
writings of Lessing, Kant and Schiller.——
(Aristotelian Society series; v. 8)
1. Kant, Immanuel——Aesthetics 2. Schiller,
Friedrich——Aesthetics 3. Lessing, Gotthold
Ephraim, *1729–1781* 4. Aesthetics, Modern
I. Title   II. Series
111′.85′0922   BH151

ISBN 0–631–15819–7

Library of Congress Cataloging in Publication Data

Savile, Anthony.
Aesthetic reconstructions.

(Aristotelian Society series; v. 8)
Includes index.
1. Aesthetics, German—18th century. 2. Lessing,
Gotthold Ephraim, 1729–1781. Laocoon. 3. Kant,
Immanuel, 1724–1804. Kritik der Urteilskraft.
4. Schiller, Friedrich, 1759–1805. Über die ästhetische
Erziehung des Menschen in einer Reihe von Briefen.
I. Title.   II. Series.
BH221.G32S28 1987   111·.85·0943   87–20872
ISBN 0–631–15819–7

Photoset, printed and bound in Great Britain by
WBC Bristol and Maesteg

Contents

Foreword

Teaching aesthetics in the University of London over the past few years it has struck me forcibly how much the best introduction to the subject is provided by its classic texts. Only, in my experience, too often study of them does not yield the returns it should, and this is not simply because the student lacks the necessary sophistication or is too pressed for time to mine the ore that they contain. Rich though they evidently are, the texts themselves present a very sealed surface to the reader and are commonly felt to speak from within a set of presumptions and in a language that repels rather than invites engagement of the critical intellect. In so far as helpful commentaries exist – and it is surprising even now how thin on the ground they are (a reflection perhaps of the widespread contempt in which the subject has for too long been held in the English-speaking philosophical world) – they have tended to limit themselves to the useful, but preliminary, task of exposition. Assessment, involving as it does engagement with the commentators' own conception of the truth in these matters, is harder still to find, and I should be surprised if my frustration in knowing where to send pupils for help was not shared by others who face the same situation. I offer this volume as a contribution, though a far smaller one than I should have liked, to remedying the deficiency.

I have chosen to concentrate on Lessing, Kant and Schiller because their main writings in aesthetics, very different though they are, all attempt to present a major theoretical position of philosophical interest in a systematic and consequentially thought-through way. Lessing's concern is the most restricted: it is whether the medium in which the artist works does not impose a priori constraints on how he may achieve success in his chosen domain; Kant's is far broader, the issue of the legitimacy of aesthetic discourse in general; Schiller's, at heart more practically oriented, the exploration of the idea that the development of aesthetic sensibility is fundamental to any state that can practise liberal politics. But far apart though they are in ultimate aim, they all have two other notable features in common. The first is that the way their positions are intellectually constructed and defended is obscured by the style in which they are couched – no surprise in the case of Lessing and Schiller, who would not have claimed to be more than philosophical amateurs, and no surprise in that of Kant either, the ultimate professionals' professional; the second is that in each case many weight-bearing beams of the structures they develop and explore are merely gestured at or left to the reader to supply for himself. So the arguments cannot simply be dusted off and presented to the curious passer by; they have to be laboriously retrieved from materials that are for the most part to hand but only dimly visible. In each case this presents a genuine philosophical challenge. In each case, and whatever the end result, it is a challenge attached to subject matter of the greatest interest. Hence my title: *Aesthetic Reconstructions.*

Since I am concerned with serious self-contained texts, I do not make any attempt to confront the thought of one author with that of the others. When they do write with each other in mind – Kant of Lessing, and Schiller of Kant – they do so against the background of misconceptions of each other which would be fruitless to explore any further than emerges naturally from the expositions that I offer. If the student has to make up his mind whether Kant's criticism of Lessing's "rationalism" is well founded, or what to think of Schiller's dissatisfaction with Kant's "formalism", he will be better placed to do so as he has a picture of the targets of attack that comes to him from a source distinct from that of Kant or Schiller respectively. But that is at most a peripheral matter, and I have judged it more important to subjugate it and like issues to those of central concern to my authors themselves.

I make one fundamental presumption of the reader: that he or she has read fairly carefully *Laocoon*, or the *Critique of Judgment,* or the *Letters on the Aesthetic Education of Man*. In no way could what is offered here be a substitute for that, and I very much doubt whether these pages would make much sense to anyone without that background. My hope would be to make it inviting and rewarding to return to these classics at a later date, and to make it possible on such a return to see them in a sharper focus than could have been possible on first acquaintance. Other than that I assume nothing very much. I try to explain any technicalities or peculiarities of language as I go along, and where for the sake of convenience I have retained these thinkers' own vocabulary and modes of expression the reader should not have far to look to find paraphrase or elucidation.

In the course of composition I have benefitted from the advice of friends and colleagues in London and elsewhere. I owe a particular debt of gratitude to Dr Flint Schier for detailed criticism of the penultimate draft, and to Mrs Claire Baines and the late Mrs Jane Connard for suggesting some of the art-historical examples and discussing them with me.

King's College, London   A.S.
May 1987

GOTTHOLD LESSING:

LAOCOON

1

Iconicity and Beauty

"Ut pictura poesis" opined Horace, and in the mid-eighteenth century that commonplace of literary theory epitomized a number of critical assumptions against which Lessing directed his classic essay.[1] Of these the most notable was that within the representative arts the medium itself is utterly transparent. By this I mean that the artist's choice of medium – be it visual, as in painting and sculpture, or verbal, as in poetry and narrative prose – imposes no constraints on what he may successfully and happily represent. Anything he can felicitously depict in one representation-permitting medium, he can so depict in another, without it having any negative implications for the aesthetic merit of the resulting work. That position Lessing uncompromisingly rejects, and in its most ambitious form his opposition to it consists of two distinct strands: (a) he is inclined to hold that all traditional sorts of representative art are constrained by their media in what they can satisfactorily represent; then (b), he believes that the different arts are constrained by their media in different ways. For the most part though, Lessing's interest is fixed on the visual and the literary arts and the contrasting medium-related constraints that

---

[1] For ease of reading I adopt the following typographical convention: to speak of Lessing's essay I write "Laocoon"; to speak of the sculpture of which "Laocoon" treats I write *Laocoon*; and to speak of the character centrally represented by *Laocoon*, I write Laocoon.

affect them, whence the subtitle of his work, *On the Limits of Painting and Poetry*.

It was of concern to Lessing that this twofold repudiation of transparency had an import that went way beyond the establishment of regulative canons of good taste in the various arts. In "Laocoon" he ingeniously puts his own doctrines of medium-constrained subject matter to work for straightforwardly iconographic ends. Thus he takes it that they provide a sure way of assigning the carved group excavated in 1506 from the Imperial Baths on the Esquiline to a post-Virgilian period, and that they offer evidential support for the contention that the group was modelled on the corresponding passage of the *Aeneid* (II, 199–224) rather than the other way about. Obviously he supposed the soundness of his critical principles might serve the art historian in other cases too.

To us it matters little that Lessing's dating of the *Laocoon* group was in fact mistaken – we now set it down with fair certainly to the first century B.C., before the composition of Virgil's epic, that is, and not after it – for that error shows no more than that his principles cannot be so easily applied to the group as he had imagined. What is of far greater concern is the defensibility of the various arguments by which the repudiation of transparency is arrived at, and on the basis of which Lessing advances his own doctrines concerning the subject matter proper to the various arts. In what follows these several arguments constitute my limited concern. I make no attempt ultimately to adjudicate between the conflicting claims of Lessing's Horatian opponents and those of Lessing himself.

I

Taking it as beyond dispute that the carved group of Laocoon and his sons and the portion of Virgil's poem in which those figures appear both display artistic mastery of a high order, Lessing asks why it is that in the statue the priest is represented as sighing merely, whereas in the poem he is depicted as crying out in agony – "*clamores horrendos ad sidera tollit*". The answer is that for the artist (i.e., the painter or the sculptor)[2] to depict

---

[2] I shall generally follow Lessing in this usage. *Caveat lector*.

the priest agonizing would necessarily offend against polite taste, whereas the poet who retails the scene may not be open to the same reproach. In the course of his essay Lessing offers the reader several distinct paths to this conclusion, with the help of which he takes it that exemplary refutation of the generalized transparency thesis will be provided.

The first of these, which I shall call *Argument A*, and which will occupy most of this chapter, turns on considerations that Lessing somewhat ambivalently represents as peculiar to Greek art, either classical or Hellenistic, where the leading criterion of artistic success is held by him to be the achievement of beauty. Once the goal of beauty is written into a correct understanding of a period's art as its fundamental aim, it follows that whatever that art represents in such a way as to exclude the possibility of this aim being achieved will fail to be a work of excellence. As Lessing himself puts it, "given this [that among the ancients beauty was the supreme rule of the visual arts], it necessarily follows that whatever else these arts include must give way completely if not compatible with it, and if compatible with it, must at least be subordinate to it" II, 16).[3] Further, Lessing takes it to be uncontestable that the physical distortion of the body that would be involved in any visual representation of the priest shrieking out in agony would be incompatible with such a work achieving beauty. So, he takes it, we can immediately appreciate why the sculptors of the group so wisely refrained from "following Virgil" at this point. To have carved Laocoon as we find him in the poem would have been to condemn the work to sure failure.

Contrary to appearance, the scope of Lessing's argument is not, as it stands, restricted to Greek art, of whatever period it may be. If acceptable, it would apply to any art of which it is proper to make critical assessments primarily in terms of its beauty. If we are content to do that for Greek art there is no a priori reason not to do the same for other art too. This, of course, is what has to be the case if the argument is to serve any widely applicable iconographic purpose. Moreover, there is a clearly discernible, though somewhat submerged, strand in

---

[3] "Laocoon", (Reclam edition, 1964) Chapter II, page 16. All page references are to this edition. Translations are usually E.A. McCormick's (Bobbs-Merrill, 1962).

Lessing's thought that inclines him to the view that the artist who does not embrace what I shall synoptically call the Hellenic ideal,[4] the ideal of beauty, that is, will not be able to achieve true greatness in his work, since beauty is the proper aim of *all* fine art.[5] In that case we should have in *A* a far more ambitious argument against the visual depiction of physical disfigurement and pain than Lessing explicitly commits himself to in the second chapter of his essay.

No matter what Lessing's private thoughts on the subject may have been, we need look no further than to the most restricted application of his explicit reasoning to see what to make of it. Only to appreciate just how the incompatibility that strikes him is supposed to arise, we have to see how he conceived of beauty. About this he is unselfconsciously forthcoming. Beauty, we are told at XX, 145, "arises from the harmonious effect of the object's various elements, which the eye can take in at a glance";[6] and from this gloss it should be plain why the distorted figure that will be relied on in the representation of the priest's agony will not be a beautiful one. It is that the distortion involved will lie at odds with, logically exclude even, that harmony of parts which would constitute the figure a beautiful one. To put it in Lessing's own words, "[t]here are passions and degrees of passion which are expressed by the most hideous contortions of the face and which throw the whole body into such unnatural postures as to lose all the beautiful contours of its natural state" (II, 16/7).

A natural reaction to this train of thought is to dispute the main assumptions on which it relies, other, that is, than that which holds *Laocoon* to be a Greek work of Hellenic art

[4] Here, and in what follows, I use the term "Hellenic" to denote that style which Lessing took to have been adopted by the Greek artists of the *Laocoon* group. By "Greek" I mean Classical or Hellenistic. Not all Hellenic art need be Greek. Nor need all Greek art have been Hellenic.

[5] At II, 19/20 Lessing approves Timanthes for concealing the grief of Iphigenia's father, Agamemnon, and says that this concealment is a sacrifice that the artist made to beauty, "not an example of how to take expression beyond the limits of art, but of how one must subjugate it to the first rule of art, the rule of beauty." And here, although the context is that of Hellenic art, what one hears is Lessing, the man, and not just Lessing the historian. Another passage in which this extensive commitment to beauty comes out is at the very beginning of III, 22, on which I comment below.

[6] Lessing is here speaking of corporeal (*körperliche*) beauty, but I shall argue in Chapter 2 that nothing of significance hinges on this apparent restriction.

centrally representing the torment of Laocoon and his sons. Without laying oneself open to a charge of splitting hairs, it would be entirely reasonable to question whether (i), the priest's agony must be depicted through unnatural distortion of his body, whether (ii), bodily distortion and harmonious interplay of the body's members are always incompatible, or, even more evidently, whether (iii), beauty itself is rightly explicated in terms of a harmonious interplay of elements. For two reasons I shall pursue none of these issues. First, as we shall see in the concluding *Note* to this section, Lessing had in reserve a different, though similarly structured argument, *B*, to the same end that depends on none of these three premises; and second, if we concentrate on these matters, we shall be focusing rather on the soundness of the argument than on its validity. Yet it is only if we reflect on that that we can hope to get to the heart of Lessing's thought.

A flaw in the reasoning seems to jump to the eye as soon as we attend to the way in which Lessing makes the connection between beauty and harmony in his reflections about the sculpture. An object is beautiful if its parts are suitably harmoniously organized, and given the apparent univocity of the word "beautiful", this will hold good whether we are talking of beautiful men or of beautiful representations of men. Only as we move from one to the other, we have to remember that the parts of a man that may be harmoniously organized may not be what are represented by those portions of a picture or a statue that have themselves to be harmoniously organized if the representation is to be a beautiful one. And, one is inclined to say, it is this equivalence that Lessing needs if he is not to come unstuck. For what he is asserting is that the distortions of the body which we are bound to reproduce in the sculpture of the agonizing Laocoon are as such necessarily disharmonious and *therefore* are incompatible with the production of the finest art that aims at beauty. But, one wants to protest, the way the finest art aims at beauty is by *being* beautiful and not just by the *representation* of what is beautiful, nor even by the representation of beautiful things *as* beautiful.

Although this criticism can scarcely fail to strike the modern reader as powerful, Lessing himself would probably not have been much impressed by it. Indeed, when one looks at those passages of the text in which he speaks of Greek art as aiming at beauty, one finds nothing to suggest anything more than that the Greeks chose to represent the beauty of beautiful objects in their art. Thus in Chapter II he is confident that the Greeks secured their ends by refusing to represent anything other than beautiful things, and he comments with some measure of approval on the Theban law which strove to promote the beautiful in art by proscribing the imitation of the uglier parts of the model (cf II, 14). And of course, as long as Lessing's argument aims to show no more than that Laocoon would not have been beautiful if he were agonizing and that the *Laocoon* would not have represented anything beautiful had the priest been shown agonizing, then the criticism I have raised will fail.

Such a line of resistance will not sway many. It is plain from other passages in his text that Lessing is quite prepared to apply the predicate ". . . is beautiful" to works of art themselves, and not only to their represented content; and it is scarcely less plain that the first sort of application is not to be regarded as a simple shorthand for the second. Consider two examples. At II, 15 Lessing remarks that the visual arts are capable of effects that merit the close interest of the lawgiver, and he goes on, "if beautiful men created beautiful statues, these too had their reciprocal effect on the men, and the state owed thanks to beautiful statues for beautiful men". If, here, the beauty of the statue were nothing more than the beauty of the men it represented, it would be hard to understand why the lawgiver should interest himself overmuch with art. Calligenics, to coin a term, would lie closer to his heart. More conclusively, at III, 22, Lessing somewhat disparagingly speaks of the modern artist,[7] whose aim is not so much beauty as truth and expression, and says that "it strikes this man as good enough that through truth and expression the ugliest in nature is transformed into the beauty of art". Whatever reservations he may have had about this latter-day doctrine, they are certainly not that when he represents something ugly, the modern artist misguidedly thinks he is representing something that in fact is

[7] Hence, in part, my reference to the ambivalence of Lessing's attitude to the scope of his argument. Cf fn 5.

beautiful. It is rather that his is not the way to achieve true beauty in art, and that objection can only be made if Lessing is working with a concept of artistic beauty distinct from that of the beauty art represents.

To say that Lessing did not take these two concepts to be identical is not to say that he did not think them closely related, and it is through the presumed closeness of their connection that we come to a more interesting defence of his argument than that just mooted and set aside. This imputes to him the assumption that these two notions are necessarily related along the lines of

(1) $(x)(y)(x$ is a beautiful representation of y iff x represents y as beautiful)

and it invites him to say that this fact renders my objection to A merely formally, but not substantially, correct. What I mean by this is that Lessing may well allow that unless a principle such as (1) is conjoined with the premisses I marked before as (i) – (iii), it will indeed be impossible formally to derive the conclusion that *Laocoon* would not have been beautiful if it had represented Laocoon as suffering. But, even without the addition of (1) as a further explicit premiss, Lessing can insist that the right semantic relation does hold between the given premisses and the conclusion; they could not all be true while the conclusion was not. And this is the substance of his position. For even if it is not explicitly stated, (1) is thought of as a *necessary* truth, and as such does ensure that the stated premisses stand in the desired relation that they do to the conclusion, whether the latter is intuitively derivable from them or not. Furthermore, Lessing can perfectly well knowingly say that the accusation of formal invalidity is one that is easily avoided. All we have to do is to add (1) to the premisses explicitly given, and at once regular derivability is restored. Its omission is no more than a matter of literary grace.

All this is very nice, one may feel, but what could possibly have induced Lessing to adopt such a crazy principle as (1), if in fact he did? Certainly he nowhere states it or argues outright for it. Nevertheless it is probable that Lessing did hold (1) to be true, and probable that he was led to do so for a reason that made it very difficult for him to see how implausible it actually is. This is that (1) is a fairly straightforward instance of another principle,

(2) $(x)(y)$(observable φ)(x is a φ representation of y iff x represents y as φ)

and this, which I shall call the *Iconicity Principle*, is fairly obviously regarded by Lessing as a constitutive truth about the nature of painterly imitation. In as much as this Principle is taken to be unquestionable, so its instances will not seem questionable either. Then the defence of *Argument A* that I have mounted becomes one that it is both natural and fair to hold out for Lessing's use.

The justification I offer for saying that Lessing very probably did accept the *Iconicity Principle* is that throughout "Laocoon" he speaks of painting in terms of imitation, illusion and deception (*Nachahmung, Illusion, Täuschung*). And at XIV, 111, where he seeks to capture the crucial distinction between poetry and prose, he does so by reference to the poet's peculiar ability to write in a graphic (*malerisch*) way, one that "brings us closer to that degree of illusion which is the special province of the material picture". Once we see that there is an intimate connection between his traditional, and unexamined, conception of visual representation and the principle I registered as (2), we have good cause to think that Lessing assumed it to be true.[8] A connection is not hard to find.

If the paradigmatic visual representation of y must create in us the illusion of being presented with y, the object that represents y is readily thought of as having the capacity to present us with just the same visual impressions as does y itself. And what has this capacity will standardly be what has exactly the same visual properties as y itself. Hence, on this view of visual representation, it is not easy to resist the belief that those things that represent y as φ must themselves appear to be φ, because they are φ. That gives us the right-to-left reading of (2). From left to right is simple. A repesentation that has a given visual property will create a visual impression of the same kind as any object that has that visual property. So if the essence of representation involves illusion, the illusion the

---

[8] "Good cause", and no more. Notoriously, belief is not closed under deduction.

representation will create will be of something that has just the same visual properties as it. By some such route as this, (2) can come to seem virtually unassailable.[9]

On this reading then the greatest weakness A has to face is not its invalidity but the implausibility of its concealed premiss. For the *Iconicity Principle* that generates (1) as a special case is thoroughly discredited today, even if it was not in 1766, when Lessing was writing. And the reluctance that the modern has in following him at this point presents a challenge. This is to know whether some consideration can not be found which might both appeal to Lessing and which could also serve to replace the overblown assumption (2) in its function of protecting A against the initial accusation of invalidity that was raised against it. Here two different possibilities present themselves.

The first concentrates on substituting for (2) a more restricted principle, (2′), that concerns itself only with art that is expressive or graphic (*malerisch*), painting or sculpture that in Lessing's words (XVII, 122) aims "to make the ideas a woken in us by the work of art so vivid that for a passing moment we believe ourselves to be experiencing the true sensible impressions of their objects". Such a move might well be congenial to him, since he is under no absolute constraint to believe that all and every figurative painting has to aim at the creation of illusion. Indeed, Lessing might well protest that I have already overstated his commitment to (2) in my gloss on XIV, 111, since to say, as he does, that material painting is *besonders fähig* (particularly capable) of illusionistic effect in no way implies that it can only depict anything through recourse to it. (Only we shall soon see that the real Lessing can not easily afford to take this attitude.)

Following this train of thought we might consider replacing (2) by

(2′) $(x)(y)(\varphi)$ (x is a φ representation of y iff x graphically represents y as φ)

---

[9] Further justification for thinking that Lessing did embrace (2) is provided by his willingness to argue in Chapter III from the durability of the artist's material to the static nature of what he can represent in that material. Again it is hard to see how he could have swallowed this idea unless he was already deeply committed to the *Iconicity Principle*.

and proceed to derive the required (restricted) principle for beauty (1′) as before, that is, as a substitution instance of the reconstructed *Iconicity Principle*, thus:

(1′) $(x)(y)(x$ is a beautiful representation of y iff x graphically represents y as beautiful)

It can be no more than a moment or two, though, before the thought dawns that the very thing that might urge the restriction of the original principle to graphic representations must oblige Lessing to abandon the biconditional versions of (1′) and (2′) as they are here recorded, for the concession that has been made in allowing the existence both of graphic and non-graphic representation in order to maintain the plausibility of some such principle or other can not but bring with it awareness that as read from left to right (1′) and (2′) are indefensible. At best we might put in their place the corresponding right-to-left readings:

(2″) $(x)(y)(\varphi)(x$ is a φ representation of y if x graphically represents y as φ)

and

(1″) $(x)(y)(x$ is a beautiful representation of y if x graphically represents y as beautiful).

Even so, we may still wonder whether Lessing might not suppose that he can still have what he wants. For the earlier defence of A, on which we are now trying to improve, only ever needed to rely on one half of each of the original biconditionals (1) and (2). So can not Lessing now go ahead with (1″) and (2″) in their place, no longer open to the objection that they are quite unsustainable? If he does, then the argument he might want to run could, in a slightly abbreviated form, perhaps look something like this:

Ass.	(a)	Greek visual art aims at beauty	Axiom (II, 16)
(i)	(b)	The graphic representation of Laocoon's agony involves the graphic representation of Laocoon's body as distorted	Premiss (i) of A
(ii)(iii)	(c)	The graphic representation of Laocoon's body as distorted is incompatible with the graphic representation of his body as beautiful	Instances of premisses (ii),(iii)

Ass.	(d)	*Laocoon* graphically represents Laocoon as beautiful only if *Laocoon* is a beautiful representation of Laocoon	From (1″) via (2″)
(ii)(iii)	(e)	The graphic representation of Laocoon as distorted excludes the beauty of *Laocoon*	From (c) and (d)
(i)(ii)(iii)	(f)	The Greek masters could not have successfully represented Laocoon as agonizing.	From (a) and (e)

Regrettably, though indisputably, (e) in this scheme cannot be validly inferred from (c) and (d), for the half of the biconditional that is needed to make the argument work is precisely the half that is unsupported by the restricted version of the *Iconicity Principle* I have for the while encouraged Lessing to embrace, viz:

(1‴ $(x)(y)(x$ is a beautiful representation of y only if x graphically respresents y as beautiful)

Only that is just what Lessing was obliged to sacrifice to preserve some credibility for the principle to which he appears so attached. So while it would be understandable enough if the proposed line of reasoning were to seem persuasive – particularly if clothed in greater style than here, 'if's and 'only if's being difficult enough to keep track of at the best of times – it is not one that Lessing can be recommended to adopt. Its very weakness may further incline us to say that the real Lessing might well have met less resistance from his contemporaries by relying on the unemended defence of *A* (resting on the original biconditional recorded above as (2)) rather than on its bastard offspring. It was for this reason that I suggested that he should not be overready to narrow down the reading I offered of XVII, 122.

The alternative defence of his argument that I mentioned promises rather better. It recommends Lessing to forget entirely about deriving (1‴) or anything like it from any generalized version of the *Iconicity Principle* – the only function of which, so far as the present argument goes, has been to supply a special premiss about beauty – and urges him to make out a case for the needed contention about beauty in its own right. Surprisingly enough, perhaps, there is to all appearances a seemingly attractive way of doing this, and that is to offer a reworked version of (1') now as a peculiar necessary truth supposedly elucidatory of what I earlier called *Hellenic* artistic beauty and which Lessing believed exemplified by the *Laocoon* group.[10] Whatever our views about the correctness of (1'), they will not touch this new proposal, which I write as (3), subscripting the particular canon by which beauty is judged.:

(3) (Representational works of Hellenic art w)(y)(w is a beautiful $_{Hellenic}$ representation of y iff w graphically represents y as beautiful).

and this claim is once again offered as a biconditional because first, it is alleged as essential to the conception of Hellenic beauty that it be achieved through the graphic representation of beautiful things, and then second, that providing only that the principle is expressed as one that applies solely to works of art that embrace that particular canon of beauty, it will also be sufficient to achieve beauty that they graphically represent beautiful things. Once again we find here a reflection congenial to Lessing in that we preserve a two-way link between the concepts *Hellenic artistic beauty* and *Hellenic representation of something beautiful* without reducing them to one.

It is crucial to this suggestion, be it noted, that the initial quantifier be restricted to range only over figurative art that accepts the Hellenic canon. Unless that stipulation is observed the half of the biconditional we are going to need to stand in for the missing (1''') above will be false. Of course there are non-Greek works of art and also non-Hellenic Greek ones that graphically represent something as beautiful without themselves displaying Hellenic beauty in their art.[11] But that is an irrelevance here. (Of some such work it may even look as though it comes up to the Hellenic ideal, but still that won't make it Hellenically beautiful because for that we need the Hellenic canon to be built into the correct understanding of the work and its history of production. That is not guaranteed by looks alone. Even neo-Gothic architecture does not aim at

[10] Recall that this is a stylistic term as I use it and that it must apply for Lessing at the very least to most *actual* Greek art whether of classical or Hellenistic provenance. This is required if Lessing is not to prejudge the dating issue that he is importantly concerned with.

[11] There may of course equally be non-Greek works that do display Hellenic beauty.

beauty $_{Gothic}$, but (cases of pastiche aside) just at beauty $_{neo\text{-}Gothic}$.

If Lessing were to adopt this suggestion and accept, as I believe he should,[12] that our understanding of beauty in art needs always to be judged in relation to the identity of that art's style, then he has what he needs. For the following piece of reasoning is free of the faults that lame its predecessor, and is arguably attractive in its own right. This time I write it out more fully, though still informally, and relativize the premises to the Hellenic canon where necessary.

Premisses:

(1) *Laocoon* is a work of Hellenic art centrally representing Laocoon
(2) *Laocoon* graphically represents Laocoon's agony only if *Laocoon* graphically represents Laocoon's body as distorted
(3) The parts of bodies that are distorted are not harmoniously organized
(4) A body is beautiful iff its parts are harmoniously organized
(5) To be artistically successful representational Hellenic art needs to be beautiful
(6) Works of representational Hellenic art are beautiful only if they provide beautiful $_{Hellenic}$ representations of their central figures
(7) A representation of something is beautiful $_{Hellenic}$ iff it graphically represents its central figure as beautiful
(8) For observational properties so related that the possession of one implies the possession of another, a graphic representation of something as possessing the former must graphically represent it as possessing the latter
(9) A work of art that graphically represents something as being not-φ only if it does not represent it as φ

Here premisses (1)–(4) recall that the main assumptions of the original *Argument A*; premisses (5) and (6) record assumptions Lessing might be supposed to make about art that accepts the Hellenic canon; and the last three premisses express unargued theoretical presumptions concerning the notion of graphic representation as it applies to that art.[13] With these granted, the

---

[12] I defend this claim in *The Test of Time*, (Clarendon, 1982), Ch 8. For this to be correct we need not expect to find the concept one that these early artists had a fully articulated grasp of. '

[13] Christopher Janaway has observed that it is very difficult to understand how one might graphically represent something as being not-φ, and that for the purposes of the argument one might like to pass directly from the claim that a body is represented as being distorted to its not being represented as beautiful. If we could, that would be well and good, and then maybe the questionable premisses (8) and (9) could be dispensed with. My trouble is that I see no readily generalizable way in which the transition could be derived except as propounded above. Lessing would not do very well simply to

conclusion is seemingly derivable that if *Laocoon* were to represent Laocoon as being in agony, it could not be a successful Hellenic work of classical or Hellenistic provenance. Thus:

(3,4)	(a)	Bodies that are distorted are not beautiful	3,4
(3,4,8)	(b)	*Laocoon* graphically represents Laocoon as distorted only if *Laocoon* graphically represents Laocoon as not beautiful	(a),8
(9)	(c)	*Laocoon* graphically represents Laocoon as not beautiful only if *Laocoon* does not graphically represent him as beautiful	9 by EI
(2,3)	(d)	*Laocoon* graphically represents Laocoon as in agony only if *Laocoon* does not graphically represent him as beautiful	2,(b),(c)
Ass.	(e)	*Laocoon* centrally represents Laocoon as in agony	Ass.
(2,3,4,8,9,(e))	(f)	*Laocoon* does not graphically represent Laocoon as beautiful	(d),(e)
(2,3,4,7,8,9,(e))	(g)	*Laocoon* is not a beautiful Hellenic representation of Laocoon	7,(f)
(6)	(h)	If *Laocoon* is an instance of beautiful Hellenic art, *Laocoon* graphically represents its central figure as beautiful	(6)
(1,6)	(i)	If *Laocoon* is an instance of beautiful Hellenic art, *Laocoon* graphically represents Laocoon as beautiful	1,(h)
(1,6,7)	(j)	If *Laocoon* is not a beautiful Hellenic representation of Laocoon, *Laocoon* is not beautiful Hellenic	(i),7,MTT
(5)	(k)	If *Laocoon* is not beautiful Hellenic, *Laocoon* does not succeed as a work of Hellenic Greek art	5,MPP
(1–9, Ass)	(l)	*Laocoon* does not succeed as a work of Hellenic Greek art	9,(j)(k)MPP
(1–9)	(m)	If *Laocoon* graphically represents Laocoon as being in agony, *Laocoon* does not succeed as a work of Hellenic Greek art	Ass., (l),CP

In the end then not only do we here have an apparently valid chain of reasoning; we also have one that is freed from too

---

assert as an independent *ad hoc* premiss that a graphic representation of something as distorted rules out the graphic representation of it as beautiful. That is something for which he would presumably think one should be able to provide an argument or to found in deeper-lying general considerations.

close dependence on a *Principle of Iconicity* that Lessing would be hard pressed to defend against all the world. Moreover it is an argument that avoids equating the beauty of art with the beauty of what art represents, while nevertheless relating these ideas in a way that serves Lessing's end. For all this though, there is a price to pay. This is that as far as the wider iconographic purposes go, we have no ground left for extending them any further than the bounds of art that accepts the Hellenic canon. But since Chapter II of "Laocoon", in which *Argument A* is at home, is itself explicitly restricted to consideration of Greek art, perhaps this is a price that Lessing might be willing enough to pay. As we shall see later on, he has no doubts that what he would here be giving up would be salvaged for him by those other justifications that he is anxious to offer for the rejection of the transparency thesis he finds so contentious.

It is an interesting feature of this reconstruction of *Argument A* that it still permits the real Lessing to speak truly – though this time maybe not so wittingly – should he say again that the original charge of invalidity was at most formally correct. For it looks as though the Premisses (1)–(4) that recall the main assumptions of the original argument cannot all be true and the conclusion false, once it is admitted that Premiss (7) offers us a genuinely necessary truth about the notion of Hellenic beauty. Of course, someone might object weakly that it cannot be a necessary truth because the Greeks could in theory have adopted different aesthetic canons than those they did adopt. Only that thought is neither here nor there. True enough, the Greeks could have adopted different canons, only then they would not have created the art they did create. That art, and this is the only art Lessing is discussing, was essentially Hellenic in its conception, and the only way the Greek artist was able to achieve beauty in his work was by making it conform to the appropriate Hellenic canon. So if Premiss (7) is true of the works Lessing was concerned with, it is necessarily true of them. Since the same is true of the remaining premisses on which the reconstructed argument now rests, under the reconstruction, the desired semantic relation is preserved between Premisses (1)–(4) alone and the ultimately derived conclusion.

It is at this point, and not before, that it becomes an interesting matter to decide whether the premisses on which the argument now rests – in particular Premiss (7) – are in fact true. Relativized as they are to art that accepts the Hellenic canon, that becomes something for the art historian rather than the philosopher, and I shall have nothing to say about the issue. Everything of importance will turn of course on its being a truth that there was indeed a unified style in which classical and Hellenistic sculpture was created and which conceived of beauty as Lessing thought it did. It is, I think, fairly plain that Lessing would not have expected any of his contemporaries to have found these suppositions dubious, and for that reason it might be a fair assessment of the argument I have developed so far to say that against the opponents that he had to face Lessing at this point still remains master of the field. Were he to enjoy the hindsight that is granted us, his successors, he might find himself gratified and not a little surprised.

Note. That the real Lessing might have preferred a defence of *A* to rest on the *Iconicity Principle* I wrote as (2) than on considerations special to Greek art that I went on to offer him is suggested by another argument, *B*, that we find in his Chapter II, and which I alluded to earlier on. It is an argument that appeals to much the same structure as *A*, although its constituent premisses are different.

At II, 15 Lessing contrasts the ultimate aim of science, which is truth, with that of art, which is pleasure. A few pages further on (II, 20) he considers a hypothetical statue of Laocoon shrieking out in pain. On that account the state is repulsive (*eine abscheuliche Bildung*) and one from which we turn away "because the sight of pain arouses displeasure". Putting these observations together, we have an argument that differs from *A* in not being effectively restricted to Greek art, even though that is the art which in context is being discussed. Consequently the use of the argument does not have to pay the price I said would be exacted by reliance on Premiss (7). Nor is it open to objection on the part of those who would want to contest the assumptions (i)–(iii) above, since it does not rely on any of them. But despite these differences the same apparently illegitimate move is made here as was made in *A*, in passing from a claim about what men in great pain are like – repulsive, this time, rather than distorted – to the very same claim made about representations of men in visibly great pain. Again, I think it makes sense to account for Lessing's willingness to argue nonchalantly in this way by attributing to him a firm belief in the *Iconicity Principle*. For just as (1) was an evident substitution instance of (2), so too is

(4) *Laocoon* is a repulsive representation of Laocoon iff *Laocoon* represents Laocoon as repulsive.

This time however there is no way in which, to avoid the implausibility of the claim, we can hope to relativize it to Hellenic art as we did for (1). As Lessing sets out his argument, there is no such restriction to be placed in the kind of art whose ultimate end is supposed to be pleasure. Failing that, (4) will have no support at all unless it is assumed to be derived from (2) and from the kind of consideration that I suggested Lessing thought made that principle irresistible.

In Lessing's defence someone might say that we do indeed often react to depictions of suffering just as we react to suffering itself, and that this is not so very surprising since in a representation of suffering we see the victim suffer as we see him suffer in life itself. Only there are several reasons why this reflection cannot be of very much help. For one thing, Lessing conceives of his argument as being of wide (unlimited even) generality, and one that should discourage the artist from *any* attempts at the representation of violent suffering. Such generality would not be forthcoming if the argument were to go forward as here proposed, for all that can be allowed is that we *often* turn away from the victim of the depicted suffering, not that we *always* do so. Sometimes after all, we may pity him. Second, the very way in which the supposedly helpful observation was put invites the retort that one does indeed see the victim suffer *in the representation* and that in doing so one remains aware that it is a representation that one sees and not life itself. It is often this very fact that enables us to experience and even enjoy emotions which otherwise we would repress or reject. In *Monsieur le Consul* Lucien Bodard describes a popular Chinese melodrama in which one Emperor of the Han dynasty upholds the cruel demands of duty that oblige him to put his daughter to death for some dereliction of filial piety. He observes: "Les Chinois de la salle pleurent, alors qu'ils ne pleurent pas dans le vie." The phenomenon is not a rare one.

This last observation is particularly damaging for Lessing's treatment of the hypothetical *Laocoon* case itself. It draws our attention to the truth that once we are aware that what we see is a depiction, we can no longer be so sure that the representation of pain will in fact be found unpleasantly distressing. Whether it is may well depend on our attitude to the sufferer himself. In the case of Laocoon, if our sentiments are at heart those of Pallas Athene, perhaps we shall feel some grim satisfaction that the priest has got his just deserts, and even take some pleasure in seeing them eternalized before us in marble. In which case, the representation of pain may not violate the ultimate end of art conceived of as Lessing conceives it. (The reader may find this a less far fetched suggestion than it may now appear in the light of remarks I make later on, in Chapter 3, on the topic of projective imagination).

Nor can Lessing hope to get very far here by restricting the prohibition he places on the artist to the representation of *bare* pain, where we have no antecedent attitude to the sufferer which may guide our (now uninhibited) response to the display of his torment in art. In many such a case our interest in the work is properly described not just as an interest in how the suffering is represented, but more fully as an interest in how the suffering is represented *in the medium*. The thought that the artist has successfully overcome the problems to which his choice of medium gives rise can well be a source of pleasure that is not submerged by the nature of the topic he has chosen to depict. This is not to deny that there are cases where the topic does outweigh these more purely aesthetic considerations – a fair example, I think, might be provided by some of the work of Francis Bacon – and there Lessing's argument might have some purchase. But what leverage this admission has is of limited use. It can not be taken as providing any well-founded injunction against the choice of any particular subject matter; at most it provides a warning about the way in which a given subject matter should be handled – not in such a way as to render aesthetic attention impossible. Since this (arguably vacuous) conclusion applies as much to poetry as it does to art, this outcome of the less restrictive variation, *B*, on *Argument A* cannot realistically hope to serve the anti-transparency cause for which Lessing originally designed it.

II

No one prepared to allow the success of *Argument A*, its soundness even and not just its validity, need think he has conceded very much. The most it licenses Lessing to assert is that Greek artists needed to avoid graphic representation of violent suffering. That does nothing to show that every, or indeed any, art is limited by its medium, or that different arts are limited in different ways. Not saying anything about poetry, the argument is restricted to the visual arts; and because in the only remotely acceptable version it limits itself to Greek art that adopts the Hellenic canon of beauty, it is not calculated to persuade the unpersuaded that the restrictions on artistic success it identifies do not derive more from the particular style that these artists adopted than from the medium in which, within their adopted style, they explored the visual world as they did.

Nevertheless there may be an interesting asymmetry to be found between artist and poet in the restricted Hellenic domain, and whether, setting out from *Argument A*, Lessing can establish one and thereby some small part of the general anti-transparency thesis he is after, must depend on what he has to say about the *Aeneid* passage he takes to have inspired the Rhodian sculptors Pliny identifies as Hagesandros, Polydoros and Athenodoros (XXXVI, 189). Only be warned. For the sake of the argument we must be content to treat that Virgilian passage, like the statue, as conforming to the Hellenic canon too, written if you like by a poet who, implausibly enough, must be supposed to be Hellenic at heart if only Mantuan born. Failing this supposition, we should not properly or instructively be comparing like with like.

One way not to proceed would be to represent Lessing as denying that the poet can ever aim at beauty in his verse, and thence concluding that for Virgil not to achieve it in his depiction of the shrieking Laocoon is no failure, although it would be one for the sculptor in the corresponding statue.

Lessing does indeed enjoin the poet not to occupy himself with beauty, but that exhortation, which we shall explore in the next chapter, only concerns the content of his work and not its aesthetic character. Just as in the visual arts Lessing took the term "beautiful" to apply to the works themselves other than as a shorthand description of their depicted content, so too in the literary arts it is plain that the term applies to what the poet writes and not primarily to his descriptions of beautiful things. Thus Lessing has no hesitation in saying of Sophocles' *Philoctetes* that it achieves beauties of which a timid critic would not even dream (IV, 29), and no qualm later on (XIII, 109) in speaking of "some of the most beautiful depictions of Homer" as not providing suitable material for the artist. Lessing is quite happy to allow that the poet limns works of beauty, and ready to allow that in adopting this as his aim he shares a common end with the artist. Only here there is alleged to be no incompatibility between the achievement of *poetic* beauty and the representation of physical pain, hence no resulting restriction on the depiction of physical pain in the poet's verse. It is on the two reasons that Lessing offers for this thought that we need to rely in taking *Argument A* to its ultimate goal.

The first of these consists in the fact that the poetic treatment of Laocoon's trials in the *Aeneid* do not bring to mind how Laocoon will actually have looked when in the serpents' toils. "If Virgil's Laocoon screams, who pauses to reflect that a large wide open mouth is needed for screaming, and that such an open mouth is ugly?" (IV, 26). So, one is to conclude, poetic beauty is compatible with the verbal depiction of suffering, whereas in painting it is not. The reasoning here is weak. First, a purely *ad hominem* observation. We saw above that when Lessing distinguishes the poet from the writer of prose, he does so by reference to the poet's ability to awaken in us impressions that persuade us that we are experiencing what is described (XVII, 122) "the poet, Lessing says, should always write graphically". And if we are to take this exhortation seriously, then it must be that for Virgil's lines to be beautiful a graphic description of Laocoon's agony is what is required and not simply the relatively detached "*Clamores horrendos*" etc. of the *Aeneid* that Virgil offers us. In that case the lesson Lessing wants us to draw from Virgil will be badly learnt, for no asymmetry between poetry and painting can be derived from comparing a deficient (non-graphic) case of the one with an outstandingly graphic example of the other. If the poetic description had indeed been comparably graphic what reason have we to think that it would not affect us just as does the lively depiction of pain in the visual arts?

Waive this objection. Let Lessing rather contemplate saying, against the tenor of XIV, 111 and of XVII, 122, that the painter is bound by constraints of graphic art while the poet is not. That way at least we do not run the risk of depreciating Virgil as I have just been guilty of doing. The thought now is that in either case, visual or literary, the graphic depiction of pain will be offensive; only in poetry there is no absolute requirement on the writer to remain within the bounds of the graphic, whereas in art there is. Yet to take this line invites disaster. Lessing's only ground for supposing that the painter is forced to concern himself with the graphic was one which regards the *Iconicity Principle* as elucidatory of the nature of pictorial representation as such. And we saw in the last section that the success of *Argument A* turns on giving up this implausible thought, and adopting in its stead a weaker principle that restricts itself to the elucidation of the idea of graphic representation alone. Now of course a painter who embraces a graphic style of painting, for instance that which I called Hellenic, is bound to observe the constraints that that imposes on him if he is to work successfully within the style. But in this he is in no different a position than the poet who chooses the graphic course. Once it is recognized that he too, like the poet, has a choice of concerning himself with the graphic or not, the hoped for asymmetry between the two arts is wanting. Likewise the contention that any particular art is essentially constrained by its medium.

Lessing's other route to the anti-transparency conclusion has nothing to do with considerations about the peculiarly graphic nature of painting, but concerns the fundamentally episodic nature of narrative poetry and drama. Exactly what this argument is is rather obscure, and it is well that Lessing makes two distinct shots at it, one in his discussion of the Laocoon episode in the *Aeneid* and the other in his extended reflections on the *Philoctetes*. Both passages appear in Chapter IV of "Laocoon".

In his discussion of Virgil, Lessing points out that the poet is better able than the artist to draw on the force of earlier (and later) episodes in the story he recounts to control and temper our response to the representations of the priest's pain. Because he has already brought the far sighted patriot and warmly loving father sharply before our minds, "we do not refer his screaming to his character, but just to his unbearable suffering. This suffering alone we hear in his cries, and the poet has no other means of making it sensible to us" (IV, 27).

What Lessing means here is something rather ill expressed by his words. It is that we do not take the priest's crying out as displaying a defect of character, a deplorable lack of manly self-control or feminine weakness (cf III, 24; IV, 40); rather we see him as a man of admirable worth who suffers intolerable pain. So when Lessing says we do not refer his screaming to his character, he risks misleading us. For in one way we do just that; we see his screaming as that of a man of a certain firm character, and this is exactly what we rely on to distinguish Virgil's Laocoon from say the painter's representation of what above I called *bare* pain in a distorted body. The fact that it is the pain of someone whom we already "know and love" mitigates our response to his unbearable suffering.

If this is how Lessing wants to be understood, there is nothing in what he says that should disturb the artist. He will say that when he paints or carves his image of Laocoon, he represents a man who has just the same moral character as the poet describes. He does not have to depict episodes in which the man's firmness of temper is actually displayed for this to be true. What makes it so is the nature of the man himself whom the artist chooses to depict. Once the spectator recognizes the subject for the man he is, his response to the representation of his suffering cannot but be tempered by knowledge and appreciation of his character. Of course the painter may acknowledge that there are occasions when character is fashioned by the poet in the development of his narrative and that the only source of our knowledge of his subject's moral strength derives from episodes that the reader works his way through. But the moral to draw from this reflection is not that the painter cannot properly represent suffering in his work, but that when he does he must take care to choose victims about whom the spectator is *already* well informed, or about whose character enough can be intimated in the depicted scene to inhibit our reacting to it as we would to a depiction of bare pain. And it will be recalled that in the *Note* to the last section the painter has already made some minimal concession on the subject of representations of that kind. This would be an appropriate place for him to urge the poet to do likewise.

I described Lessing's argument as obscure. What is obscure about it is how the thought that the poet's ability to cause us to hear Laocoon's unbearable suffering alone in his cries is to underwrite the judgment that Virgil's work is beautiful, whereas in the sculpture the same suffering is guaranteed to block that judgment. Help here is found in the discussion of the *Philoctetes*. That play is a tragedy, and as far as Lessing is concerned it is essential to the success of tragedy that it have the ability to arouse pity. For him this is "the sole end of tragic theatre, and [in consequence] its heroes must show feelings and express their suffering and allow bare nature to run her course" (IV, 37). I take it that Lessing would allow that when these things are successfully achieved we find beauty in tragic art, and the problem for the dramatist in his quest of beauty is to combine the representation of suffering of his hero with the arousal of pity in the audience. Indeed since the dramatist makes use of actors who may actually scream before us on the stage, makes us hear and see the screaming itself with the almost inevitable repulsion that that brings (cf IV, 28), his task is if anything more difficult to achieve than it is for the poet. But as the *Philoctetes* demonstrates, the difficulty is not insuperable. Applying this thought to Virgil's description of Laocoon then, it appears that Lessing's idea must be that what makes the passage a beautiful one is its capacity to combine a striking account of the priest's suffering with the arousal of our pity or sympathy. And what we have to ask is whether the painter cannot avail himself of the same means as does the dramatist – and perhaps to a lesser extent the poet – in the presentation of visible suffering and pain.

I see no immediate reason to think that he might not. After all, what Lessing tells us in explanation of Sophocles' genius is how he manages to find an unexpected array of means to evoke pity and sympathy for his protagonist, so that in the end our attitude to seeing his suffering is already sufficiently preformed by our knowledge of his circumstances and of his plight. This is just the same sort of thing that Virgil is supposed to be making use of in the *Aeneid* when he presents Laocoon to us as someone for whom we already have a warm admiration. So there is no apparent reason for the painter not to avail himself of just the same stratagem as does the dramatist if he wants to depict violent pain and suffering in a beautiful canvas. As before, he only needs to insist that what the discussion of the literary arts teaches us is that in the pictorial representation of physical violence and pain, the painter or sculptor should select a subject to whose suffering we are predisposed to respond with as much pity and sympathy as we do when we meet him in the most successful tragic drama and poetry. However this is not to draw distinctions among the arts that work in different media. It is to insist instead on their close affinity.[14]

At this point it is fair enough to ask whether I am not being inconsistent in allowing Lessing the conclusion of *Argument A*, that the Greek painter who aims at beauty must eschew the representation of physical pain, yet at the same time denying that he shows there to be any disanalogy between him and the poet or dramatist, whose writing may indeed be beautiful even though it depict a physical suffering that should not tempt the artist. The reply is short. There is no inconsistency, for the reason that Lessing is operating with a concept of artistic beauty that applies in different ways to graphic representations in the different arts. Thus in the case of the Hellenic sculptor or painter, we saw that beauty of a representation consisted

[14] Although it won't take Lessing to his very strong conclusion, it can be said in his defense that he is responding to one significant difference between the nature of the kinds of art with which he is concerned. The painter is, in his visually available depiction, bound to show a great deal other than what he concentrates attention on in order to depict just that. The poet by contrast is not so placed. And what is, so to speak, intrusive in the painter's case risks being aesthetically unsettling. He therefore faces a stiffer challenge than the poet, in that he has to make the intrusive material (the gaping mouth, say) contribute aesthetically to his end. While this may not be clearly impossible to achieve (*pace* Lessing) the difficulty it gives rise to might caution prudence in the painter's choice of subject matter. How urgently it does so will depend on the extent to which the painter can call on the resources of the spectator's imagination in the appreciation of his work, and that is a topic that I take up in Chapter 3.

simply in its graphic representation of something beautiful, and this is what ruled out the hypothetically agonizing version of the *Laocoon*. But in the literary arts Hellenic beauty in the graphic representation of pain is a graphic representation of pain that inspires sympathy and pity. Since different standards are being used in the several arts there is absolutely nothing objectionable about the Hellenically-minded painter saying to the Hellenically-minded poet that if he abides by painterly standards he cannot represent painful scenes with beauty, but that if he, the painter, adopts poetic standards he will succeed as well as the poet in the beautiful depiction of these things. Disanalogy between them, however, there is none, since the converse of this thought is equally defensible.

However, immediately the tenor of what I have been saying is put in these terms, Lessing's champion may think he sees his way through. For he will say that these hypotheticals, involving the imaginary exchange of roles between artist and poet, have necessarily false antecedents, and that they must therefore be rejected. For the painter to adopt the poetic standard he would have to be able to capture the whole *course* of Laocoon's suffering, and that he cannot do. Nor can the poet properly be asked to delineate the painterly beautiful in his verse, for that requires him to occupy himself with *bodies*, which are not his proper subject matter. Each artist therefore must achieve beauty in his own way, and that necessity will preserve the asymmetry between the arts expressed in the rhetorical question: "Who will not allow that that the artist did well not to have Laocoon cry out, and the poet just as well to have him do so?" (IV, 27) To examine this new defence of the anti-transparency position is matter for the next chapter.

2

Beauty and Subject Matter

At the end of the last chapter I suggested that if Lessing is to establish any instructive disanalogies between the critical canons that apply to art and those that apply to poetry, he must show that the way the artist achieves beauty in his work is not available to the poet, and likewise that the poet's way is closed to the artist. Nothing less than this will do, for without it the acknowledged success of the argument that restricts the Hellenic artist in his choice of subject matter will stand no chance of bearing any more nourishing theoretical fruit.

Here we approach the intellectual core of the "Laocoon" and find Lessing advancing two notorious claims either of which will, if sustainable, take him forward in his pursuit of an a priori refutation of the arts' claims to transparency, that is, of the idea that the medium within which the artist works imposes no constraints on his selection and handling of subject matter. Of these two claims one is more restricted in its ambition than the other, and concerns the idea of beauty. For ease of reference I shall simply call it the *Beauty Thesis*. Its fellow will be the *Subject Matter Thesis*, and addresses itself to identifying the proper place to be held in art and in poetry by the representation of the body and of action. In this chapter I discuss each in turn, and I take up first the more restricted of the two.

I

The *Beauty Thesis* maintains that beauty has no place in poetry. Not, we saw, that poetry may not itself be beautiful, but that the beauty of poetry, be it beauty $_{Hellenic}$ or beauty $_{Other}$[1], can never require that physical objects, in particular human bodies, be graphically represented as beautiful. So, for instance, whether in our discussion of the various Greek arts we say that they all aspired to the same state, that of being beautiful $_{Hellenic}$, or whether we think they aimed at quite distinct goals, of being say beautiful $_{Hellenic\ (visual)}$ or beautiful $_{Hellenic\ (poetic)}$, we have to acknowledge that they will achieve success in different ways, painting and sculpture by the graphic representation of beautiful objects, poetry by the graphic representation of events that evokes such feelings as pity and sympathy (cf IV, 37). Moreover, Lessing now asserts this difference is not merely a contingent one; it is *conceptually* excluded that the poet should concern himself with the graphic representation of anything as beautiful at all. That lies beyond his power, and he could not successfully adopt the painter's stance even if he would. We shall come to Lessing's grounds for this startling assertion in a moment. But first we need to know how limited in scope it must be even when it is protected against two immediate objections.

Remembering that Lessing rejects the transparency thesis by holding (a), that all arts are constrained in what they represent by their medium, and (b), that different arts are constrained by their media in different ways, it is apparent that the contrast between painting and poetry under discussion, needs to be a strong contrast and not a weak one. I call a strong contrast one that affirms of one art that it has to meet a standard that another art cannot match; a weak contrast is one that affirms merely that one art may – though need not – embrace a standard that another art can not adopt. Here only an argument that established a strong contrast will suffice, since on the basis of a weak contrast alone Lessing will have nothing that would yield claim (b) of his anti-transparency thesis, let

---

[1] As in the last chapter I use subscripts to designate styles in relation to which the beauty of the individual work is to be judged.

alone claim (a). The most he would have would be an observation about limitations on a single art, and that could not supply the desiderated conclusions.

Now the *Beauty Thesis* maintains that any poetry as such can not graphically represent beautiful things, but it does not say anything about painting except that it may do so. If we are looking for a strong contrast, we shall therefore have to cast the thesis as applying solely to art of a sort that *must*, if successful, represent beautiful things; and it is dubious whether that claim could really be made out for art in any style other than that which Lessing identifies as the visual Hellenic one. Thus, so far as the actual extent of his argument goes, it is very limited in its reach. And while there could well be styles of visual art other than the Hellenic that aimed at beauty$_{Other}$ by requiring the graphic representations of beautiful things, to allow that the present argument extends to such possible cases does nothing to enlarge its range within the domain of the actual representational art we know. It does not touch art that aims at beauty$_{Other}$ by the graphic representation of things other than beautiful ones, and it ignores that art which aims at beauty$_{Other}$ by means of representations that are other than graphic. In these cases the only contrast one could hope for would be a weak contrast: and some of the time one would not even find that.

This is not to say that over the range of Hellenic art Lessing's argument is a failure. In particular two accusations that are likely to be levelled against it cannot be made out. The first is that everything turns on the correctness of Lessing's definition of beauty as "arising out of the harmony of several parts of something that can be taken in at a glance" (alternatively, "that are surveyable at one go") (XX, 145), and that that definition is fundamentally mistaken. Whether what this objector says is true or not is neither here nor there, for even if Lessing has not got right what beauty really is, it is open to him to say that the occurrence of the word "beauty" serves only to designate a certain property of objects, namely that captured in the definition, and that it is that property he is claiming poetry to be incapable of graphically representing things to possess. It is that property, he can say, that the Greeks so cared about in the things around them, and it matters not at all for the substance of "Laocoon" whether this property is or is not that of beauty itself. Of course we might have to change the expression of some of the claims Lessing makes if we should decide that the objection is substantially correct, but as far as he is concerned that need involve no more than the substitution in his text of some less misleading word. All confusion here will be avoided so long as we bear in mind that the elucidatory phrase or definition is at worst stipulative about the use of Lessing's term "*Schönheit*".

The other preliminary worry in that, stipulative or not, the definitional phrase I cited actually fixes on the beauty of bodies – *körperliche Schönheit* is what is defined – and it will be said that it can scarcely come as a surprise that the only things that possess that quality are bodies. In so far as Lessing's argument is to rest on that contention his thesis is therefore entirely vacuous.

What ruins this complaint is its lack of generosity. Admittedly, Lessing does introduce his definition as explicative of the beauty of bodies, but it would be nearer to his overall intentions to see this restriction as deriving from his conception of what property it was he was concerned with. Rather it is a consequence of that property being what it is that it can pick out a feature that bodies have, not a reflection of some concern of Lessing's about a property that he can discern at the outset to be possessed by bodies and by bodies alone. If he really were at pains here to define a specifically bodily beauty there would be a point to doing so only if there existed another sort of beauty that might be characterised in some different way. But Lessing gives his reader no hint that be believes the natural world to contain any other sort at all, let alone one that might be accounted for in a different manner than that which he here describes.

With these two matters out of the way we may approach the *Beauty Thesis* itself. Following the elucidation of beauty as deriving from the harmonious effect of things whose parts can be surveyed at one go, Lessing continues:

> it demands therefore that these parts lie next to one another. Since [by the *Subject Matter Thesis*] things whose parts are juxtaposed are the proper objects of painting, it, and it alone, can depict the beauty of bodies (XX, 145).

By implication the poet, whose proper concern is with actions and sequences of events, is ill advised to attempt the graphic representation of bodies, and since that is where beauty lies, the representation of beautiful things *as* beautiful eludes him.

The proper question to ask Lessing here must be whether his presumed connection between those things that can be taken in at a glance and things whose parts are juxtaposed will take him where he wants. For taking his expression *"auf einmal"* literally, we should typically be able to judge things to be beautiful providing only that their parts lie more or less on a plane, profiles, say, façades of buildings, views and so on. What seem to be excluded are the judgments we make of a body or a building or a dress and indeed of much sculpture in the light of our experience of them *as we move around them.* True, in these cases the parts of the objects are all juxtaposed, but that itself does not allow their organization to be taken in at a glance or at one go. For that we need to see how the parts fit together from several points of view, and to view the whole synthetically, in the light of our enjoyment of several discrete views of it. Since only the acceptance of some such thought as this will make it possible for Lessing to say that the property of beauty he describes extends to bodies rather than just to aspects of them, and since he reckons he has picked out just that property of bodies that so preoccupied the Greeks, he is, for iconographical reasons if for no other, bound to accept this adjustment to his position.

The moral to draw is not that the idea of taking things in at a glance has no place in the description of the beauties that Lessing identifies. It does; only he has slightly mislocated it. What is important cannot be the *temporal* unity of the glance, but its *experiential* unity. By this I mean our ability to unite the various elements of the things we judge by allowing what we perceive at one moment to be aesthetically informed by our experience of the previously perceived and still expected aspects of the same thing. It is this that Lessing needs to concentrate on rather than our ability to perceive them all together at the same time, as can be seen by reflection on the case of music which brings out the point particularly sharply. Music or melody has to be distinguished from the sequences of sound that make it up, and what we rely on to draw the distinction is the idea that while the melody, like a sequence of tones, is heard sequentially, unlike them, it is heard in such a way that we experience the single tones in the sequence as related to each other in our sensibility, and hear the weight that one note bears as function of the weight that other notes nearby it are experienced as carrying. As long as we make non-molecular judgments of this kind we shall be able to discuss what we hear in musical terms, and once we find that the distance in space or time does not psychologically admit of such synthetic experience, there the reach of musical judgment peters out. Analogously, it is just this concession that Lessing needs to make about the interpretation of his expression "*auf einmal*" if he is to succeed in his claim that it is primarily bodies that qualify as beautiful. And, of course, without this capacity to experience the various parts of an object informing our perception of one another, distinct from simply seeing them all together (or perhaps somehow imagining them all together) at the same time, we could not even judge to be beautiful those things such as profiles and façades that Lessing's actual definition of beauty best fits. Even there, where everything can be taken in at a glance in virtue of the particular form of organization it enjoys, the capacity for the non-molecular viewing of one part or detail in the light of others that surround it and which present themselves to the eye at the same time is absolutely required for any minimally sensitive aesthetic response to them.

So far, so good. We can rescue Lessing's contention that bodies are beautiful without doing great violence to his elucidation of the notion of beauty – whether we agree with it or not.[2] But in doing this, we inevitably make room for the poet to say that the restriction of beauty to those things whose parts are *spatially* juxtaposed is now quite arbitrary. True, bodies and profiles, buildings and landscapes, are all things whose parts are spatially juxtaposed, but the only reason for this notion of juxtaposition to appear at all was that Lessing too hastily assumed that what could be taken in at a glance must be things

---

[2] It is not just that no great violence is done. If anything a considerable improvement is offered to Lessing's own account of beauty. For the way we now propose to understand "*auf einmal*" does bring to our attention one central limitation on the range of things it makes sense to speak of as beautiful. Even though he articulated the thought incorrectly, he deserves credit for seeing that some appeal to what can be taken in at one go is going to have to find its place in any acceptable elucidation of the concept.

that fall within one view, and that things that fall within a single view must have their parts in spatial juxtaposition. Once the move away from the unsatisfactory extensional and temporal interpretation of "*auf einmal*" is made, however, and those words are given an intensional reading instead, we see that spatial juxtaposition of the parts that are judged to lie harmoniously together in a thing of beauty is not imposed either. And, the poet will go on, since such unity of parts as is called for must be provided by the mind rather than by the material configuration of the object judged, and since the mind has a capacity for the unitary experience of what is temporally discrete, there is no reason yet supplied for denying that the actions and sequences of events that poetry depicts are just as good candidates for the qualification "beautiful" as are bodies themselves. This said, the asymmetry between art and poetry that the *Beauty Thesis* purports to establish is no more than an undemonstrated matter of faith.

II

This argument is irrefutable; and its effect is finally to deprive Lessing's original *Argument A* of any power to contribute to the rejection of transparency, even in the most restricted of domains. The interest it has is confined to what it can teach us about graphic visual representations in Hellenic art and no more. At this point it would be urgent for any full appraisal of Lessing's thought to examine the tenability of the one assumption he makes about which very little scepticism has so far been expressed; that is the assumption that *Laocoon* is indeed a work of Hellenic art. Not of course, that *Laocoon* is not a work of Greek provenance; but can we really believe that among such works there does exist a unified style of visual art of the kind that Lessing stresses in his discussion of the group, and within which style the *Laocoon* was executed? Art-historically at least the suggestion smacks of the heroic.

If we set this issue aside though, it may be supposed that Lessing can easily enough shrug off the current setback. As he presents the *Beauty Thesis* in Chapter XX it presupposes the truth of a second doctrine, the *Subject Matter Thesis*, which identifies the proper objects of painting and sculpture as bodies, and those of poetry as actions. Conversely, it also affirms that it is contraindicated for the artist to occupy himself with actions or for the poet to concentrate on the delineation of bodies. If Lessing can sustain this idea the *Subject Matter Thesis* will itself establish an asymmetry between the arts in a way that is quite independent of the *Beauty Thesis*, and, what is more, will do so in a way that is both detachable from considerations peculiar to Hellenic art and, to all appearance, in one that is more closely medium-related than its predecessor. So the *Subject Matter Thesis* promises a considerable advance beyond anything we have yet seen along the path to a general anti-transparency conclusion and runs less risk of falling foul of art-historical material. Of course, this is not to say that the doctrine does not have its limitations. It does; only they cannot be identified without our first having a clear view of its pretensions.

The official statement of the position is found at XVI, 114:

> If it be true that painting uses quite different means or signs for its representations than poetry, to wit, figures and colours in space as against sounds articulated in time; and beyond doubt that the signs have to bear a happy accommodation (*ein bequemes Verhältnis*) to what they signify; then it follows that signs can only express (*ausdrücken*) objects, or parts of objects that are juxtaposed, and successive signs, objects or parts of objects that succeed one another.
>
> Objects, or parts of objects, that coexist are bodies. Hence bodies and their visual properties make up the proper topics of painting. Objects, or parts of objects, that succeed one another are above all actions. So actions make up the proper topic of poetry.

Quite what this "dry chain of reasoning" (XVI, 115) is to establish emerges uncertainly from these lines. From what Lessing goes on to say in the next few sentences, it is evident that he does not intend to imply that it is a conceptual impossibility that poetry should represent bodies, or that painting should depict actions. Only he says that such representations would be allusive only (*andeutungsweise nachgeahmt*) and not direct. The painter can suggest action through his representation of bodies, and the poet suggest the presence of bodies through his depiction of actions.

Better than that – *express* them – however, they cannot do.

The use of the world "express", and not the straightforward "represent" that we might have expected, must alert us to the thought that Lessing's claims are offered with some limitation in mind. Indeed, it is only if we impute to him the repugnant view that all visual representation has to be construed in terms of illusion that we could otherwise understand his reluctance to think that sometimes one might directly, and not just allusively, represent a temporally extended process in two dimensions – as is perhaps attempted say by those sentimental drawing room images of the seven ages of man so popular in the last century. Similarly, we see no trouble for the poet in depicting a body simply enough by the usual mechanism of reference and description. Yet it is remarkable that when Lessing applauds Virgil for refraining from depicting Dido, he does so by saying "Dido is no more to him than *'pulcherrima Dido'* " (XX, 153). If reference and description alone had the power to constitute *expression* in poetry, there could scarcely be any more potent expression of beauty than that.

I conclude that Lessing is to be seen as fixing his attention on direct, non-allusive, representations of a certain sort, and about these alone offering an argument of uncertain power to the effect that their content, be it in art or in poetry, will be partly determined by the nature of the signs that these representations are obliged by their medium to employ. So before we can start to assess the thesis itself we have to decide what it is for a representation to be an expressive one. Also, of course, we shall have to form a view of the modal strength of the easy accommodation doctrine that appears to underwrite the alleged asymmetry between the two major sorts of representative art as they confine themselves to expressive non-allusive depiction of their respective subject matters.

We saw in the last chapter how Lessing took the notion of graphic writing to constitute the essence of poetry (XVII, 122; cf also XVII, 125 and XIV, 111). It is notable also that he sets down the aim of "modern" artists at III, 22 as truth and expression rather than beauty. And it suggests itself to me that these two ideas are linked for Lessing in that a representation is thought to express its object if, and only if, it depicts it graphically. In effect, to be graphic and to be expressive are to his mind one and the same thing. And this idea is generically expressed by Lessing at XVII, 122 as the capacity a work of art has, through the vivacity of the ideas it arouses, to induce us to believe that we are sensibly aware of the depicted objects. "For the moment of deception the artist gets us to forget the means (words or brush strokes) he uses to this end." Furthermore, the central importance of *belief* to the idea of expression is further attested by Lessing's saying later on (XX, 152) that all the learning that informs Ariosto's description of Alcina's beauty (*Orlando Furioso*, VII, 11–15) is of little help to the reader who demands only that "he believe he sees a beautiful woman before him and experience the soft throb of blood that the actual perception of beauty occasions".

We must not say here, as in the context of *beauty* I suggested we might, that if we do not like Lessing's account of expression we should treat it as stipulative of the use he wants to make of the word "express". If we did that we should find that graphic art does not extend nearly as far as he needs it to. In painting, at most *trompe l'oeil* work would qualify, and in poetry, we should risk finding no candidates at all. Moreover, were we in all seriousness to believe ourselves actually experiencing the events the poet describes, it would often become impossible to account for our undoubted ability to abstract from them and to continue with the work we are engaged on. Sometimes even the only decent thing to do would be to stop reading, as do Francesca and Paolo in *Inferno, v*; only contrary to what Lessing would be bound to suppose, what moved them had little enough to do with modesty.[3] So, to find a more fitting

---

[3] Noi leggiavamo un giorno per diletto
    di Lancialotto come amor lo strinse:
    soli eravamo e sanza alcun sospetto

Per più fiate li occhi ci sospinse
    quella lettura, e scolorocci il viso;
    ma solo un punto fù quel che ci vinse

Quando leggemmo il disiato riso
    esser baciato da cotanto amante
    la bocca mi baciò tutto tremante

Galeotto fù il libro e chi lo scrisse
    Quel giorno più non vi leggemmo avanti. (*Inf. v*, 127–138).

extension for the idea, and to give Lessing's argument the scope it needs, we must put in place of his belief-based account of expressive representation something rather more lifelike. (Incidentally, it should also afford him a better appreciation of Dante than his own theory permits.[4])

Cast in absolutely general terms, and leaving specification for later on, it is an appealing thought that the artist or writer proceeds graphically in his work to the extent that his audience is brought by the accurate perception of the signs vividly to imagine the sensible features of what they depict. While remaining recognizably close to Lessing's own suggestion, this gloss differs from what he offers in three important ways.

(a) It makes no reference to belief, and thereby not only makes room for the notion of the graphic to acquire a reasonable extension, but also displays sensitivity to the demand that appreciation of the poet's work involve a feeling for how he achieves his effect *in the medium*. Lessing is over-hasty in depreciating such an interest (cf II, 12/13), and his tendency to ignore it is reinforced by his concern with illusion, or belief in the actuality of the representation, which he perceives would be incompatible with a sharp awareness of the words that induce it or the brush strokes that compose the image that we see. Hence his demand that we forget the words for the moment of deception (XVI, 121)[5]. There is every reason not to follow him here, and I see no unacceptable weakening of his position flowing from not doing so.

(b) On Lessing's view it would be difficult for us to confront graphic art without taking ourselves to be involved as participants (passive maybe, but participants none the less) in the represented scene. For if we do believe ourselves to be experiencing the sensible impressions of the objects that are

---

[4] Of course Francesca and Paolo could be imagined to stop for some other reason than modesty, say to satisfy a voyeuristic curiosity – but any alternative to the real one, which excludes their believing themselves to be in the presence of the erotically engaged Lancelot and Guinevere, is equally silly.

[5] At this point it is particularly clear how tense the relation is between Lessing's conception of graphic representation in terms of illusion and his espousal of non-transparency when that is conceived of as a claim about the physical medium in which the artist works. Whether the same tension persists when we move away from the physical medium and think instead of the demands of *category* (cf Section III below) is another question.

represented, we can scarcely do other than think of ourselves present at the scene. Now sometimes we do do this, and Lessing can admit that it is important that we do, only this is not always part of our experience of graphic representation and does not derive from the generic nature of the graphic itself. On my alternative account, we can say that what Francesca and Paolo did in reading their tale of Lancelot and Guinevere was simply to have vividly imagined the described situation (*il disiato riso/esser baciato da cotanto amante*), and not to have thought of themselves as witnesses present at it. Imagination, unlike belief, is quite neutral with respect to thought about our own position.

(c) On the revised view, we are better able than was Lessing to treat poetry and art in parallel, and then go on to establish an asymmetry between them, if we can. Once we fix the graphic or the expressive in terms of belief, in the case of art we are pretty well bound to say that we erroneously take the statue or the picture for the man or the scene it represents. Yet in the case of poetry we can not begin to say that we take the words for the depicted objects or actions – except possibly in those rare cases of the onomatopoeic evocations of sounds themselves – so instead we should be led to say that belief is simply occasioned by the awareness of the words. Once the belief requirement is dropped though, this disparity vanishes. We say that in either case we are brought by awareness of the signs to imagine the sensible detail of the scene, without any suggestion that we take the signs for the scene at all. In neither case need we overlook in our appreciation of the artist's work the relationship between the marks he lays down and the images they constitute. Of course there are differences between the ways in which the imaginative effect is achieved in the different arts, as we shall see later on, but these are not consequences of the essential nature of the graphic imagination itself. Nor will these differences ever bring with them the idea that a commitment to the graphic and the expressive in representational art must involve the acceptance of thoughts that are recognizably false.

With this adjustment made, we can turn to the second issue I mentioned, that of determining the modal strength of Lessing's judiciously, but infuriatingly, vague doctrine that in graphic representation there must be an easy accommodation between the signs and the represented object. This question can only be resolved as we find a reasonably plausible interpretation of the doctrine itself, and then ask ourselves how strong it can be taken to be.

So far as interpretation goes, we know from the first quotation from XVI, 114 that particular cases of easy accommodation are found when the character of the painter's signs (their spatial coexistence) is matched by the graphic coexistence of the bodies he represents. We also know that we find the same easy accommodation of signs to significance when the character of the poet's audible words (their successiveness) is matched by the graphic successiveness of the actions that are delineated in his poem. From our discussion in Chapter 1 of Lessing's position on the topic of iconicity, it is almost inevitable that we should think of him as proceeding to these specifics from a general principle that sees it as a necessary feature of the graphic representation of something that is perceptibly φ that the same property φ should characterize the poem or the painting that effects the depiction. Thus we can see the easy accommodation doctrine well expressed in the familiar (though still modally inexplicit) sentence (2″) of Chapter 1:

(2″) $(x)(y)(\varphi)(x$ is a φ representation of y if x graphically represents y as $\varphi)$

Here the easy accommodation is fully explicated in the regular occurrence of the same predicate in the relevant places left and right of the connective, and it arises out of the demands we make on a representation if it is to achieve graphicality as I have described it in belief-free terms.

Now, what sort of necessity are we to suppose this sentence to enjoy? Because Lessing himself does not help us much about this the only way forward is to settle the issue dialectically, offering interpretation of his thought under the guidance of apparent truths. To begin with, consider the strongest version of (2″), namely that which sees it as a *de dicto* conceptual truth, and suppose it to be offered absolutely generally in regard of the observable properties of objects falling within the range of the predicate variable. Such a reading is not inviting. In the first place, the source of the alleged conceptual necessity is quite mysterious, since the capacity of the artist's signs to cause one to think imaginatively of this or that sensible property of an object seems, as far as logical possibility goes, fluid and not rigorously tied to the qualities of signs that have this power. We are little inclined to say that thoughts of a particular sort (graphic imaginings) not only are brought about in this particular way – whatever it is – in our world, but would be brought about in just the same way in any alternative world whatever. In this case there is nothing on display, or even under the counter, which offers us any reason for saying so weird a thing.

Closer to our actual experience, we can see that the principle does not hold in full generality anyway, since even in our own world it is frequently false. Consider an example that involves colour. Often the colour that something represented in a painting appears to be, and hence, let us suppose, is represented as being, is a function of how things around it are painted, and not of the colour that characterizes the relevant representational sign when that is taken by itself. Yet by the unrestricted *Iconicity Principle* (2″) this could not be so, since it is demanded that if the colour of the object is graphically represented as being blue-green say, the corresponding portion of the canvas should itself be blue-green. In fact it may happen that no portion of the canvas is blue-green. As the Impressionists knew, the apparent colour effect is brought about in a far less direct and simple way, and the reader will easily be able to fashion other examples of the same discrepancy at will.

A weaker reading of (2″) than this is yielded by taking it as a psychological law of a kind. Then even if it is not a conceptual truth about graphic representation that there should exist this easy accommodation of sign to thing signified, the correlation of the two partners is still required if human perceivers are to find representations they come upon graphic. Here at least, puzzlement about the motivation of the claim is avoided. Only as it stands, it still can not be true. The very example of colour just cited shows that in full generality the contention is false to our actual experience. And if we concentrate on those cases that Lessing takes as paradigmatic, the painter's representations of bodies, we shall find that commitment to the psychologized version of the *Principle* will render even graphic perspectival representation far more difficult than in fact it is. How could I paint a wall on the oblique that the viewer sees as rectangular while using signs that mark out a rectangular patch on the canvas? It cannot be done. (It is not open to Lessing to say that what is represented here is an oblique-looking rectangular wall, and that I paint a correspondingly shaped patch on the canvas, for as has so often been observed, that is not how rectangular walls look when obliquely viewed. For the most part they still look rectangular.)

Maybe this difficulty is not overwhelming. To meet it, and at the same time retain the suggestion of nomologicality, Lessing might try saying that what is strictly required by way of law for successful graphic representation is not that the signs themselves display the properties that the represented object is shown as having, but that the signs *appear to the viewer* to display them. Thus in the colour case, while there is no blue-green segment of the canvas that matches the blue-green colour of the depicted object, it does appear that at the relevant spot the canvas is blue-green. Similarly when we see the wall in the representation as rectangular, it strikes us that the non-rectangular portion of the canvas that carries that sense itself appears rectangular. Moreover, Lessing might go on to say that even though we could no longer be hoping to arrive at the desired conclusion about the proper objects of painting as derivable from (2″), but as proceeding instead from the new sentence

$(x)(y)$(Observable φ)(if x graphically represents y as φ, x appears to be φ),

there does still remain a regular connection between the signs themselves and what is represented for (2″) not to be too misleading. Unless there are special factors at work, what produces in the perceiver the appearance of the sign being φ is the fact that the sign *is* φ. In the particular case in which he is interested, that is, in the case of the representation of bodies, the situation is generally normal, and it is not so very irresponsible to present the argument as moving directly from the signs to what they signify. Under pressure to be more precise Lessing could happily enough make the suppressed step explicit.

This then is an option at his disposal. But there is both theoretical and textual reason to think that he might not wish to rest much weight upon it. The most serious obstacle to accepting the new sentence as a matter of (even approximate) law is that very often what guides us in seeing something graphically in a picture as being of such and such a nature is our knowledge of what sort of thing it is that is represented, and not the way the canvas independently appears to be. One might say that graphic imagination tends to move from a theoretical conception of the represented object to its vivid realization rather than to that realization from an awareness of the canvas as it is on its own account. Of course, the realization of the vivid image is dependent on the canvas conforming to that image, but "conforming" here can imply no more than that the canvas enables the graphic image to be achieved. An example brings this home. De La Tour will graphically represent a warmly glowing candle, and we see it as warmly glowing because of the illumination it appears to throw over the faces of the men gathered round it. When we describe how the canvas appears to be however, we find that there is nothing there that appears to be warmly glowing at all, certainly not the patch of bright colour that represents the candle's flame. And it cannot do anything to support such a contention to say that we need to see that patch of colour in the context provided by the reddish pigment used for the faces of the men, because it is no part of *that* context that the red is used to represent the reflection of the candle's flame on their weather-beaten skin. The context is not a representational one at all, it merely consists of the spatial relations of one colour patch to another. So once we abstract from its representational content the canvas is no longer plausibly describable in terms that the revised (approximate) psychological law would appear to require.

Moreover, as a matter of historical record, it would be unjust to impute to Lessing off-hand commitments to psychological laws, particularly when cast in such simplistic manner as the proposal just considered. At IV, 35 he says in tones whose modernity may well startle latter-day ears that

> nothing is more misleading than general laws about our feelings [experiences] (*Empfindungen*). Their web is so fine and interwoven that it is scarcely possible even for the most assiduous observer to pick out a single strand and to trace it

through all crossing strands. And even if he were successful, what good would that be? There is no such thing in nature as a single feeling; with each one come thousands of others at the same time, the very least of which so completely alters the master feeling as to heap exception on exception, with the result that the supposedly general law is finally restricted to a few instances.

True, Lessing is here talking in the context of a thesis of Adam Smith's about our emotional response to others' suffering, but there is no reason to think that he would not want to apply the same remarks to other aspects of our experience as well. And it is noteworthy that the form taken by my more abstract theoretical objection to the revised version of the lawlike-oriented interpretation of Lessing's thesis was indeed to impugn its generality with the help of counter-examples, prospectively leaving standing only isolated and unsystematically connected cases conforming to the general pattern.

If we can find a third way of reading the easy accommodation claim then that treats it neither as a conceptual truth nor as derivable from a regular psychological law, we should clearly do so. And one such way may be to record the doctrine not so much as a principle from which particular conclusions may be derived, but as a summary of particular observations that result from the workings of determinate psychological mechanisms of perception built up through our commerce with graphic representations of one sort and another. On this third way of taking him, Lessing will be saying that there are kinds of graphic representation which, for explicable reasons, we find have to conform to the pattern of the open sentence one gets from (2″) when the quantifiers are dropped, and that when the artist addresses himself to these, he will find himself obliged to abide by the demand that has grown up for accommodation of the signs to the thing signified. Otherwise he will miss his graphic effect. Here a reason will have to be given in each case why accommodation is demanded, and any attempts to establish (2″) in full, or even substantial, generality will be abandoned.

When we look at the structure of XVI as a whole, and abstract from Lessing's rather misleading formal presentation of his argument, I think we can see him moving forward in just such a manner. He is concerned with two cases only, that of painting and that of poetry, and with their respective predilection for bodies and for actions. He displays no further concern to advocate or establish any more general accommodation thesis. Rather than being content to derive the claims he makes about the two arts from any general principles, he offers special reasons, different in each case, for thinking that what artist and poet can achieve by way of graphic effect will be constrained by the nature of the medium in which they work, or the signs they use. Taken in this way, what Lessing has to offer is more hopeful than the sentences I initially quoted from the beginning of XVI may suggest. Moreover, his suggestions are relatively immune to counter-examples of the kind I have drawn on above, and which would otherwise seriously disconcert him. On this way of taking him then it is no longer the accommodation doctrine itself but the particular reflections he offers about the different arts that guide him in saying what he does about the limitations that are imposed on their authors' choice and handling of subject matter. These reflections we must now look at in their detail, and I shall consider the case of painting and sculpture first and go on to that of poetry thereafter.

III

The argument then is going to be this: graphic art is unable to depict actions and events because, for psychological reasons, the signs it employs do not permit us to see these things in them. What it is about the signs that makes this impossible is their juxtaposition, and to approve this claim of Lessing's we need to make it persuasive that there is a genuine psychological difficulty in seeing in juxtaposed signs anything other than bodies or such things as can be viewed whole at a single moment. Furthermore, if Lessing's ultimate conclusion is to be that the limitations on the artist's subject matter are imposed by the medium of his art, the juxtaposition of the signs he makes so much of has to be a feature of them that works of painting and sculpture *necessarily* possess. Were it otherwise the conclusion that would emerge in the end would risk being far less strong, not that graphic art is bound to eschew the depiction of actions and events and bound to concern itself with the representation of body, but merely that such graphic art as is in fact juxtaposed must accept these restrictions.

So, postponing any description of psychology for a moment, let us seek an understanding of "juxtaposition" that is as strongly connected with the idea of art as may be. Once that is firmly in place the psychology can probably be fairly quickly dealt with. Undoubtedly Lessing's idea is that juxtaposition of signs is something forced on the painter by his working in colour (paint) and on the sculptor by his working in stone (or metal or wood). And from the words that he most frequently uses it is plain that he takes what is executed in these media to be juxtaposed in that the identifiable material constituents of the work making up its signs stand next to one another in space or, to put it more precisely than he was concerned to, that they are related by the ancestral of contiguity. So, for each material part of a work of painting or sculpture, it is necessarily contiguous in two or three dimensions with any other arbitrarily chosen constituent of the same work, or contiguous with some part that is contiguous with that part, or . . . etc. Thus effectively to say that the artist's signs are juxtaposed is to make the claim that his work is necessarily continuous.

Only it is not true that all works of visual art are continuous and that no gaps ever exist between their various material parts. While we can certainly admit that the vast majority of paintings and sculptures we and Lessing know are of this sort, roughly paintings that lie within the unbroken bound of a canvas's edge, and sculptures cut or moulded in a single block of matter, there are undoubtedly cases which are not. To take a recurring example, in an Annunciation we may find the painted figures of Virgin and Archangel detached from one another and placed on either side of an altar, or the carved figures of the two set upon a balustrade flanking the steps up to the choir, as for instance at Santa Maria dei Miracoli in Venice. Here the contiguity condition is unfulfilled, and the required necessity of Lessing's claim under threat.

Occasionally it will be plain that such apparent counter-examples are easy enough to defeat. So we can point out that the space between the parts of the carved or painted work itself constitutes part of the work, or better put, has a representational significance of its own. This is certainly so in Santa Maria, where the priest or server – and now, sadly, only the admiring visitor – who mounts those steps feels himself almost miraculously hallowed by passing through the space that lies between Mary and Gabriel, as he most certainly would not if he thought of himself as merely passing through the physical space that separates the two carved figures representing those persons. Similarly with seemingly non-continuous frescoes that artists like Tiepolo or Veronese will paint to overcome breakdowns of continuity that are imposed by the architectural furnishings of a wall, making those furnishings part of the depicted scene, with the effect that real windows double as windows in the representation, and a real pilaster becomes a pillar in the picture behind which something of what we see on either side of it is obscured.

But these are plainly sophisticated devices, not regularly employed. There is nothing impossible, or even uncommon, for a single painting to be broken up by wall furnishing that has no representational significance, and nothing strange or remotely difficult to understand, about divided Annunciations where the space between the pictorial elements is mere material space. (With Annunciations it is particularly clear that this is happening when, imagining the two halves put together, we find that there is already sufficient continuous space represented between the two figures to make any addition achieved by separating the two halves otiose.) So although the purely spatial reading of "juxtaposition" is notably improved by abandoning extensionality and requiring not continuity simpliciter but representationally significant continuity instead, it will still not capture all the painting and sculpture that we and Lessing are familiar with.

Although Lessing constantly speaks in spatial terms, talks of figures and colours *in dem Raume* and uses the spatial verb "*nebeneinanderstehen*", an alternative would be to take the notion of juxtaposition as fundamentally temporal, meaning more that the material parts of the artist's work must all coexist in time than that they should be spatially continuous. Here extensionality is reinstated, and the breaches in the continuity condition that could not be mended even by abandoning it would not matter, since where we do come across representationally non-significant breakdowns, the discontinuous parts of the same work will still all exist at once. It is uncertain even whether Lessing would find much to disagree with here despite his preoccupation with spatiality, since put together with the requirement noted above, that to be aesthetically judged a work of art needs to be synthetically (*auf einmal*) graspable, the coexistence condition will bring with it pressure on the spatial proximity of the work's signs. For as discontinuity increases so surveyability in thought – and not just surveyability in the field of vision – is made more difficult.[6] Hence to interpret "juxtaposition" in temporal terms is not altogether to abandon Lessing's concern for the spatial relationship of signs.

To make this change does not leave everything of importance untouched however. Most strikingly, it becomes impossible now to defend the claim in terms of which Lessing's main thesis is couched, that it is the medium of art that imposes the restrictions on its subject matter. There is nothing at all impossible about the supposition that the day should come when paints are on sale that change their hue in the course of an afternoon according to the intensity of light that falls upon them. So the painter may then be challenged to use a pigment that moves from Titian red to silver-grey to represent in some graphic detail the progressive ageing of a woman's hair within that span of gallery time. Likewise for the possibility of development of the sculptor's materials with unfamiliar sorts of instability. In such cases we should have no particular reason for insisting that the new kinds of work were executed in a new medium unknown to earlier artists. The painter would still be working in paint of colour, and the sculptor in metal or stone. Hence the media we know cannot be said to enforce juxtaposition as a matter of a priori necessity. And as the example of the ageing woman shows, it would be overambitious for Lessing to claim that the medium of paint rigorously forbids

---

[6] By the expression "surveyability in thought" I mean only the ability that our perception of the signs has to be informed by our experience of their fellows. As above, talk of "synthesis" here is also to be understood in this way, rather than in the more pictorial way familiar to one from the A version of the *Critique of Pure Reason* and elsewhere, which suggests that we hold together in the mind at one and the same time different images or ideas or "representations" of perceived objects.

the successful graphic representation of change or of sequences of events. Here we meet a further limitation on the power of the *Subject Matter Thesis* to establish full-blooded anti-transparency of the kind Lessing wanted.

Maybe this is no more than we have to accept. And perhaps the damage is not too great. For there is another possible answer to the question "Where does the juxtaposition of the artist's signs stem from?" that Lessing could accept, and which would leave him with something better to say than that the artist who happens to execute his work in coexisting signs can not graphically represent anything other than bodies. What I have in mind is that this restriction derives not from the medium, but from a particular category of art in which painter and sculptor usually opt to work, and that this choice of category forces onto their productions those temporal and spatial relations between the signs that the works of art Lessing was concerned with all have.[7]

Now of course it would be of no use to say that the category in question is defined in terms of the extensional relationships between signs that have gone into the explication of *juxtaposition*. For then we should have only the tautological assertion that of necessity art whose signs are juxtaposed, is juxtaposed. But independently of this undesirable consequence there are two good reasons against offering such a specification of category anyway. The first is that when the artist elects to work in a particular category, the category's specification must itself offer the promise of sufficiently interesting *aesthetic* achievement to motivate the choice. But if all that goes into the specification is that the signs must be coexistent and normally be continuous, too little will be revealed to make choice in favour of it intelligible. Second, and more important, the category specification we come up with ought to be full enough for the artist working within it to determine whether what he does within the limits it imposes can be aesthetically assessed,

---

[7] I take the term "category" from Kendall Walton's "Categories of Art", *Phil. Review*, 1971. To do the best possible for Lessing I have been forced to devise a category that both traditional painting and traditional sculpture fit as distinct species. Innovative art could well belong to a different category. Even though I would not ultimately expect this particular specification of category to figure in any full taxonomy of the arts. I am sure that Walton is right to think that the notion of category is indispensable.

whether what he produces is in fact synthetically graspable. Now in the spirit of attempting to specify the category by purely extensional means and talking just about features of the signs, the best that could be done would be to say that the signs produced must enjoy *sufficient* persistence in their coexistence and possess *sufficient* continuity. Otherwise synthetic graspability will be made impossible or too difficult for all but the fanatic. Only when the question of how sufficiency of persistence or continuity is to be determined is posed it becomes clear that covert appeal to something quite other than the extensionally describable properties of the signs is being made, to wit appeal to what it is that those signs represent. For how long signs need to persist to be properly graspable in the imagination and now closely juxtaposed they need to be, is partly a matter of what it is that they represent. Roughly speaking the greater the complexity of their representational content, the longer will be the minimal permissible persistence of the signs and the greater will be the pressure on them for spatial compactness. Hence, I claim, allusion to the content of the work has to be made if the category is to be adequately specified. That way at least, a purely tautological derivation of the necessary juxtaposition of the signs will have to be avoided.

My suggestion is that the category of art with which Lessing is solely occupied here is that which *puts all its (visually) recognizable representational content on display at once*. We might perhaps call this the category of *the iconic*. This covers all the art that Lessing has in mind. Not insisting that all the signs should be surveyable by any one individual at once it avoids difficulties that would otherwise be raised by the three-dimensional arts and those two-dimensional works that trade on exploitable ambiguities of their signs. It offers a rich contrast with music and poetry of the kind Lessing wanted. It is full enough in intellectual content to offer comprehensible motivation to the artist to work in the category. Lastly, it does permit the generation of informative necessary truths about the relations of signs among works that belong to the category. Thus, if the artist puts all the directly recognizable representational content of his work on display at once, he is bound to make the signs that convey this content all exist at once. Furthermore, as we saw, subject as his work is to the demand for synthetic graspability, he is bound to have a concern for the spatial continuity of his signs which can be overridden with impunity only if there is some aesthetic significance to be gained from the breakdown, or if it is forced upon him by the material context of his work. To think that it is open to him to do anything else in a systematic fashion is to write down the need for synthetic graspability, and effectively to take less than fully seriously the truth that what the artist produces he produces under the concept *art*.

We have reached a point then where, although the idea that the choice of medium can generate restrictions on subject matter through relations between the signs that the medium imposes has been abandoned, it is still reasonable to think that at least the most important of those same restrictions may emerge from the iconic category of art that painter and sculptor standardly employ. Because the category does generate the juxtaposition of signs that Lessing noticed, it is a further possibility that these restrictions may get explained in just the way that Lessing supposes. To see whether this idea can be made out, we have now to turn to the psychology that was set aside a little while ago. Gratifyingly enough, it appears to be a relatively easy matter to say why it is that bodies, and bodies alone, should be the proper objects of the graphic art that is constructed within the category defined. To appreciate this, we have only to take note of one relatively understressed feature of the way in which the artist achieves graphic effect, and to remind ourselves of one familiar metaphysical truth about the nature of observable processes.

In painting and sculpture graphic effect that comes anywhere near Lessing's demand for illusion can only be achieved where what we see is represented *in the signs*. The image-based thought we have of the object has to realize itself in vision at a particular point on the canvas or in the stone. Anything else that the artist gets us to think of with vivacity, be it within the frame of the work (as in the case of the harrowed countenance of Agamemnon beneath his cloak in Timanthes' picture (cf II, 19)) or beyond the limits of the work (as with the King and Queen in Velasquez' *Las Meninas* (Prado, Madrid)) will be better thought of as allusively suggested, however powerfully and precisely thought of as something that the picture represents by its signs, but not in them.[8] These cases, about which more will be said in Chapter 3, Lessing thinks of as peripheral to his main concern.

The metaphysical truth I alluded to is that an object involved in an observable process of change has to be in different, mutually exclusive, observable states at different successive moments. There is only a change from one state to another provided that at one moment the changing object is in a state that at a succeeding moment it is not in. So, for instance, a woman's hair can change from being Titian red to being silvery grey only if at one moment when it is not silvery-grey, it is Titian red, and at a later moment, when it is not Titian red, it is silvery-grey.

If we put these various matters together, we arrive at the following highly plausible claim, and one that lies very well in Lessing's mouth. For art belonging to the category of the iconic, there is an insuperable psychological obstacle to the achievement of graphic effect in the representation of change, or indeed anything other than that of physical objects as being in some determinate state or other. Subject to the juxtaposition relationships that are imposed with the adoption of this category, there are two, and so far as I can see, only two, ways in which the painter or sculptor might represent a process or a change – as opposed to a moment of a process or a change that is under way (as Fragonard does, for instance in *La Balancelle* (Wallace Collection, London) representing the girl not as swinging from A to B, but as in swing from A to B). In one way he will situate one and the same object at two different places in his canvas and represent it once as being φ and once as being ψ, where the idea to be conveyed is that the object is represented at different times and has changed from being φ to being ψ. When they have interested themselves with the representation of change, this has been the standard way for artists in the Western tradition to depict change or actions involving lapse of

[8] Things can be represented by a picture that are not represented in it. Thus we may say, using a *that*-clause, Velasquez represents that the King is sitting for his portrait and that he is wearing something blue. This is, in my usage, part of the representational content of the picture, though it need not be shown in the picture. The tentative specification of category in terms of *(visually) recognizable representational content* is meant to exclude what is represented by the picture but not in it.

time. There in the predella, for example, are Cosimo and Damian, just about to be slaughtered, and a little further to the right in the same painting there they are again duly decapitated. The artist has shown us their martyrdom. Alternatively, and as far as I know with very little significant precedent in our art, the artist has the theoretical possibility of getting the spectator to see the same figure in two incompatible ways, first say as φ and then as ψ, rather as we sometimes see the same sign in a Roman mosaic as the leading edge of a cube, and then as non-leading edge. The shift of aspect that we experience might then facilitate our seeing the representation on occasion as depicting a change of the object from one state to another. Perhaps the most common cases of this that we actually find are in those postcards or matchboxes that display the ogling model successively clad and then naked as the card is turned from side to side. (The manufacturer's aspiration would, I suppose, eventually be to develop the technique to the point at which he could say that the model was graphically shown stripping off.)

I say that both of these alternatives conform to the juxtaposition constraint, and while this is obviously enough so for the first of them, for the second it may sound surprising. But it should not do so. The reason is that while maybe no one can see the represented object at one and the same time as being both φ and as being ψ (and as shifting aspect from φ to ψ), none the less the figure is at one and the same time on display as being both φ and as being ψ (and as shifting aspect), though of course it is not on display to any one viewer as being both φ and ψ at one and the same time. And I contend that these two are the only ways in which change over time might be represented within the juxtaposition constraint since any other way we might have of visually representing change, as in a film or in a strip cartoon, or in a flip-though picture book, will involve a representational content that is not all on display at once. One part of it will be displayed to all the world, and then another part, while the first part becomes inaccessible and makes way for the images that follow.

It is clear that Lessing should say that neither of the two alternatives I have outlined will count against his dictum that painting can only make use of a single moment in the depiction of actions" (XVI, 115), since although we might find ourselves well able to understand representations of either sort, in neither case shall we be able to experience them as graphic. The obstacle to our doing so is slightly different, but undeniably real in each case. In the first of them graphicality in the representation of change will demand that we should first see the represented object as φ and then as ψ, and that when we see it as the one, we do not see it as the other. Now, when the subject of change, Cosimo, say, is represented for us twice, at different points of the canvas, while we may pay little attention to one of the representations we cannot help being aware that there are two, and therefore can not experience the one as giving way to the other. (The same difficulty will defeat the sculptor who places the two figures back to back, where even if we do not see them both at once, as we do in painting, we still are aware that both coexist). What would be needed then would be to get the viewer to experience what he sees as the yielding of one state to the other, and while it is not absolutely impossible to engineer this within the limitations of the iconic category it is so difficult to arrange as hardly to be worth trying.[9]

The other possibility might seem more hopeful, only its effective absence from our tradition of pictorial representation should lead us to expect to find it beset with difficulty. Here what is required is that the viewer directly recognize the depicted objected as changing from being φ to being ψ, without being able to pin that change down to any observable underlying change in the canvas or the stone. Again this is no logical impossibility, as we can see from the way in which a painter like Monet can sometimes draw on instabilities of visual aspect-fixing in creating an illusion of water shimmering in the picture,[10] or the sophisticated and successful postcard

[9] Not *logically* impossible. We could set signs spinning on the faces of a large cube, all visible to someone or other at one, and for each spectator create the illusion of movement, say. That would be a juxtaposed work by these standards. But why go to these lengths? It's more fun at the flicks.

[10] Anyone preferring to say that Monet shows us water ashimmer rather than shimmering (and who spots a difference here parallel to "not as swinging, but in swing") may like to consider the exploitation of aspect-shifting used in Op Art. There it would sometimes be difficult to refuse to say that we see something as moving from one state to another.

manufacturer achieve the illusion of his model stripping off. But these are quite exceptional cases. In general the psychological requirement that has to be fulfilled before we can see a change is that the signs themselves register a change, and to do this time is needed in which one sign can be replaced by another, in my example for the sign that starts off as Titian red to change to being silvery-grey. Immediately this is conceded, we have left the realm of juxtaposed painting and are approaching the art of film or some other, non-iconic, kind.

IV

Lessing has won a certain intermediate victory then. He has given us good reason to think that save for a limited number of exceptional cases of peripheral artistic importance juxtaposed representations are bound to encounter great psychological obstacles to the graphic depiction of change over time, and hence of actions and sequences of events. Consequently the painter or sculptor working in his familiar category of art will be well advised to occupy himself with objects as they are, or as they can be seen to be, at a single moment and not as they are, or appear, at successive moments. But if this victory is to serve his further purposes, he has also to make out the converse claim as it concerns the poet, viz that the poet cannot express bodies and is well advised to confine himself to the graphic representation of actions and events. This we know that Lessing believes, but with what justification remains to be seen.

An essential characteristic of poetry is that its works are not "juxtaposed", but "successive", by which, preserving symmetry, must be meant that its signs do not allow the display of all their directly given representational content at once, but only sequentially. Taken in this way even if we thought of the signs of a poem as constituted by the words as printed on the page, they would not be juxtaposed for the simple reason that except in the rarest of cases their understandable content cannot be gathered at once. This contention will be even more solidly based for anyone who notes Lessing's own inclination to elucidate poetry in terms of sound (cf XVI, 114), and who agrees with Paul Valéry that we can only make sense of the idea of poetry in connection with that of a voice, and hence of a temporally extended reading of the signs.[11] Then poetry is quite securely successive, for the understanding of its signs that an audience comes to must be so organised in time that it roughly coincides with the delivery of the words. Since in a reading one line gives way to another, even when the audience is thought of consisting of many different members it will be well-nigh impossible to envisage all the representational content of the poem being conveyed to any assemblage of them all at once.

Just as Lessing offers a psychologized account of the impossibility of juxtaposed art representing action or change, so too for the obstacles that confront poetry in the representation of bodies:

> The poet, who can only show the elements of beauty after one another refrains from the representation of bodily beauty as such altogether. He feels that these elements cannot possibly have the same effect when ordered successively as they do when they are juxtaposed: he feels that the concentrating look we want to subject them to after their enumeration does not yield a coordinated picture; that it goes beyond the power of the human imagination to represent to itself the effect on us of this mouth, these eyes and this nose all together, – unless we can recall a similar composition in nature itself or elsewhere in art. (XX, 145).

What is important to remember here is that as Lessing takes himself to have shown that in the case of art the painter cannot achieve graphic representation of change over time, so in the case of poetry it is the graphic delineation of bodies that purportedly lies beyond the poet's capabilities. Of course any half-competent poetaster can represent bodies alright, and Lessing is scathing in his criticism of lesser lights than Homer

---

[11] Paul Valéry, "Opening Lecture in Poetics", in *Aesthetics, Collected Works XIII* (New York, 1964), p. 100. "A poem on paper is nothing but a piece of writing, subject to all the uses to which such writing can be put. But among its possibilities there is one, and only one, that creates the conditions under which it will take on the force and form of action. A poem is a discourse that demands and introduces a continuous connection between *the voice that is* and the voice *that is coming* and *must come*. And this voice must be such as to command a hearing and call forth an emotional state of which the text is the sole verbal expression. Take away the voice – the right voice – and the whole thing becomes a sequence of signs connected only in the sense that they are traced after one another".

who think that this is just what they have to do. So in praise of Homer himself we find him commenting on *Iliad*, v, 43/7 that "we see the clothes in the poet's description of the robing: anyone else would have depicted the robes down to the last fringe, and shown us nothing of the action itself" (XVI, 117).

To judge whether the reasoning is plausible we should pause for a moment over the way in which Lessing takes it that graphic effect is achieved in poetry. All that has been said on the subject so far is that the artist of whatever kind proceeds graphically as he lays down signs the correct appreciation of which involves his public in vividly imagining the sensible features of the depicted objects. In the specific case of the visual arts though, we have said that this effect must be achieved in such a way that what is imagined should be perceived in the signs themselves, but evidently no such demand can be imposed on the poet except in the very most restricted of cases. The signs cause thoughts that are evidently not rooted in the sound of the reader's voice in the way that what we see in a picture is rooted in the pigment laid upon the canvas. (It is interesting to ask why there is this asymmetry. Could it be because what we directly see are objects rather than appearances, whereas what we directly hear are sounds and not the objects that are their sources?)

If in poetry, we cannot appeal to anything like the seeing-in phenomenon that is so indispensable in the visual arts, how are we to draw the distinction that Lessing calls on both in art and in poetry between what is directly expressed and what is merely allusively suggested? The only device I can think of adapts a distinction of Richard Wollheim's between two ways in which imagination proceeds,[12] actively and passively, and elucidates the graphic representations of poetry in terms of passive, and the allusively suggested, in terms of active, imagination. In my usage, imagination is passive when the thoughts to which a reading of a poem gives rise are tightly controlled by the words

---

[12] In "Imagination and Identification" in *On Art and the Mind* (London, 1974). The distinction Wollheim draws defines imagination as passive in its thought of something when in order to be imagining that thing it is obliged to entertain a particular determinate thought. Thus to be imagining myself reciting the *Aeneid* I have to think of myself starting off "*Arma virumque cano . . .*" My own use of the distinction diverges from his slightly at this point.

that are read, so that if I read them with full understanding I have to have these thoughts; on the other hand imagination is active in so far as understanding of the words leaves me latitude in what thought to think. Thus when the poet gives me to understand that things are ordered in such and such a determinate way in virtue of the words he uses, his figures of speech, the cadence of his line and his patterns of rhyme, what he conveys will be graphically or expressively put to the extent that it would be a failure of my understanding of him not to have just *these* thoughts. On the other hand, when a writer does no more than suggest a framework within which imagination runs free and does not indicate how the details are to be filled in, then no matter how vivid are the ideas that I have as I allow imagination at work, what I think is not graphically expressed in the poem so much as allusively suggested by it.

With the distinction between the graphic and the allusive drawn along these rough lines, it can seem entirely reasonable for Lessing to say that it will be practically impossible for the poet to achieve graphic expression of bodies. The reasoning he can use follows very closely the train of thought quoted from XX, 145. If what we are aiming for is a graphic depiction of a body, we shall require the sensible image that the words provoke to be relatively full, in that our thought must be passively generated by what the poet writes. Merely to indicate the odd detail will not do, for in completion of the whole too much will be left to imagination in its active function, and then the figure will turn out to be suggested rather than expressed.

This much said, it might appear quite impossible to achieve graphic success in the poetic delineation of bodies. Yet to think this would be a mistake. Even in comparatively short passages expressiveness can be achieved on occasion. To take the simplest case, provided that the body in question is a fairly regular one it is relatively easy to convey in a few words how it appears. Consider a uniform cube, baize green in colour and of a velvety texture, having two inches long edges. In a brief description, suitably tailored for style, pretty full sensible information might be vividly conveyed in such a way that the imagination is almost entirely passive and the thought maximally graphic over a limited range. So there is no absolute barrier to the poet expressing bodies, any more than there was to the painter expressing events. Only it should be clear that for bodies that he might have any serious interest in depicting his task is going to be exceedingly difficult. The moment he departs from regular figures, or from figures of a type that are so familiar to us that the use of certain words inevitably leads us to think of them – and the last sentence of the quotation warns us not to put too much reliance on that – the only way the poet can proceed without permitting his reader to exercise his imagination fairly actively is to extend the indications he gives about the body he wants to express, and then it will take longer and longer for him to provide his reader with the cues he needs to provoke adequately full and vivid thought.

It is at this point that Lessing correctly says that the human imagination quickly enough finds its limits and ceases to be able to coordinate the information it is given. One can of course go on till doomsday supplying information that renders the theoretically constructible image fuller and fuller, only a theoretically constructible image is rarely one that we can synoptically achieve,[13] and that for two obvious reasons. First a limitation is imposed on what we can construct by what we can remember. As one reads a poem and gives one's attention to the line being pronounced, so the capacity to hold before one in persisting sharp focus the lines that have preceded quickly diminishes. Second, and more subtly, we have to beware of treating poetry any less holistically than we treat art. As there, so here the force of any single piece of information that the poet gives will be tempered by the way in which it lies together with information he gives us about the same and other objects elsewhere in the poetic context. So not only does the graphic expression demand of the reader that he have an excellent memory for details left behind as he reads on, but it also demands a high degree of sensitivity in the readjustment of previously entertained thought in the light of detail that is introduced only later on as he makes progress through the work.

By themselves these truths about our psychology ensure that graphic representation of bodies in literature is something

[13] Compare Lessing's remarks at XVII, 126/7 on Virgil's non-graphic, didactic (*dogmatisch*) account of a good heifer at *Georgics*, iii, 51–62, where the achievement of a synoptic lively image is not what he is aiming for.

Lessing is right to hold beyond the compass of most poetic talent. And when we compound the difficulties by remarking the pervasive vagueness of language that is liable to leave more and more work to be done by the active imagination and to cut down even further the employ of imagination that is passive, we may very well say that the undertaking of expressing bodies is as little worth the candle for the poet as the graphic expression of actions and sequences of events was shown to be for the painter.

V

As far as the negative claims about art and poetry go everything is apparently well then. All that is outstanding now for the erection of the required strong contrast between the two of them is the positive reflection for poetry parallel to that which was granted for art, *scilicet* that the poet is significantly better at home with the graphic representation of events and actions than he is with that of bodies. If Lessing can establish this then the *Subject Matter Thesis* will be made out (within its limitations) in a way that is genuinely powerful enough to upset his Horatian opponents.

Just as in the case of painting Lessing argues that it is the juxtaposed nature of the signs that facilitates the synthetic construction of the image, so for poetry his claim is that the successive character of the poet's words and the images they give rise to, is what makes for the expressibility of actions and events. Only the first of these two claims is far more plausible than the second, and it is quite impossible to share Lessing's innocent enthusiasm for the analogical reasoning he espouses to make his point. Pursuing the analogy of art, Lessing argues that those obstacles to the depiction of events that the artist encounters do not arise for the poet; nor does he face those difficulties that thwart him in any attempt he makes to express bodies in his verse. To Lessing it seemed evident that the very lapse of time that is required for the poet to be able to retail events and actions is for him an aid and not a hindrance to the achievement of the graphic image. The idea is fundamentally that the events that are graphically brought before the mind's eye by the reading themselves take place over time, and, as it were, the verse keeps pace with them, whereas bodies are inevitably left behind by it and fade away as they drop out of view.

Even though Lessing does not fully articulate this thought it is clear enough what he is getting at. Only once we take it at face value, we see it running into a difficulty that makes it practically useless. This is that it trades quite illicitly on an assumption of events enjoying a kind of atomicity that can be reckoned on to excuse them from making their appearance in poetry via any synthetic exercise of the imagination. Lessing seems to think that we shall succeed in thinking graphically of events that the poet recounts without having to temper the way we think of one event in the light of how we think of others, without in fact having to think of them as being together. For unless this were so, the poet would be just as much hampered by the limitations of memory and the holistic aspects of imagination as he is when he comes to attempt the graphic expression of bodies. That some such assumption as this does underlie Lessing's thought can be seen from the way in which he speaks of his favourite examples of graphically represented events, of Pandarus' hunting (XV, 112/3), of the robing of Agamemnon (XVII, 117), of the construction of Achilles' shield (XVIII, 134), for all the time he speaks as though one constituent event of these activities is entirely detachable from the others. But in fact it is quite impossible for the imagination to treat them so in the formation of its graphic thoughts. One only has to reflect that each event is an event *in a sequence*, and that imagination can only conjure up the sequence *as such* if it recalls vividly where the sequence starts and just what its composing moments are and are like. Here what Lessing has to say about the limitations of memory and synthetic imagination applies as much to the representation of events as it does to that of bodies.

A second point is equally telling, even though Lessing thought that it was obvious how it should be met. It is that as he himself says "actions cannot exist by themselves, but must attach to certain objects (*Wesen*)" (XVI, 114). The natural inference to draw from this truth is that the graphic delineation of objects can not be achieved except through the graphic delineation of objects that the events in point involve. Yet if we are already persuaded that the graphic depiction of bodies is a practical impossibility for the poet, how can it be any less impossible for him to express the single event, let alone the sequence of events, that involves them? It cannot. All the difficulties that Lessing believes to infect the poet's attempts to capture the body as the artist does must equally attach to each of those moments of which sequences of events are constituted and which the poet has to bring vividly to our mind if he is to respect Lessing's exhortations.

Lessing's own reaction to the realization that events are dependent on bodies is swift and far reaching in its consequences. It is to say that the poet need only *suggest* the bodies, just as the painter in his representation of bodies in action pictures only the most pregnant moment, from which preceding and later moments are easily comprehensible. "Likewise, he says, in its progressive imitations poetry can only use a single quality of a body, and has therefore to choose that one from which arouses the most sensible image of the body relevant to its purposes." (XVI, 115)

The effect of this recommendation is certainly to do something to relieve Lessing from the pressure of the two criticisms just made. If the poet in his expression of action is allowed to suggest the body involved in it by means of a suitable partial description, then the fact that it is beyond the practical scope of imagination to achieve more than this in the construction of an image that is determinately laid down by the poet will be of no account. The objections lapse. But of course only so long as we are still prepared to regard the outcome as graphic. Here Lessing faces a dilemma. If the poet does not abide by the demand to be graphic he will run the risk of being a mere prosaist (XVII, 122); on the other hand if he does not abandon the directly expressive for the sake of the allusive and the suggestive he will have no proper subject. Then the only true poet would be he who kept silent.

Evidently the only thing for Lessing to do is to relax the notion of the graphic as it applies to poetry – to say, that is, that in so far as the poet is concerned, expressive writing must involve the reader's *active*, as well as his passive, imagination. True, the poet thereby gives up some measure of fine control of his work, but at least he does not deprive himself of voice. Now it is clear that this remedy to his problem is one that Lessing is in fact willing enough to accept. That emerges from his approval of Homer's practice of describing objects by a single qualifying adjective (XVI, 116), on the basis of which the reader is given enough to go on to conjure up the lively image of the events that he needs to. Only this concession (or emendation) has its consequence. And that must be that by this relaxed view of what it is for poetry to be graphic, the obstacles to the truly poetic description of *bodies* are now no more real than are the obstacles to the expression of events. What we say about the one, we can equally well say about the other. Once the expressive in poetry is detached from any (even distant) analogue of the idea of seeing-in that binds the painter, the limitations neither of synthetic imagination nor of memory operate to exclude or enjoin any particular choice of subject matter. And this is important; for its effect is to deprive Lessing of the strong contrast between the arts that he is looking for to upset the transparency claims of his opponents. While we have agreed that the painter can not graphically express events, but can express bodies, the poet now is ultimately free to select his subject matter at will, provided only that his reader is able to conjure it up vividly in his mind's eye. The anti-transparency contentions are thus in the end no better supported by the *Subject Matter Thesis* than they are by the *Beauty Thesis*.

This weak contrast is the best Lessing can have, I suggest. But it is surely pertinent now to ask if he can really have even that. For what is it that obliges the painter to paint graphically? Not, we saw in Chapter 1, the idea of representation itself. Nor, as we shall see in Chapter 3, is it that there is no enrichment to be brought to a painting by the spectator's application to it of his *active* imagination, which will take him beyond what he can see in the signs. Rather it must be simply that in painting graphic effect has to be exhausted by the notion of seeing-in. But when it is allowed that it is practically impossible for the painter who adopts this sort of expressive depiction as his exclusive goal to paint anything other than bodies and the way they appear, it is a real question that every practitioner of representational art is bound to ask himself, why he should ever want to limit himself to the narrow compass that this particular choice of style imposes. As we shall see, some of the very most interesting thoughts Lessing has about imagination and the richness of visual art inevitably imply abandoning this constricting limitation. In the end the artist who takes Lessing seriously on these topics may well feel that the *Subject Matter Thesis* need constrain his art as little as it does the poet's and then that even a weak contrast between the two is ultimately difficult to maintain.

3

Transparency and Imagination

In their different ways the arguments examined in the two previous chapters have been limited in their scope. *Argument A* of Chapter 1 attempted to erect distinct canons of good taste in art and in poetry conceived within the Hellenic mode, and the *Beauty Thesis* and the *Subject Matter Thesis* of Chapter 2 looked no further than to art of one medium or another that was representationally graphic to secure the same conclusions. In the third chapter of "Laocoon" however, in the course of his discussion of the *Laocoon* group itself, Lessing presents a rather more general argument for the contention that the artist is subject to constraints that do not bind the poet – more general in that it supposedly reaches to any representational art whatever, and not to art of the graphic variety alone. True enough, even if his reasoning is successful here, as it has not really been before, it will not fully establish the anti-transparency claim in either of the two forms I originally presented it. None the less, the interest and breadth of vision that the argument enjoys in its own right makes it well worth discussing irrespective of its eventual fortune in Lessing's essay.

I

The reflections in point concern the role of imagination in the proper experience of the visual arts, and once again they are designed in the first instance to persuade the reader how improper it would be for the authors of the *Laocoon* group to represent the priest as crying out. Adverting to the sculptor's necessarily limited concern with a single moment of the whole action, and the painter's even more limited concern with a single viewpoint from which the action can be presented, Lessing goes on (III, 12):

> It is evident that the single moment and the point of view from which the whole scene is presented cannot be chosen with too great a regard for its effect. But only that which gives free rein to the imagination is effective. The more we see, the more we must be able to imagine. And the more we add in the imagination the more we must think we see. In the full course of an emotion no point is less suitable for this than its climax. There is nothing beyond this, and to present the utmost to the eye is to bind the wings of fancy and compel it, since it cannot soar above the impressions made on the senses, to concern itself with weaker images; shunning the visible fulness already represented as a limit beyond which it cannot go. So, when Laocoon sighs the imagination can hear him scream; but if he screams, then imagination can move neither to a higher plane nor to a lower one without seeing him in a more tolerable, hence less interesting state. Either it hears him groan, or it sees him already dead.

To assess the force of these lines we need to recall the context from which they are taken. At the beginning of the chapter Lessing has briefly considered the proper end of art and identified it as pleasure achieved either through beauty or through truth and expression. It quickly becomes plain that for him the best measure of the artist's success is given by the way his work responds to these demands as it is exposed to deep and extended scrutiny, and not just as it strikes the fleeting glance of the man whose closest attention is given elsewhere. It is this commitment to the extended view that introduces the appeal to imagination that we find in the quoted passage; for it is that which is supposed to afford the artist and the spectator the resource they need to fend off the prospect of loss of freshness and dulling of pleasure that repeated extended viewing of the single work is liable to bring. That, I take it, is how we are to read the otherwise (to me) incomprehensible sentence "the more we see, the more we must be able to imagine". Exercise of imagination on the part of the viewer will keep the oft seen work alive for him, failing which it will lose its appeal and measure up poorly to the test of pleasure achieved by beauty or by expression.[1]

It would certainly be wrong here to be put off by Lessing's assumption about the importance of the repeated and extended view. There are, indeed, art forms that do not attempt to engage men's deepest interest and that see themselves simply as accompaniments to something more engrossing – *Tafelmusik*, manuscript illumination, Pompeian fresco, to name but three – but it would be no loss to Lessing to admit that his argument from imagination may not apply to these rather marginal sorts of art. For one thing, not all of them are cases of figurative art – and it is only there that the transparency thesis applies and is to be contested: for another, these arts are very possibly parasitic on the existence of those others for the enjoyment of which the engagement of the spectator's close interest is essential. It is even plausible to say that where art aims at greatness rather than just at excellence of its kind, it must engage the closer and deeper view, and it would be no derogation from Lessing's most extensive aim to say that *great* painting, unlike poetry of equal stature, has to observe restrictions that are forced upon it by the way imagination enriches it when we attend to it in the proper manner.

Imagination, then, works to prevent the finer art from palling. And we are told in the immediately preceding sentence that what is especially important for imagination to be effective is that it should be given free rein. That may well strike us as curious. For it is natural to envisage someone who allows his imagination free play as he stands before a statue or a canvas to be phantasizing about the subject, somewhat in the style of Walter Mitty. So, for instance we might for a minute suppose Lessing to be suggesting that when I confront the *Laocoon* group in the Vatican, it should somehow be an index of that work's stature that as I do so it is particularly easy for me to think of myself as some heroic Grand Captain about to enlist the help of the assembled tourists gathered round and storm up the

[1] I take it that expression is graphic, in the sense discussed in Chapter 2, and that truth is included under it for Lessing in virtue of his assumption that what is graphic induces belief in the real presence of the depicted object.

beach to the rescue of the wretched priest and his sons. But of
course nothing of the sort was in Lessing's mind; and there are
at least three good reasons why to think of the exercise of
imagination in this vein would unfit it for the role that he
intends for it.

First, the encouragement of phantasy of the Mittyish kind is
all too private. Allowing our thoughts to wander in this way,
we too easily escape the control of the artist and his work. For
the content of private phantasy is just what *we* make it and in
so far as it plays freely it is hardly answerable to the work that
sparks it off.[2] Since its richness has its source in what is not a
shared and public matter, but depends only on the individual
psychology of the phantasist, however engrossing he may find
it, no credit for the pleasure can attach to the work, or through
the work to its author.[3] Second, private phantasy can only be
developed as our concentration detaches itself from the work
that provokes it. It is then the phantasy that engages our
attention properly speaking and not the work. But for Lessing,
the free play of imagination has to coexist with, *fortify even*, the
attention we fix on the work, and thus be of a kind that is
resistant to the temptation to private phantasy. Last, it is
commonly observed that where phantasy is encouraged by a
work of art and is of a kind uncontrolled by the artist, it is not
something that speaks in favour of the work *qua* art. We think
it too weak at a certain point to hold our attention in its own
right, or else we see it as implicitly abandoning pretensions to
artistic consideration altogether, and serving some more
dubious end. In either case we regard the invitation to this
exercise of imagination as a defect and not a strength.

So, straightway we are required to find a different way of
taking Lessing's talk of imagination's free play, and one that
permits of exercise within the artist's control, that is in a way
that makes it answerable to the work that invites it. Only then
will the richness that the imagination brings in its engagement

---

[2] Not all phantasy in art is private though. Sometimes phantasy may be provoked
under the control of the artist for a particular aesthetic purpose. My negative remarks
about phantasy in what follows are aimed exclusively at phantasy of the private kind.

[3] The nicest way of putting the demand for publicity is surely Fielding's at the start of
Tom Jones: "An author ought to consider himself not as a gentleman who gives a
private or eleemosynary treat, but rather as one who keeps a public ordinary, at which
all persons are welcome for their money".

with the artist's representation be genuinely attributable to the work and properly bear upon its critical evaluation. Similarly, it is only on that condition that reflections about the content of imagination as provoked and controlled by a representation of a particular scene bear with any critical relevance on the artist's selection of and manner of handling his subject matter. Hence only thus have they any hope of supporting Lessing's claims about the divergent nature of art and poetry. The challenge, of course, is to see how close we can come to finding a specification of the free play of imagination that meets this demand.

At the very outset one might doubt whether this challenge can be met, since there may appear to be something paradoxical about the requirement that the spectator exercise his imagination *within the artist's control.* Does not the actuality of the one, the exercise of imagination, exclude the possibility of the other, the control of the artist? However, it is not here that the greatest difficulty lies. In one way, and a way that arises at a point in the dialectic well before Lessing himself need even mention the topic, it is plain that the spectator cannot but exercise something that Lessing is happy enough to speak of as his imagination just as the artist directs. As he faces the marks on the canvas or the words on the page, the viewer or the reader is caused to entertain determinate, though unasserted, thoughts by what the artist has laid down. In so thinking of the scene depicted, and rooting the thought at each point in the marks that are set there before him, he may perhaps be thought to exercise imagination.[4] Furthermore, he does so correctly (for the most part) as he entertains the thoughts that the artist means him to do. At points where he diverges in his thought from the artist's control, or where his thoughts wander away from what the canvas or the text will support, we say that he has misunderstood the work before him. Then he is not using his imagination as he aims to – assuming of course that his aim

---

[4] Here and in the rest of this chapter I shall adopt as relaxed a notion of imagination as may be. In fact I think that this involves far more than has a good claim to the title, as I argue in "Imagination and Pictorial Understanding", *PASS*, 1986. But for the purpose of allowing Lessing the greatest freedom in this very general argument, we want to pick up as wide a variety of thought as possible as might be supposed relevant to our comprehension and enjoyment of the figurative arts. That it is not always properly called "imaginative" should be neither here nor there for Lessing's ultimate ends.

is to appreciate the work as it demands. So here, in the simplest of cases, we can see that the control of the viewer's imagination is something that is quite proper – essential even – for the artist to pursue.

Only cases like this can be of little help in understanding Lessing. For one thing, they are chosen from areas of our experience of figurative art which is the very most immediate. It is that which is in play when we make the most straightforward identification of subject matter in a picture, or give the intellectually least demanding account of a statue. Nothing as bland as this will comfort the artist who proposes to rely on the power of imagination to preserve the interest and freshness of his work in the eyes of those who honour it with their protracted attention. If this is all imagination can do once shorn of the achievements of phantasy, the artist must reconcile himself to swift exhaustion of his work.

Secondly, even if imagination here does operate within the artist's control it cannot be said to enjoy *free rein*. In the first place it is unspontaneous in that there is very little the reader or viewer can do to prevent himself from having the prescribed (straightforward) thought that recognition of the represented scene consists in – provided only that he is sufficiently familiar with the category of art in point, that he has a reasonably developed view of the world's contents and that there is nothing much amiss with his sensory apparatus. Ready primed, imagination steps in willy nilly to provide them. In another way too, imagination is unfree in this sort of case, for as I have described it, it is closely tied to the canvas or the page. Everything in the immediate experience is pinned down to the signs provided by the text. So that far from being in free play, imagination is doubly restricted. And it is here that we may more pressingly sense an air of paradox than before: for while there is no great difficulty in the spectator exercising his imagination in a way that the artist controls, it may seem far less clear how he can do this in a way that leaves his imagination free at the same time, whether we think of that freedom in terms of spontaneity or in terms of thought that is not directly answerable to the signs that the artist lays down.

Nonetheless I believe it is plausible to think that there are ways in which this may be achieved, where even if imagination is not perhaps set free beyond all control, neither is it entirely constrained; and three such kinds of case in particular merit discussion. To give them labels I shall call them exercises of imagination that are *exploratory*, or *projective* or *ampliative*, and in respect of each the question will arise of what help it can be to Lessing both as a means of staving off the dulling of pleasure in ambitious works, and more distantly, as providing a route to the establishment of distinct regulative canons of good taste in the various arts. My discussion of each will revolve around its exercise in visual art, but this should not in the end make assessment of Lessing's comparisons between the arts impossible.

Exploratory Imagination. The kind of imagination just discussed, and set aside, has been that in which recognition of the representational content of a depiction is psychologically direct or immediate. Although directness of recognition is in part a matter of degree, and although different people will not always directly recognize the same things in a picture (even when in the end they do agree in their understanding of it), it stands in evident contrast to recognition of another sort on which we usually depend for a great deal of our pictorial understanding. This is the recognition that we arrive at, often laboriously and painstakingly, as we try to make the best overall sense that we can of the signs that the artist lays down, and say what it is that is represented in the canvas. To achieve this we frequently have to start off from what we recognize directly and then find a fuller and richer description of it that we ultimately come to see as fitting what the picture shows us. So, to take an example, in a Goya in the Museum at Agen we may directly recognize a monk slumped in a chair, but not know quite what to make of his repose. That becomes clear only when it strikes us that the band around his neck can be nothing but a garrote, and thus his repose, the repose of death. The shock we experience is delayed, and delayed because imagination (or less committally, thought) has had to explore the possibilities in making sense of the signs, and had to travel beyond what it directly and immediately recognized. Without its exercise, we would not see that the picture depicts an attitude of death, hence without it, full understanding of the picture would be precluded.

An equally clear instance of the exercise of exploratory

imagination is in providing us with understanding of motivation. Thus in Gérard David's *Adoration* (Musée des Beaux Arts, Rouen) that we understand that the orchestra of angels around the Virgin are playing their music *in adoration* is something that we come to recognize only because of our direct recognition of who that woman and that child are. Without that knowledge we could not identify the motive that underlies the depicted angelic activity and could not arrive at a correct description or even a correct visual experience of the representational content of the picture. Nor, of course, could we enjoy the emotional response to it that the picture demands.

The contrast between these two sorts of understanding, the direct and the indirect – or better, the more and the less direct – serves to bring out how, in the latter case, though not in the former, imagination has a kind of freedom. Here it enjoys a freedom of spontaneity in that I exercise it at will in the light of a desire to make full sense of the work before me, as I also freely decide how far to pursue my exploration of the scene in making what I judge to be full sense of it. In its exploratory aspect, imagination operates in accordance with the spectator's sense of satisfaction or dissatisfaction with what he makes of the work. Direct understanding, by contrast, does not wait on any such sense; it precedes the will and does not respond to it. Then too, the imagination that is exercised in answer to the interpretative drive is directed by the viewer. The actual route he takes in search of full comprehension is one that is very largely up to him to fix, even though its goal is not. Of course it will sometimes happen that this freedom of direction is restricted by the artist determining that one element of his work has to be made sense of before another can fall into place, but for much of the time the route to understanding that the spectator takes is his to choose.

While being free in this way, in the other way I mentioned the exploratory imagination will be constrained. Once its aim is described as finding a full and rich account of what the painter has depicted, the result of our exploration is bound to the signs that the artist lays down. *This* (and here we insert what direct *and* indirect recognition have achieved) is what the artist has to show us. Anything else, we might want to say, that detached the output of imagination from the signs would loosen our understanding from the artist's control, and as such a step is taken deliberately, will move our thought more in the direction of private phantasy, or as it is taken inadvertently, will make for misunderstanding and misapprehension of what the artist offers us in his work.

It may be protested that I have far too easily assumed that control of thought through being rooted in the signs is one and the same thing as control of imagination by the artist. It will be said that we often seek the best overall sense of signs by appeal to matters that the artist himself did not contemplate, or could not have contemplated. The answer to this criticism may be brief here. It is that the best, or more exactly, an optimal, reading of his work is only to be found in a reading of the signs that could in principle have been offered by the artist himself, as well as by the later (or contemporary) spectator. The mere fact that the signs can tolerate what seems to a later eye a more gratifying overall construction than they could to the eyes of contemporaries cannot itself be sufficient ground for taking that as a better reading of the signs. The sense of satisfaction and dissatisfaction I alluded to in guiding interpretation has to be thought of as satisfaction in the understanding of the work that is offered, and it should be common to both parties to the transaction, artist and audience, that the best sense of the signs is one that would correctly explain their original laying down as well as one that finds an aesthetically replete sense for them. Failing that it is difficult to make sense of art as a public and social institution at all.[5] As an historical claim about what Lessing himself would have thought, this seems uncontestable. To him, it would be a grotesque idea that an interpretation of his work that the artist himself could not have envisaged might be defended as canonical. This should be plain when we remember that his remarks about the place of imagination in the understanding of sculpture are addressed directly to the artist: it is he who has to make room for it and control what its content shall be. It is not something that the viewer can be left to generate (entirely) for himself.

Is it correct to identify the exploratory work of the

---

[5] For greater detail here see R. Wollheim, "Criticism as Retrieval", Supplementary Essay IV of the Second Edition of *Art and its Objects* (Oxford, 1980), or my *The Test of Time*, (Oxford, 1982), Chs. 3 and 4.

imagination with what Lessing takes himself to be writing about? In one way the identification is appealing, for what has guided my description has been the idea that it lies within the competence of the artist to construct pictures or statues that reveal their content to the viewer little by little, and not immediately and all at once. So, in such cases the viewer has an incentive to return to the work and to give it his close attention over an extended period. Only by so doing will he in the end come to feel that satisfaction with his understanding of the whole that is held out as a promise to him when he views it for the first time, and the initial lack of which serves as an irritant that he seeks to neutralize through closer acquaintance and extended scrutiny. And this accords well with what Lessing writes, since the idea provides a clear way in which the artist is able to combat the threat of his work palling over time. He safeguards it against that fate by ensuring that it demand exploratory attention, and that the full array of satisfactions that it yields is not to be enjoyed except through this exercise of imagination.

In another way though, it may look as if what I have been describing is still at odds with what Lessing was thinking of, for in the passage I quoted he is quite explicit in saying that the imagination *adds* (*darzu denken*) to what the artist offers, and he illustrates his contention about the importance of imagination by examples that involve future or past events which are not in fact shown in the canvas, not visible from the single point of view with which the painter is supposedly concerned, and not visible from the single point of view from which he represents the momentary event. Only it is difficult to come to any clear decision about how serious this objection is. In the first place Lessing is far from expansive about how he thinks imagination is to be put to work, and nothing that he says indicates that it must operate in one manner only, the one, that is, which is illustrated by his chosen examples. Second, we should not overlook how very easy it is, even if mistaken, to think of what I am here calling explorative imagination as indeed *adding* to the picture or the statue something that is not shown there by the artist. I have been at pains to write of it as *discovering* what the depiction has to show us, but for someone who assumes that *direct* recognition will provide all that the picture actually displays, it will seem evident that the fuller interpretative description that we come to by attentive and exploratory viewing is something that we ourselves somehow furnish on top of that. Then, when such a man comes to give examples of imagination at work it would be easy and natural to choose cases in which this is indeed just what happens. Lessing's discursive elucidation of the working of imagination here is so exiguous that it is impossible to tell whether this conflation is one that he would easily make. Then, third, for someone so fixed on the idea of *graphic* representation as was Lessing, it would be easy to assume that everything imagination discovers that goes beyond what can be immediately seen in the picture is not something that is so much discovered in it as superadded to it. So for instance, when in *Las Meninas* we see Velasquez painting on the canvas that is turned away from us a portrait of the King and Queen, we enlarge our description of what we see along these lines, even though we do not see that portrait in the picture. The portrait itself is not shown us even though we recognize that it is there. In such a case as this, we still need to say that the exploratory imagination *discovers* what the picture we confront represents, only in doing so we abandon the idea that everything that is represented is directly shown.[6] Again it would be easy, but mistaken, to think that here exploratory imagination does add rather than discover, and tempting to think of Lessing making that mistake. (That it is a mistake can be seen from reflecting that we shall want to contrast this output of imagination, which tells us what is depicted if not shown, with that which involves itself with what is neither depicted nor shown, and which falls to the ampliative exercise of imagination's powers. Were we to speak of both as additive, the distinction would be hard to draw. In the latter case there is indeed addition, as we shall see, but the mere fact that Lessing talks of addition and cites examples which can only be described in that way cannot definitively exclude an interpretation of what he is saying in terms of exploratory understanding, which discovers while it does not add.)

[6] Cf Chapter 2, footnote 8.

Projective imagination. That Lessing was certainly aware that the imagination does sometimes operate other than in an exploratory way, that it takes us beyond both what is shown and what is not shown but nonetheless represented, is evident from his recurrent contrast between what is shown and what is suggested. This contrast can be drawn on in filling out our generous and relaxed typology of imagination's working that will complement (a), its function in phantasy, (b), its function in the recognition of what is directly shown and (c), its function in the exploratory identification of represented content.

In his "Imagination in the Experience of Art" (*Royal Institute of Philosophy Lextures*, Vol VII, 1973) R. K. Elliott draws attention to one way in which we feel it proper to experience Grünewald's *Buffetting of Christ* (Alte Pinakothek, Munich). That picture, it will be recalled, shows us a vicious-faced Roman soldier, arm uplifted, about to strike the defenceless Jesus. What it does not show us, not in the picture or even outside it (comparably with the way in which Velasquez represents that the King and Queen are present beyond that part of pictorial space appearing within the frame), is the blow that is struck. However, Elliott interestingly suggests that a common experience of the work is for the spectator to project himself into the picture by identifying with the soldier, and in imagination completing the blow that we see is about to fall. In this case he strikes the blow himself, and acquires a disconcerting self-knowledge in recognition of the pleasurable satisfaction that he experiences in doing so. Elliott goes on to ask whether the imagination might not here "contribute precisely what is necessary if the painter is to communicate his meaning" (ibid, p. 91).

What the example suggests is that there may be an activity of the imagination proper to the understanding of art that engages the spectator with the action of the depicted scene through encouraging him to project himself into it (either as actor, as here, on other occasions as passive participant), one that is not tied to the signs in the same way as before, but which, none the less, still lies within the power of the artist to control. If it can be made out that such an activity of the understanding can indeed evoke responses that are importantly thought of as true to the work, and if it is clear that they are as much phantasy-resistant as the work of the exploratory imagination was previously shown to be, the suggestion will be one that can sensibly be offered to Lessing.[7]

That such experience can be entirely proper to the work is to my mind suggested by the fact that it is sufficiently common and sufficiently predictable. Once it is known to be common, and is realized to be relatively surely foreseeable, then providing that it regularly occurs in a given case it must, failing special explanation, be presumed to have lain within the artist's intention that it should occur, or at least be imputable to him through recognition by the spectator of the artist's adoption of what are mutually understood means of evoking the responses that he does. As for predictability, one very special feature of the sort of imaginative activity that Elliott describes does much to facilitate this, and that is its very lack of spontaneity.

What I mean by saying that imagination here is unspontaneous is that we find it difficult to resist being pulled into the work through identification when once we are deeply engaged with it. In the Grünewald case the thought of delivering the blow in the soldier's person is one that presents itself to us without it being sought out as something to be unearthed and discovered. What makes it inevitable that we have the thought is that we can scarcely identify the action before our eyes without thinking it through to term and thinking it through to term as participants; and for the artist to encourage, control and make use of such thought, he need only have the knowledge of which sort of initiated activities are liable to present themselves to our minds in just such a way as this. With this knowledge in hand, he can predictably control the way in which his audience will think beyond the scope of the signs themselves, and truly then be said to enrich his work with a significance that derives from an experience that the imaginal projection brings with it.

From this description it should also follow that projective

[7] In his "Imagination and Pictorial Understanding", *PASS*, 1986, Richard Wollheim contests this suggestion on the grounds that it would involve us each in giving a different (and hence false) account of the picture's content. In its place he suggests we imagine more impersonally, and univocally, *the spectator* present or acting in the scene. I am myself unpersuaded by the objection, but even if it is correct the impersonal projection of the spectator into the scene would still fall to the exercise of projective imagination.

imagination is phantasy-resistant. We noticed before that phantasy tended towards privacy and unpredictability, and that it was in large measure voluntary. It also tended toward incompatibility with that engaged attention to the work on which just critical assessment must rest. Here, though, things are quite the reverse. The projective imagination operates within the artist's control, and only does so once the spectator's mind is fully engaged with the work. Furthermore it is relatively passive in its operation in that it has little choice in regard to its actual content up to the point at which predictability ends. Private phantasy, by contrast, is constrained by no such limitation. So on these two scores we have no cause for concern. But still we might wonder how good a case can be made out for saying that it was anything like this that Lessing had in mind when speaking of imagination in the terms he does at III, 23.

It certainly speaks in favour of this interpretation that it encourages us to be ready to speak of imagination as *adding* to the viewer's experience of the work. We have found here that he cannot think of himself as just discovering what the text has to reveal, but needs to engage himself with thought about what the work does not put on display. Only when we have something like this available will we be able to do anything like full justice to the illustrations that Lessing himself gives of imagination's working and to his demand that the artist leave room in his work for it to take the spectator beyond what is shown, to climaxes of emotion or to termini of sequences of events, the nature of which the artist is explicitly prohibited from attempting to depict. Indeed, the very strongest arguments for attributing this interpretation to Lessing is that it alone seems to make good sense of the critical conclusions that he wants to draw from his discussion of the subject. As I have put it, the events that encourage projective imagination are in the clearest cases those which have a natural terminus and which the mind is inclined to think through to term.[8] It will be obvious that if the terminus itself is represented, the imagination cannot have any scope for play of this sort. As Lessing puts it:

[8] In so far as a full typology of situations that encourage projection finds different sources for it than these, Lessing's argument will be less surely able to rely on it. How great an obstacle for him this is I let the reader judge.

there is nothing beyond this – and to present the utmost to the eye is to bind the wings of fancy . . . shunning the already represented visible fulness as a limit beyond which it can not go.

So, if the artist is to draw on this resource of imagination, he will be compelled to avoid the representation, recognizable either directly, or through the exploratory imagination, of climactic moments or termini of sequences. Then, finally, such a reading of Lessing's idea has a better capacity than the last to give some body to his insistence that imagination be given *a free rein*. Here imagination operates in a way that is importantly free from tight control by the text. It is not limited in justifying all of its thought by reference to some aspect of the signs, so that we can say that this is what we straightway see in it, or that this is what we recognize they ultimately have to show.

But are there not countervailing considerations too? It could be objected that if Lessing's exhortations are to be universally applicable, they could not be carried through. Only in *some* cases do we think that the imagination is at all challenged to work in this projective way. In the case of portraits, say, or in pre-Romantic landscapes, it is certainly not; even though there is room enough for the exploratory imagination to engage the spectator's extended interest. Second, the freedom of rein that the imagination can be acknowledged to have is of very limited scope, since its operation is, as already noted, liable to be involuntary, and its content and terminus to be highly directed. Third, one may wonder, if this is how we are to understand his remarks about the way imagination works, then how should we take the observation that the more we imagine. the more we think we see? To each of these worries I fancy a reply is not hard to find.

To start with there is absolutely no need for us to read Lessing's advice as being universal in its application. After all, he is considering only cases of representation where we are concerned with a series of events that have a natural terminus, as in the *Laocoon* case. Here he suggests only that the artist pull out the stops that are available to him, and that one in particular, grounded in the activity of the spectator's imagination, is liable to be very powerful. If he is right in his critical reflections, it would be of use to the aspiring artist to be made to realize that when he chooses subject matter of certain sorts and does attempt to pull out all the stops, he had better not commit himself to ways of handling his subject that are incompatible with its engaging the spectator's closest attention. Second, we know that however we take it, the freedom of imagination the spectator does enjoy cannot be absolute, for then it would tend towards unacceptable phantasy. All that has been remarked is one phantasy-resistant way in which imagination's freedom from the signs is available to the artist to draw on in endowing his work with ample richness.[9] That imagination has here little freedom to determine its content, and little freedom to pursue identification beyond the predictable terminus of the incipient represented event, does nothing to invalidate this observation.

The third source of resistance would be serious only if we insisted on reading Lessing's remark that "the more we imagine, the more we must think we see" as being equivalent to "the more we imagine, the more we must think we see *in the picture*". That would be unduly restrictive, since the very strength of the present proposal is that it takes us *away* from the signs, and thus guarantees that if we do see more, we do not see it *in* the picture. In speaking of *Las Meninas* we saw that this cannot be a demand that is upheld even throughout the range of the exploratory imagination, where we are admittedly concerned with what we discover to be represented for there we saw that the artist represents that something is the case without showing it to us as being that way. If the strong reading of the puzzling sentence is not insisted on there, then we should not demand with any great insistence that it be upheld here either.

This does not mean that we can give no content to Lessing's thought here. We can, but we need to remember how likely it is that his way of expressing himself is conditioned by his fixation with the centrality of graphic representation and his belief-centered construal of that, which I have criticized in Chapter 2. My suggestion is that he speaks of imagination as encouraging us to think we see more in a picture because that is the natural

---

[9] It should perhaps be stressed that the exploitation of this resource of imagination can not be by itself sufficient to enrich the work for the spectator. Whether it does or not will depend on what is achieved through it. "Pulling out all the stops" must be taken along with the qualifications *in the right manner*, and *to proper effect*.

way in which we would express our belief that we are seeing something. But since we have diluted the insistence on belief to the point where we say only that the thought we have must be a vivid and passive one (and in the case of graphic visual representations be rooted in the signs), it should not be a distortion of what Lessing wants to say when now he moves beyond the graphic, that we shall "see more" as the thoughts we have that take us beyond the picture are suitably detailed, vivid or intense. If the projection that occurs is one that involves me as a merely passive participant, then very likely it will involve me with the thought of how the events I witness appear; if, as in the Grünewald, I am an active participant, then the demand will be met through the intensity of my emotional involvement with the scene as I live it through.

Setting these three objections aside then, we have to ask whether this projective function of the imagination can defensibly be brought to the notice of the aspiring artist who wants to guard his work against the prospect of palling. The reply must be that it may, so long as the experience that it engenders is one for the spectator to value. And there are a number of reasons why we should think that while it certainly is not always so, in the best of cases it evidently can be and indeed, is so. To mention only two, it enables the viewer to increase his self-knowledge in eliciting from him emotional responses that he does not recognize to be within his normal repertoire. Then, at a further remove, it challenges him to come to terms with his feelings, and find a place for them in the psyche that is not one in which they remain dangerously outlawed. It is a familiar hypothesis that when the presented image that releases violent feelings in projection calls them back to itself, and to the immanent order that is actually on display, a step is taken towards their mastery and integration. The promise of either of these two gifts can not but be an incentive for the spectator to engage himself fully with the works that offer them; and while his repeated and extended return will not now be justified by the thought that he has not yet found in it all that such a work has to show, the suspicion that he can only slowly and in a piecemeal way work through his feelings, elaborate them and find a secure place for them, may well encourage him not to regard that as the only rational motivation for lingering with the best projection-facilitating art he comes across. He will want to return to the finest of such work to make its beneficent influence fully effective.

Ampliative imagination. The third member of my trio shares features of the other two. Like them it is resistant to private phantasy, and like them its direction lies within the artist's control in that its exercise is demanded by the full comprehension of the work. Then, like the explorative imagination, it is spontaneous; it is up to the spectator to initiate and interrupt, and up to him to select the route by which it proceeds. Like the projective imagination, and unlike the explorative, it involves thinking through episodes of a sequence that are not themselves shown in the work; unlike the projective, and like the explorative, it does not involve the viewer in coming to think of himself either as active or passive participant in the scene. Unlike either however, the ampliative imagination is predominantly active, enjoying a far larger degress of inventive freedom than they in the detailed content of its thought.

After this one wants an illustration. What could possess all these features? Why not the *Laocoon* group itself? As far as Lessing is concerned, I see no reason why he should not think that working on this narrative scene the three cooperating artists extended an invitation to their public to envisage how the scene depicted could have come about and how it could have continued beyond the moment of action on which initially they fix their attention. Concerned as he is with the graphic and the expressive, Lessing would be very open to the thought that the viewer is often challenged to visualize how a scene that is presented could have come about, and challenged also to think through in its sensible detail how it might have developed. This conception of the work of understanding certainly accords well with the actual examples that he gives, and also does justice to his concern that imagination be given a free rein. Here at least, where the viewer has to think through for himself the possible run up to and follow through from a depicted scene, and is not given any guidance in doing so by the artist except what direct and explorative imagination come to discover in the representation, imagination is freer of control than it is in either of the other two cases. That alone must speak in favour of this reading. Still, one wonders. Is it right to say that so thought of, ampliative imagination is as it needs to be phantasy-resistant? More challenging perhaps, is it even right to think of what the imagination has here been described as supplying as at all important to a full and proper understanding of figurative narrative art? To these two questions I would like to return a tentative affirmative answer.

As for illegitimate phantasy, that will be largely ruled out by insisting that in these cases the viewer is not concerned to project himself into the action at all. It is further checked by the depiction of the scene placing boundaries to the way in which the future or the past may be envisaged. The artist has to rely on his audience sharing with him some common knowledge of the events involved – as he does in the case of Laocoon and his fate – so that he sees the various represented figures as having come to occupy the stance they do from some agreed but indeterminately specified anterior situation which imagination is challenged to fill out. This common knowledge of past and future forms a framework beyond which imagination may not stray if it is to assist comprehension and appreciation of the work. Within these limits, however, it does not follow instructions that the artist is in a position to give; hence it is genuinely free, and genuinely active. Only not in the service of unrestrained phantasy of the Mittyish kind.

What of the other claim, that this activity – or something very like it – is proper to the perception of figurative art, and enters into a full appreciation and understanding of its works? It would of course be absurd to claim that this is something that always does, or always could, play a part in replete understanding. Neither does it, nor could it. But there is a notable kind of case in which it is arguable that the exercise of ampliative imagination as here described can be important. This is when the artist is dealing with a well-known story, and when it is bound to be pretty much common knowledge among those he is painting for at what point in the familiar sequence of events the scene he has represented is set. So the viewer knows what is going to happen next, and what has already occurred, and his knowledge itself will impinge on his reflective assessment of the narrative artist's success in depicting his chosen scene. If what he shows does not conform plausibly with an understood past or an understood future, if there is no way of visualizing one or the other consistently both with the known story and continuously with the represented present, then that will count against the success of the representation as it is offered. Correspondingly, it may count in its favour that the way in which the scene is represented assists the viewer coherently to visualize a run up to the scene and an outcome of it that, while familiar enough in outline, are rarely thought through in their details.

In narrative art of this kind, then, it can be a contributory factor to painterly success that the ampliative imagination should be able to exercise itself satisfactorily. It will fairly naturally be bound to make the attempt to do so given the assumed familiarity with the stories and legends from which the artist takes his subjects. Nevertheless, the viewer enjoys a large measure of freedom in finding ways in which to match what he visualizes both with that he knows about the tale or the history and with what the artist presents. It would be a task for the skilled master to draw upon the possibility of this spectatorial imaginative activity within the framework of conventions that he knows his public assumes him to be adopting and to do so in such a way that the enrichment that it brings with it is one that feeds back, as it ultimately must if it is not to be extravagant and divert attention from the work it is supposed to serve, into the representation that he presents to view.

Before moving on, I should forestall one objection that is bound to be made. It is that this is not in fact how we do look at narrative painting. Our interest hardly ever extends to the visualization of scenes that are not directly shown. My first reply is that this is in part a matter for historical investigation. Even if this is not today how we look at paintings of the genre (and remember how distant from us that genre actually is), it is hard to believe that such an interest did not play some part in explaining the appeal that narrative art had for the cultivated German gentleman of the mid-eighteenth century. In part, however, my description of the working of ampliative imagination has concentrated on the idea of visualization of scenes that are *not* shown, in mirror to Lessing's own concern with what is graphic and expressive. So for him to approve of my elaboration of the little he says about imagination, it would be important to acknowledge the graphic elements in what we ampliatively imagine. Thus, for instance "when Laocoon sighs, imagination can *hear* him scream; but if he screams, then imagination can move neither to a higher plane nor to a lower one without *seeing* him in a more tolerable and hence less interesting state". The verbs "hear" and "see" that I have emphasised draw attention to the way in which Lessing at least, conceived of imagination working beyond the edge of the picture or sculpture in much the same way as he takes it to work within it. The description offered here of the way that ampliative imagination works has sought to capture this.

Even if Lessing himself has a misleading way of thinking about narrative art – misleading in supposing its structure to depend ultimately on literary (or at least narrative) rather than pictorial interests – a far richer account of what the ampliative imagination offers can be given that abandons the obsession with appearances while still avoiding collapse into phantasy, and still maintaining a large degree of freedom on the part of the spectator. For what is shown us in the picture may encourage thought about what is not shown, though the thought is not graphic, and encourage it in a number of distinct ways. To see how Lessing's suggestions can be enriched once we abandon the constraints imposed by insistence on graphic appearances, it will suffice to mention two examples.

Fra Angelico's Prado *Annunciation* is remarkable in presenting within one picture two temporally distinct scenes. In the foreground, to the right, beneath the familiar colonnade is the Annunciation itself, while there in the garden to the left, somewhat in the background, the Archangel is seen driving out Adam and Eve from their earthly paradise. It would probably be ground common to Lessing and the modern viewer to say that the presence of the Expulsion in the scene brings sharply to our mind a question that few other Annunciations do: "Why is it that mans needs the promise of redemption that the angel brings to Mary?" Now *Lessing* might go on . . . so we think of Eve's original acceptance and eating of the apple, of Cain's murder of his brother, of the adoration of the Golden Calf and so on, as we know them in the story, and thus imagination works graphically beyond the represented scene to enrich Angelico's painting as it presents itself to us. By contrast, *we* might rather say that what enriches the work is not so much the vivid thought of these legendary events as the thought of man's real iniquity to man and of our own failings, and that it is only these that can serve to account for the true richness that the painting has. Only by moving away from appearance in amplificative imagination, only by thinking about something other than how the story may be visualized as going, shall we give the picture its due and give it the chance to work as deeply on us as it aims to.

To take this step away from anything Lessing suggests is not however to take a step towards phantasy. For these more abstract thoughts are still directed by the artist even if in their detail he can have known nothing of their content.[10] It will have been his purpose to get his viewer to think of sins he recognizes as his own, whatever they may be, and through achieving this, to give the work a force it could not otherwise have. The picture does not now control the detail of imagination at all, and the viewer's imagination – if that is what we can now still call it – is correspondingly given freer rein than was the case under Lessing's more graphically oriented regime.

Take another example. In Jean-Louis David's *The Lictors Returning the Bodies of Brutus' Sons* (Louvre, Paris) we are shown the anguished Brutus present at, though not seeing, the return of his sons upon their bier, struck down at their father's own command. Here we say correctly that Brutus' anguish is represented, but it is not represented that he have any particular thoughts. Nor I think are we ourselves invited to identify projectively with him and empathically feel what he must feel. Rather it seems that we stand outside the whole, and imagine to ourselves what the thoughts of a man in such a situation might be, and need to elaborate them in some detail if the painting is to draw out our sympathy for him as it can.[11]

---

[10] Note that this is not inconsistent with the view that the best interpretation lies within the artist's control and within his intentions. For he may often intend that we entertain thoughts within a certain range but leave it indeterminate what they are. In thinking the thoughts we do, we follow his intention, even though he can not say in detail what it is that we are to think.

[11] The situation is of course more complex than my description suggests. David, *le Robespierre du pinceau*, wants us also to admire Brutus and the Revolutionary virtue that sacrifices private love to public order. Not viewing the Revolution quite with David's enthusiasm, our sympathy for Brutus is also tinged with horror.

Again it is not a matter of imagining the graphic detail of earlier or later scenes, but of imagining possible thoughts for the represented characters in their situation that is required. Imagination is still ampliative in that it involves thought about what is not shown, and as before it is on a free rein within bounds that are determined by the artist. And this control, which ultimately takes us back to the canvas, is what protects our thought against any inclination it might otherwise have to untoward phantasy.

Leaving all attempt at further description aside, it is arguable that the ampliative function of imagination and thought serves Lessing's various needs better than the other two competitors. And we find some suggestion that it is this (taken in the rather narrower graphically oriented guise I first introduced) that Lessing has in mind when he advises the artist to restrict his subject matter to stories of figures chosen from among those that are universally known:

> The artist has this advantage too [*scilicet* of quickly capturing his viewer's interest] when his subject is not new to us, when we recognize at first glance the intent and meaning of his entire composition, and when we not only see his characters speak, but *also hear what they are saying*. The greatest effect depends on first glance, but if this forces us into laborious reflection and guesswork, our desire to be moved is immediately cooled . . . We do not like what we see, and what the artist wants us to think, we do not know. (XI, 95/6, my emphasis).

This passage, far removed in the text from that from which I set out, does suggest that provided the ampliative imagination works fairly effortlessly we find it enhancing the picture. (Cf "*also hear what they are saying*".) Furthermore, it seems to work in just the way in which Lessing talks about the *Laocoon* case itself. The imagination does add to what the artist shows us, and it encourages us to enlarge our response to the work through thinking about what occurs before and after, as well as during, the represented moment.

Then, too, if such appeal to the imagination can, when skilfully employed, enrich our appreciation of art, even if within a rather limited genre, it would be unwise for the ambitious artist to neglect it, not to make room for it if he can in the works of that genre that he executes. For one thing, if he ignores imagination altogether, he will cut down the resources he can draw on to engage our emotions with those involved in the represented scene. And if he does not ensure that imagination plays within bounds that are relatively immediately understood, he will run the risk of turning his public away from his work and making its members cross and angry. Once, however, imagination is set in motion, the viewer will find that as he comes to fashion its content, he will perhaps be drawn repeatedly back to the work from which he sets off to control the detail of his own thought against what the artist has offered him. Ampliative imagination and thought is on a free rein within boundaries that the artist sets, and as its detailed elaboration is felt to enrich the work, so the working out of what those details should be within imposed limits inevitably calls back the viewer to the canvas from which he started out. Thus ampliative imagination, like the other two varieties, has its part to play in retaining interest under repeated and extended acquaintance.

II

Of each application of imagination three questions have to be asked: Is it necessary that the artist make appeal to it if his work is to retain his public's interest? When appeal is made to imagination, have we any reason to think that the representation of emotional climax is to be discouraged? Does appeal to imagination force on to art restrictions on the handling of content that are not likewise imposed on poetry?

The first issue has largely found its answer as we have gone along. In each way, what the spectator imagines in his search for understanding and appreciation of the single work *may* make it more interesting for him than a relevantly similar work would be that offered imagination little scope. But of course it will not follow from this that when imagination is allowed small scope the resulting work is bound to pall. In part this will be an empirical matter, and there is no more the commentator can do than to point to common features of experience which will remind his reader how probable it is that claims with universal pretensions advanced in Lessing's name are overstated.

Here it would surely be particularly apt to recall how often we find some great beauty in art that calls us back to it time and time again, even though its appeal is not mediated by the thought that we have more and more to discover about it or that it invites us to develop something that it suggests rather than straightforwardly shows. Its dense crystallization of values to which we are attached may itself be enough to explain its capacity to retain our attention and our love.

Someone who is inclined to pooh-pooh this commonplace may not even be a stranger to the experience. Instead he may lie tightly in the grip of a mistaken thought about the products of art, the thought that they are, like some objects of practical desire, of a kind that once enjoyed or consumed can have no further value for us. Then it is only natural to think of the artist who desires his work to survive as seeking to build into it a sense of incompletion, which he challenges the spectator to make good by the exercise of imagination. Only to cling to this thought is to ignore what a long line of acute thinkers have sought to criticize in a rather convoluted way by pointing out that the aesthetic is essentially disinterested (Kant), or that it liberates us from the will (Schopenhauer), or more recently, that it belongs to a distinct order from all practical interest (Valéry). A remark of Valéry's may stand for all of them. Contrasting the satisfaction of practical desire, which extinguishes the initial desire, with the satisfactions of the aesthetic, he writes, "in the aesthetic order, satisfaction revives need, response renews demand, presence generates absence, and possession gives rise to desire". Were Lessing to argue for the impossibility of fashioning imagination-independent art that does call us back and back to it, and back and back to the same familiar satisfactions, he would be neglecting one salient feature that much great art enjoys, that which Valéry called its aesthetic infinity.[12]

Anyone at all sympathetic to Valéry's description of aesthetic experience must acknowledge that its aptness has a serious consequence for Lessing's major thesis. Once we allow

[12] I am sure that Valéry's point about the aesthetic infinite is detachable from the contrast with practical desire. However the connection between the two ideas is deeply rooted in traditional thought about the topic. We find another instance of it in Schiller's *Letters*, IX.7, on which I comment in Chapter 7 below.

that imagination need not always have a significant role to play in retaining the viewer's attention and in explaining the strength of his attachment to the famed work, it will not be possible to argue that all the finest representative art *must* submit itself to constraints that the operation of imagination imposes. A sculptor determined on the presentation of Laocoon's scream (or some other climax, or simply what in Chapter 1 I called bare bodily pain) may say that if only appeal to the imagination can be bypassed then the only reasons Lessing has to scorn his efforts will be those that have already been shown to be deficient. If this artist's endeavours are doomed to failure, it must be for reasons that escape Lessing.

Let us however set criticism aside and ask our second question, whether the operation of imagination is as restricted as Lessing claims it is. It must be plain that each of the three types of thought on which I have concentrated is reasonably independent of the others. They may be exercised severally or jointly, and which aspect of imagination is most appropriate can only be determined by the particular work that the viewer approaches. Appeal to imagination will thus only impose restrictions that stem from the particular function that is called for in the particular case. If Lessing's thought is that *any* exercise of imagination that serves to revive and retain interest in figurative art imposes constraints on the handling of subject matter, then he must make out that *each* type of imagination's exercise brings its own constraints with it. Only this demand is not at all easy to meet.

As we have already seen, the claim is easiest to sustain for the projective imagination. To engage that the painter will have to represent an action that is already in train, but not yet complete. The representation of climax would then impede the spontaneous exercise of projective imagination altogether. As Lessing puts it, however, it is as if, were the climax actually shown, imagination would only find something less interesting to occupy itself with, and we see him justifying his advice to the artist to refrain from representing climax on the grounds that the most moving element of the sequence would already have been provided. This reasoning must be at fault, for if there were an alternative reward available in favour of which a choice might possibly be made, it could scarcely be one obtainable from the exercise of imagination in its *projective* role. Its energies are exhausted in one direction alone, so to speak, so that if it does not involve the spectator by getting him to complete the blow in the Grünewald case, or arguably to face Laocoon's scream as a passive participant in the case with which Lessing is concerned, then it is probably not involved at all. The rationale for refraining from representing the scream or the striking of the blow is then simply misrepresented.

Abstracting from this slight inconvenience, it should be noted that to make wide use of this last reflection Lessing would need to supplement it by considerations that show appeal to the projective imagination as being regularly more rewarding than appeal to imagination of the ampliative kind which imposes no such restriction. For then, when the artist contemplates the composition of some narrative work that might possibly involve the representation of climax he will regularly be moved by the calculation that a richer way of handling his subject matter could always be found as long as he selects some non-climactic moment of the action, and, in his working of it, makes way for the benefits that exercise of the projective imagination is able to bring. The trouble is though that there just is no way in which any such general argument can be mounted. If ampliative imagination works in the various ways I have described, the interest that it will generate for the work that encourages it will depend very much on the interest that the depicted subject itself has for us and of the ideas on which it touches as we elaborate it. Independently of that there is no way of deriving a claim that any exercise of ampliative imagination would be bound to be less interesting or rewarding than anything that could be supplied through projective imagination were room made for that instead. Yet without the support of some such strut a general prohibition on the representation of climax conceived as derivable from consideration concerning the nature of projective imagination will be seriously undermotivated.

What it is correct to say is that when the tyro is composing his work he needs to have some idea of the possible benefits he can bring to his public by encouraging its members to exercise imagination either projectively or ampliatively. In either case there will likely be gains, but it cannot be said, independently of knowledge of the particular subject matter and of the way in which imagination would be encouraged to work in the versions envisaged, whether greater interest and depth will accrue from handling the topic in one way or the other. This is not of course to say that on some occasions that the two may not work together and that when they do the ampliative imagination will be subject to constraints that the projective imagination imposes, but although that is something that the artist may want to bear in mind, it is of no particular theoretical significance, and can teach us no lesson that we have not already learnt.

So much for the projective imagination and the contention that its employment carries with it restrictions on subject matter. What of the two other cases? It is easy to see that nothing of substance can emerge for Lessing from reflection on the nature of the exploratory imagination. He wants us to think of the violence or the pain or the climax of an emotion as something that the imagination adds, and through adding to what the work shows, enriching the spectator *as the representational content of the work itself does not.* Only we know now that exploratory thought can only discover what the work does representationally contain. So were it the exploratory imagination that brought us to the realization that what was represented was a climax or was a case of violence – as, say, in the example of the Goya garrotting – the figure would indeed need to be represented as at a climax, or as in pain, and this would go directly against the recommendation that Lessing is trying to defend. Succinctly, if imagination obliges the artist to eschew a subject, it cannot be exploratory imagination, for that will enforce the representation of the subject, only in a way that makes it not immediately recognizable.

The only way in which I can envisage anyone defending Lessing on this interpretation of imagination's working is by saying that it just is not a possibility that the prohibited scenes should be other than immediately recognized for what they are, so that the artist would find that, if he represented them, there would be no room for the viewer to discover slowly, by exploration, that what he admired was in fact a scene of climax. But no such assertion could withstand much scrutiny. Even when we set aside examples that belie it (as does the Goya), it will suffice to remember that bodily expression of pain or any other attitude can be counterfeited, and that counterfeited pain or violence can be represented in art as well as the real thing. We may have to rely on information provided from context to tell us which in fact we have, and what is really going on in the work, and where appeal to context is needed for full comprehension of the work, there as much room is made for the exercise of exploratory imagination as one might desire. Thus any reason Lessing might have to inveigh against the exploratory imagination leading us to discover climax must have some other basis. He offers none.

Lastly, can Lessing hope to ground the constraints he believes need to be imposed on the artist in the nature of ampliative imagination? The only hint he gives about what he might say here is found in his second chapter, in his discussion of why Timanthes did well in *Iphigenia's Sacrifice* to hide the grieving Agamemnon's sorrow beneath his cloak. "It is an example of how one should subject [expression] to the first law of art, the law of beauty" (II, 19). True, the recognition that it is a grieving father that is depicted is a matter for exploratory imagination to discover, but what the artist did well to hide was not that, but the details of his grief, and that is something that we must assume ampliative imagination may well enough vividly fill out. Only the inhibition that Lessing mentions is not justified by any thought about imagination, but by appeal to considerations about beauty that we have already had cause to reject. However, it must be obvious that reflection on the nature of ampliative thought could not provide a justification for avoiding the depiction of such grief or such climaxes as Laocoon's agony. If what makes its employment rewarding is the satisfaction that we find in the visualization of and reflection on anterior events in the sequence – the causes of grief, the way the climax could have come about – then the artist might hope to achieve that by challenging the viewer to visualize and reflect on events prior to the climax by representing the climax itself. As far as the ampliative imagination goes, there is no asymmetry discernible to me between our interest in the past and our interest in the future, hence no greater call for the painter to refrain from the depiction of emotional heights than any other moments of a sequence. Interest in how those high points could have come about and how we should think of them and of those who suffer them is a real interest, and, I am inclined to think, potentially just as rewarding as interest in how any pre-climactic moment may find its fulfilment.

My conclusion then is that the nearest Lessing can come to making out a case for saying that imagination imposes restrictions on the visual artist's handling of his subject matter is in the case of projective imagination, though even there his grounds for the assertion are not well enough thought through. It is of course an entirely different question whether this truth about the projective imagination can furnish what Lessing so much wants, a genuine disanalogy between art and poetry. To make out any case for that he would need to show either that in poetry there is no room for projective imagination to work at all, or that, in so far as there is room for it, it has to function in such a way as to dispense the poet from the limitations that it imposes on the artist. Neither option looks very hopeful.

It is common to our experience of literature – even of vividly graphic literature – that scenes are described in such a way as to invite us empathically into the action. It has often been a prized ability of the narrative poet to indicate some action and allow the reader to imagine himself carrying it through with all the emotional response that the poem's hero would have felt. In some ways it may even be easier for him to achieve this than for the painter, for he is better placed than is his colleague to grasp the reader's imagination by leading him up to the significant moment and then leaving him to imagine in his own person what must follow. So the way the argument would have to work will be by finding a difference between the way in which imagination acts in the two cases. But this must be difficult, for imagination can only accept the invitation to projection in either case as it finds itself picking up a lead to a climax that is not itself depicted. This Lessing must rely on in either of the two arts since it is precisely this quasi-constitutive element of projective imagination in general that forbade the representation of Laocoon's agony in the statue, and not some contingent feature of it that might be thought applicable to art and poetry.

All that Lessing could now hope to find would be the thought that if projection must work in poetry just as it does in art, here at least, in poetry, it will inevitably be more rewarding for the poet to eschew it in favour of the benefits that ampliative and exploratory imagination might bring. But two things are wrong with this idea. The first is simply that experience tells us it is false; the second, that no demonstration that one way of proceeding is more rewarding than another can support the conclusion that the less rewarding may not also yield works of great stature. Only that is what Lessing would need to underpin his anti-transparency thesis; and it is entirely lacking.

So the third way in which Lessing hopes to establish a difference of substance between art and poetry turns out in the end to be no more successful than the other two. Indeed, what is interesting as one reflects on his discussion of imagination, is how hard it really is to make out that the art which Lessing thought of as more restricted than its fellows really is so. Appreciating how wide the call on the viewer's imagination may be in his hunt for full appreciation of what the painter offers, we see how little trammelled the artist is by having to show in his depictions what happens at a single moment and, in painting, from a single point of view. For imagination may be called on to take us beyond the bounds of the canvas's edge, may invite us to see what is not shown, may take us into the past and into the future, and may involve us personally in the action – all of which goes against the initial plausibilities. It is certain that Lessing did not clearly realize how his brilliant invocation of imagination serves to mitigate what he took to be the obvious limitations on art, and it is perhaps ironic that reflection on what he thought would underwrite a distinction and even a ranking of a sort, should teach us how elusive any theoretically interesting and critically helpful statement of disanalogies between them really is.

IMMANUEL KANT:

CRITIQUE OF JUDGMENT

4

The Problem of Taste

While the aesthetic of Lessing before, and of Schiller after, suffer present philosophical neglect, that of Kant certainly does not. Commentaries abound, and I do not propose to enter the lists with any of them.[1] My aim is to present the very most central argument of Kant's work in as unadorned and direct a fashion as I can, attempting to engage his thought as closely as possible with issues in aesthetics as we would today recognize them, and not to preserve it in the formaldehyde of his own vocabulary and his own archetectonic. This is not to say that study of the commentaries does not help one do this. It does. Only too often the student gets get bogged down in a plethora of detail and of Kantian idiosyncracy, with the result that he forgets what precise question he is trying to follow through. If I were to identify one specific encouragement to this result, it would be Kant's own failure to make sufficiently plain right at the start of the work, in his elucidation of what he calls "the judgment of taste", just how, and just how soon, the problem he thinks of as *the* fundamental question of aesthetics is thrown up. That commentators sometimes follow him in this is no surprise.

[1] Most notable in recent years have been D.W. Crawford, *Kant's Aesthetic Theory*, University of Wisconsin Press (1973), E. Schaper, *Studies in Kant's Aesthetics*, Edinburgh (1979), Paul Guyer, *Kant and the Claims of Taste*, Harvard University Press (1979), and most recently of all Mary McCloskey, *Kant's Aesthetic* (MacMillan, 1987). My own interpretation differs in many places from all of them, as will be evident to anyone who makes the comparisons.

In the first of the next three chapters I shall, therefore, concentrate on the sense and nature of that question, the question that is: How are judgments of taste possible? The second goes on to discuss Kant's answer to it, treating his proof that such judgments are indeed possible. The last contends that his answer demands, and that it is given, ulterior completion with a demonstration, based it should be said here on a significant and less than fully acknowledged revision of our understanding of the original question, that such judgments are not just possible, but also actual, in the sense of being immune to common forms of scepticism. The conclusion of the *Critique* – or at least of its main strand – is that we have every reason to think that aesthetic discourse proceeds by the warranted offering, questioning and accepting of its sentences as contingently true or false. What sorts of truths these are, metaphysically speaking, is something that must emerge as we go along.

Putting the conclusion like this may seem at once tame and alien to Kant's avowed concerns. But that the issue to which it responds was felt urgent enough at the time is evidenced by Hume's essay *Of the Standard of Taste*, and whether Kant had read that essay or not, we can easily see how it would have struck him, and why it would have made the sceptical challenge to which I represent him as responding so particularly pressing. Half way through the eighteenth century the problem Kant came to address was no longer waiting to be launched. It was already aloft.[2]

"Hume seeks an assurance that aesthetic claims are not arbitrarily subjective, and that they are decidably true or false. The assurance that he looks for is to be provided by locating 'principles' displaying a conformity between objects (often literary) and the mind, by way of pleasing or displeasing sentiments that such objects regularly evoke. Should such principles be found we should have what we want, criteria by which things may be judged to be truly beautiful or ugly, and which would warrant us in thinking that we do more than express our feelings by the use of these terms, that we do propound genuine empirical judgments in using them and not

[2] I draw here on Mary Mothersill's *Beauty Restored* (Oxford, 1984), Ch. VII.

simply a semblance of such judgments dressed up in the right grammatical form."

So, I surmise, Hume's essay might have struck Kant,[3] and striking him like this, it would have set the wheels turning. For if Hume is right there could apparently be a science of the beautiful; only Kant is clear that such an idea is mere and demonstrable illusion.[4] Thus immediately he is under pressure to provide an alternative explanation of how such judgments might be genuinely capable of truth or falsity. Here is the sceptical problem, and here in the barest outline, is a snapshot of Kant's main question: How are judgments of taste possible? But much has to be done to get that question in presentable order before we can start to appreciate Kant's own Copernican answer to it.[5]

I

The Judgment of Taste. §§1 – 22 of the *Critique* are presented in their four Moments as elucidating what Kant calls "the judgment of taste". It is usually taken that Kant is here concerned with what we should think of as an analysis of the concept of beauty, but while that may be true of much of this segment of the work it is certainly not so of the Moment of Quality. In particular it is not so of §1, which sets the tone for what follows. Consider the very first sentences of that very first section:

> If we wish to discern whether anything is beautiful or not, we do not refer the representation of it to the object by means of

[3] Hence the (scare-)quotes. The last paragraph is meant more as a caricature than as a précis. As Mothersill shows it does no justice to the reserve Hume himself has about the existence of such principles, or to the subtlety of his final position on the issue of objectivity.

[4] Cf *Critique of Judgment*, §8.6, §58.9. References here and below are to section and paragraph of section. §58.9 provides a particularly sharp rejection of the idea that we might look for empirical principles to which taste is subject. See also §33.3

[5] This is not just a gratuitous reference to the pretensions of the first *Critique* (cf B xvi, xxii fn)? Nor is it a mere Kantian piety to claim that the third *Critique* here follows in the steps of the first. For Kant, the key to truth in aesthetic discourse lies not in the conformation of the object so much as in the nature and the interests of the contemplating mind that engages with it, something that pre-Copernicans could only take as embracing unmitigated subjectivism. For Kant the inward turn was to pave the way for the revolution that will unseat the sceptic in aesthetic matters, just as in matters metaphysical and epistemological.

understanding, with a view to cognition, but by means of the imagination (acting perhaps in conjunction with the understanding) we refer the representation to the subject and its feeling of pleasure or displeasure. The judgment of taste, therefore, is not a cognitive judgment, and so not logical, but is aesthetic – which means that it is one whose determining ground *cannot be other than subjective*.

What Kant is concerned with in this passage is not the content of the thought that something is beautiful. It is with the evidential grounds on which such a thought is to be assessed as true or false, and at the same time with the grounds on which we may reliably advance such a thought as being true. About these grounds Kant discernibly makes three claims: (i), they involve a representation of the object judged; (ii), the representation is important through the effect it has on the perceiver rather than directly through its content; and (iii), the decisive effect is that of pleasure or its absence.

What these requirements amount to is easy enough to understand. When my perception of something constitutes a genuine element of my experience I have to see that thing, hear it etc., as being thus and so, as having a particular conformation. How I perceive it is what Kant calls "the representation". What evidences a claim that something is beautiful is its being perceived, and therefore its being perceived in a certain way, as structured in this manner or that. That is Claim (i). Claim (ii) is complex. There is no specifiable recurrent element of our representation given to us in perception, the same from case to case, that verifies, or warrants, or evidences what we say. That is how things would be if we were to "refer the representation to the understanding for cognition".[6] Rather, our representation, *whatever* its content may be, varying from case to case, operates to produce a reaction in us to the object and to its yielding the representation that it does. It is the occurrence of our reaction or response, stable now from case to case, that determines whether or not the object is a beautiful one. Claim (iii) identifies the stable response as that of pleasure.

---

[6] And it is the thought that there is no such observable feature that Kant encapsulates in his claim that the judgment of taste is not cognitive. That claim is not the denial that our aesthetic judgments may not be true or false, or that they can not properly be said to record knowledge (of a sort) about what we judge.

A final claim, (iv), introduced in the following section, goes on to insist that the pleasure be, in a suitable sense, disinterested.

Taken together, these four claims identify and define the judgment of taste, and while it may not yet be clear what the best formulation of the definition might be, it should be apparent however that nothing is hereby said about the *content* of what the judgment of taste judges. Consistently with this, there seem to be two alternative ways of describing it. *Either* one might say that *p* is a judgment of taste providing only that it is of a type whose correct application is fixed by those features of *experience, subjectivity* and *pleasure* that Kant labels "aesthetic" (§1.2). Judgments that something is beautiful will then constitute prime examples of the genre. *Alternatively*, and more restrictively, one could say that a particular instance of a judgment to the effect that something is beautiful is a judgment of taste only if it is made on these "aesthetic" grounds, and actually expresses the determination, the discerning, or the ascertaining that someone makes of an object's beauty on a particular occasion.

The prime difference between the two alternative ways of putting it is that according to the first, any judgment that we might make to the effect that this object or that is beautiful will be a judgment of taste. According to the second, only some will be, those, that is, which are themselves made on these privileged grounds. One can see that this latter course rules out a good many individual assertions that we make, since I might put forward as true the thought that Helen is beautiful on hearsay, or because I have mistakenly taken my perception of her sister Clytemnestra to be of Helen, on whom in fact I have never set eyes, or because that's how I explain those naval manoeuvres off the Boeotian coast, or because I wanted to excite Menelaus' jealously, or because I wanted to curry favour with Paris, and so on. None of these assertions would, on the second way of taking it, count as judgments of taste. On the first way they all would.

Is there anything to choose between these options? Does it matter? I think it is certain that as Kant often talks he has the former in mind, since "the judgment of taste" is frequently used interchangeably with "the estimation of something as beautiful".[7] But however that may be, in the quoted passage from §1 it must be the second reading that Kant is preoccupied with. We are set to consider some item about which we want to know whether it is beautiful. That immediately sets us before a particular occasion. We are told to consult the response of the subject who perceives it, and who is concerned with the truth or falsity of the judgment. We appeal to a particular experience of the kind Kant outlines. Here it is clear that we could not be considering just any assertion that the thing is a beautiful one.

Is this just a trivial matter? Could we not at the outset take Kant to be telling us in general how we are to settle such a claim, whether or not it happens to be made on these privileged grounds? For any such case, he would be saying, the thing to do is to look at the experience of a perceiver of the object, and see whether they yield him or her distinterested pleasure. But to put it like this reveals a deep lacuna in the first suggestion, and one against which the second formulation is protected. It is that the generalized way of putting it omits, and can scarcely fail to omit, to specify that the representation and the response it generates which are to count must be those of whomsoever it is who is interested in determining that the object he is speaking of is a beautiful one. No-one else's reaction is thought of as being in point. This can be brought out by a simple illustration.

Imagine the casting-director of some film anxious to assure himself that the agency has sent round the two good looking young starlets he asked for. He wants to "determine whether they are beautiful". Following the first route he might reflect that down in the agency there will certainly have been someone whose job it was to size the girls up. And surely, he will tell himself, their response will have been as Kant demands. The agency is reliable enough. So that must be alright. He makes a judgment of taste and knows that it is of a type to have the appropriate Kantian grounds. Still, his anxiety persists.

Consider now the casting director on the next door set, who has the same requirements and the same worry, but who takes the second option. To relieve his anxiety and determine

---

[7] Though perhaps the substantive "estimation" belies this.

whether he has got from the agency what he wants, he need only make a judgment of taste as *his* option specifies it. He sees that it is not good enough simply to affirm what others report, as his colleague over the way did. It won't do, as Kant engagingly puts it, to "grope about among other people's judgments" (§32.2), such as the agency's. And this he avoids, because on the second way of speaking a judgment of something's beauty can only be a judgment of taste if the representation and the pleasure that results are those of the person who actually makes the judgment. That is what is needed. Without this there will be no way of setting up the demand that is so evidently perceived by Kant as crucial, that for me to find out whether something is beautiful or not I have to see it for myself. As he puts it, "every judgment which is to show the taste of the individual, is required to be the independent judgment of the individual himself" (§32.2).

For this reason, we do well to reserve the expression "judgment of taste" for those judgments that something is beautiful which are in fact made on these defining grounds. Others may well be true; they may on occasion well be the best we can produce, not having the chance of confronting the judged person or object ourselves; none the less they will not be judgments of taste. If this is seen as simply stipulating a use, then it is a stipulation that has a very clear point, and one to which Kant shows sensitivity right at the outset.

To say that this usage of the term is stipulative, be it a stipulation of Kant's or merely of mine, in no way forestalls substantive questions about it. Two in particular have to be settled, one bearing on the issue whether what Kant sees these privileged evidential grounds as fixing is indeed fixed by them; the other concerning the point of making such a stipulation, whether or not Kant is right on the first issue.

Concerned as he is at the start with an epistemological matter, Kant would naturally answer the first question by saying that the evidential ground that we have used to define the judgment of taste is the ground we need to be possessed of if our claim that something is beautiful is to have a secure title to knowledge. Against him it might be protested that in that case Kant's sense of what we rely on to achieve this goal is unduly blinkered. For while it may be true that to make a judgment of taste is often the most direct way of assuring myself that this thing or that is beautiful, on other occasions I do so, and may have to do so, by quite different methods. Examples already used bear witness.

(a) Sometimes the object of our judgment lies beyond perceptual range. We form our opinion with pictorial or photographic aids, as did our monarchs in the past when, to be on the safe side, they required their envoys to procure likenesses of prospective foreign consorts. (b) On occasion we surmise someone now long inaccessible in the flesh, or whose former charms are now sadly withered, to have been supremely beautiful since only that could explain . . . the launching of a thousand ships, or why the now aged face looks as it does. (c) Even where I could, if I chose, make a judgment of taste, perhaps I'm just not bothered enough to do so. Suppose I learn of my mistake in taking Clytemnestra for Helen and succumb at once to Clytemnestra. I now make a regular judgment of taste about Clytemnestra as I did not before, and later on, learning that the twins were monozygotic, infer in a desultory way that her twin sister will be equally beautiful. (d) The indolent casting director may well reflect that his agency is reliable enough to transmit to him knowledge that it possesses. What does he pay those guys for, anyway? Perhaps he's just unnecessarily anxious about the competition from the next door set.

Were we to take Kant to suppose that other than by making a judgment of taste, knowledge in the aesthetic dimension is strictly speaking unattainable, we would be imputing unnecessary error to him. While secondary methods such as these may be of limited use, they are not of no use whatsoever. On occasion they may provide us with the only means we have of coming to as reliable an opinion as may be required for it to count as knowledge. But there is no good reason to deny this modest insight to Kant, for he displays very little concern for supporting grounds of aesthetic judgments other than those that define the judgment of taste.[8] Silence on his part should

---

[8] Though at §33.2 he does come out strongly against one other possibility. "If anyone does not think a building, view or poem beautiful, then, *in the first place* he refuses, so far as his inmost conviction goes, to allow approval to be wrung from him by a hundred voices all lauding it to the skies . . . He recognizes that others, perchance, may see and

not be taken for a denial that others may be available.

What is clear, however, is that where there is a choice of ground available to us, and in particular where different sets of grounds conflict, Kant holds we should prefer to base our view on a judgment of taste rather than anything else. At §32.3 the young poet is advised not to change his confident opinion of his own work when confronted by critical unanimity ranged against him . . . not at least until, with increased maturity, he comes to make a judgment of taste condemning his own juvenile efforts. Here Kant supposes that there is at least a possibility of the critics getting things right against the poet (and not because he is prepossessed in his own favour), but this shows no more than that the data on which the judgment of taste is based are not logically conclusive for what is judged. Nonetheless, for Kant, they do initially appear to provide the best evidence, or the preferential grounds, for making such a judgment, and if we can come by that and care enough about getting things right, it is plain that we should certainly seek it out.[9] In sum, in Kant's eyes the judgment of taste constitutes the paradigmatic ground for advancing aesthetic claims. If we put it like this, the charge that his view of our evidence for aesthetic claims is unduly narrow will not arise.

This brings me to the first substantive query. Is Kant right in thinking that the judgment of taste is paradigmatic? I believe he is, and offer two reasons for its being so. The first is that the alternative methods that we on occasion use are themselves only reliable to the extent that in the situations envisaged positive judgments of taste about the object in question could

---

observe for him, and that what many have seen in one and the same way may, for the purpose of a theoretical, and therefore logical judgment, serve as an adequate ground of proof for him, albeit he believes he saw otherwise, but what has pleased others can never serve him as the ground of an aesthetic judgment. The judgment of others, where unfavourable to ours, may no doubt, rightly make us suspicious in respect of our own, but convince us that it is wrong it never can." But here we should notice that Kant is concerned with a case of conflict of views, not with one where for whatever reason we ourselves have nothing to say.

[9] I say "they do initially appear to" because we shall see in Chapter 6 that reflections on the young poet force Kant to take a significantly different tack at this very sensitive point. But we can only reach the decisive shift in the structure of his thought if we first of all take it through in the way it is originally set out.

have been made. So in case (a), the portrait will provide knowledge only if, in the foreign court, favourable judgments of taste about the candidate were made, or would have been made had anyone cared, or dared. In (b), the explanation given supposes that those naval manoeuvres result from responses to Helen that would have underwritten a Kantianly specified judgment of taste. In case (c), if the absent Helen would not have produced the same response in me as did Clytemnestra, then my inference would not have given me knowledge, and (d) it is clear that our idle casting director's claim to knowledge is no better grounded than the judgments of taste he relies on his agency to have made. There are no similar dependencies to be had the other way round.

The other consideration is this. Kant can say that what makes it preferable to make a judgment of taste for ourselves where we can, is that whereas a man may in theory acquire knowledge by some other route, it will always be open to him to wonder whether he has it even on the evidence that he draws on in forming his opinion. On the other hand, if he makes a convinced judgment of taste there will be very little scope for him to doubt what he judges.[10] It is as if while the secondary routes to the aesthetic claim may yield knowledge, when they do we may nevertheless be uncertain whether knowledge is what we have, whereas if I determine that an object is beautiful by way of a sufficiently convinced judgment of taste, there is no, or certainly precious little, room for me to stand off from the judgment I make. There is no evidence that I could collect that would effectively dislodge that on which I am inclined to judge in the face of the object itself. Before he revises his opinion the young poet has to repeat his erstwhile critics' experience of his work in his own person.

The second substantive question I announced is strategic. Why should Kant be so preoccupied with these preferential grounds on which we judge something beautiful? Certainly his interest is not just to provide accurate description of the procedures we have for settling aesthetic claims. The answer must be that his central concern is to secure a legitimate place

[10] Very little, but not none. See Chapter 6, Section II and references to Kant's text there at fn 5.

in our thought for aesthetic discourse and, if I am right, in a way quite distinct from that which he could have seen Humean empiricism as offering. His strategy is to show that on the securest grounds we take ourselves to have for judging something beautiful, on our paradigmatic grounds that is, we are in fact warranted in claiming it to be so, and that the content of our aesthetic thought is therefore adequately underpinned by what we take to be our best evidence for it. Failing that, even if our talk of aesthetic matters were not judged to be empty, it could not pretend to a legitimate place in our conception of the world. On this picture, Kant's transcendental question, the question "How is beauty possible?", which I said he thinks of as *the* fundamental problem of aesthetics, comes to be answered by showing that the transition from paradigmatic ground to assertion of content in this domain of discourse is perfectly in order.

To argue in this way demands as a preliminary both that what we accept as best evidence or paradigmatic grounds for assertion and the nature of the content asserted on that evidence be correctly located and described. On my way of taking Kant, we can now see that the first of these two tasks has been creditably performed in the very first move that the *Critique* makes. Nothing I have had to say about it tends to put that in doubt. What has next to be done is to examine Kant's treatment of the second task, remembering as we do so, that even when that is complete, absolutely nothing will be settled as to whether the desiderated transition from ground to content can be satisfactorily effected. We shall have done no more, so to speak, than situate two banks of a gulf which we know must be spanned if either of them is to be of service to us in our exploration of the world.[11]

II

Analysis. I turn now to discuss the *content* of the thought that

[11] It is of course itself a matter for exploration what sort of service aesthetic judgments can perform. I hope it will become plain that Kant is under no illusion that all truths are objective ones, even if they are all phenomenal rather than noumenal. It is fascinating to see the distinction between subjective and objective as we now think of these ideas being worked out within the framework of transcendental idealism.

something is beautiful, situated in Kant's text in the remaining sections of "the elucidation of the judgment of taste", and in particular in the Moment of Quantity and the Moment of Modality (§§6–8, 18–22). Since the ultimate purpose served by the analysis is to prepare a bridgehead that can be linked to the discussion of evidence, it will be convenient to represent Kant's thought about the content of aesthetic claims in the form of a truth condition for the proposition *x is beautiful*. Then we shall be able to ask whether this proposition, having the content that it does, could be justified on evidence of the kind we have already picked out for attention. Kant himself talks of "the explanation (*Erklärung*) of [the concept] *beauty*", but if things were left in that unfashioned form the relationship that has to hold between evidence and definition would not appear so clearly. At any event, anachronistic though it may seem, a truth-conditional presentation of Kant's claims can only make them more perspicuous than they would otherwise be. It neither falsifies them nor adds unwanted obscurity.

Before broaching this topic, I should say something about methodology. In the course of his account of the beautiful Kant introduces us to a number of very different keywords: "universality of delight, apart from any concept", "the harmony of imagination and understanding in free play", "the form of finality", "purposiveness without a purpose", "the object of a necessary delight", and "finality of form". All of these have their place in his full elaboration of the concept, but they cannot all make their appearance at once and at the very outset for one very simple reason. It is that some of these notions, those I shall claim that are left over when we have set universal and necessary delight aside, arise in response to the question what beautiful things must be like in their representation (how is it that they must strike us) if the inference from evidence to content is to be sustainable. And to put the question this way supposes that we have already formed some conception of the *content* of the claim that something is beautiful that precedes the identification of these other parts of the story. Otherwise one would be at a loss to show that they are forced on us by the transition requirement. So I propose to develop Kant's explication of the concept as a two stage process. First I shall represent him as offering what I shall call an *analysis* of the proposition that *x* is beautiful in such a way as to allow the transcendental question to be fully and explicitly stated; then, at a second stage (and in the course of the next two chapters), I represent him as discovering how we are bound to find beautiful things presenting themselves to us if that question is to receive a positive answer. The end product should capture everything that he locates as belonging to the *elucidation* of the concept.

To proceed like this supposes that we can attribute to Kant some, maybe only rather dimly perceived, idea that determines what belongs to the analysis and what is better left out of it and kept for a later date. At §8.2, as he discusses the universality of delight that belongs within analysis as firmly as anything does, he gives us a hint. That universality, he says, is something that "belongs so essentially to the judgment, that no one would dream of using the expression [*scilicet* "beautiful"] unless he had this in mind as he did so" (*ohne dieselbe dabei zu denken*). This suggests to me that the analysis might pick up what is generally perceived, at no very high level of abstraction, as belonging to the meaning of the term. This leaves it open, as we need it to, whether or not there are characteristics of the beautiful (or anything else for that matter), which are necessarily connected with it and can with philosophical acumen be displayed as such, but which people do not have in mind as they speak. These then naturally find their place in the concept's more fully elaborated *elucidation*.[12]

It might understandably be objected that if what I have in mind on Kant's behalf is what most obviously belongs to our pre-theoretical conception of beauty, then my choice of the term "analysis" for it is unfortunate. For that suggests something more reflective than what Kant appears to be looking for. In reply, however, we can say that what he relies on to form the initial analysis is nothing more complicated than the very standard sort of philosophical reflection that rationalizes the way people talk, and elicits from general patterns of speech what is fairly superficially assumed by those using a certain term. It is in this way of course more theoretical and

[12] My use of the word "meaning" is thoroughly untheoretical. Another way of putting it would be to say that Kant is here concerned with what people generally take themselves to convey by use of the term.

abstract than would be a simple canvass of speakers' unreflective assertions about what they mean, but it stops far short of any claim to detect all important conceptual truths about its use. Thus Kant begins his discussion by considering how we need to think of the beautiful, (a) once the empiricist option has been ruled out,[13] and (b) in such a way as to secure a distinction that everyone is expected to make, between beauty proper and the merely agreeable. Given this undemanding concession to methodology at the start, my choice of term should be comprehensible and acceptable enough.

As I see it, this preliminary analysis is constituted entirely by the claims that summarize the second and fourth Moments: "The beautiful is that which, apart from any concept, pleases universally" (§9), and "The beautiful is that which, part from a concept, is cognized as object of a necessary delight" (§22). Each element requires attention.

Pleasure. Common to each formulation (which we are to read conjunctively and not as exclusive of one another) is the idea that pleasure appears in the analysis and that it arises apart from any concept. Despite being closely related to similar claims made above in the discussion of the judgment of taste, these two ideas must be regarded as distinct from anything that occurred there. We are now concerned not with what warrants our thinking that something is beautiful – our own disinterested pleasure in the representation – but in what it is for the object to be as we assert it to be, namely one that produces such pleasure universally. Obviously these are not the same.

The only question it is profitable to ask about the appearance of pleasure in the analysis, is what justification Kant has for taking it to figure here as well as in the earlier discussion. After all, it must not arrive entirely out of the blue. Certainly he might envisage saying that it is something that everyone will agree has to be our response to beauty and that is

[13] The targets of Kant's explicit attacks are Burke (notably in the general comment at the end of §29), and the more rationalistically inclined Batteux and Lessing, at §33.3. Kant's deepest worry about both the empiricists' inductively generated principles and the rationalists' *a priori* commitments is that they could have no force against the man who responds differently, counter to the alleged principles. They have no power against dissent.

conveyed by our saying of something that it is beautiful. Yet if that were all there were to it, this reflection might well provoke the thought that if that shows anything, it is that pleasure is rather extrinsic to the idea, a mere effect that beauty regularly produces, rather than intrinsic to, and constitutive of, it. My own inclination is to say that what legitimizes and sustains its place within the analysis is that that is how it must appear if it is to be possible for us to use our judgments of taste as warrant for anything at all, and as making anything like a full-blooded claim on the world rather than just as expressions of our own personal delight. For if we know that we set out from a pleasure in our experience that has no stable object (i.e. that isn't a response to some "Humeanly" recognizable and recurring feature of beautiful objects),[14] then there would be no hope of justifying the thought that the object that pleases me, the judging subject, will be of such and such a standing character, no hope at arriving at what Kant calls a "logical" judgment, even though we express our thought "as if beauty were a quality of the object" (§6.1).[15] Consequently the only alternative way in which a claim might be made on the world is by our committing ourselves to the object's disposition to produce occurrences of a like pleasure in others when they view it as I do.

[14] Quite apart from the fact that Kant names other targets for attack (see last footnote), there is something invidious about this use of Hume's name, since as Mothersill points out (op. cit. 181), it is pretty certain that in the end Hume doubted whether there could be principles of taste anyway. I have stuck to it though because much of his essay on taste does suppose we might look for such principles, and that our doing so will consist in finding supposedly and unexaminedly cognitive and objective features of things as "delicacy" and "elegance" which stand in a peculiarly happy relation to the mind. However his mature philosophy might have dealt with them, I do not find a clear awareness in that essay that these features are subjective in the way Kant thinks beauty is. They seem to be thought of by Hume (and earlier candidates in the canon like *concinnitas* or *sprezzatura* certainly were thought of in this way) as features that characterize objects without reference to us, "on their own account", as Kant would put it.

[15] It is interesting that Kant does not explicitly confront the question of how we are to identify what goes into the analysis. He is, as I suggestion in my Preamble, insufficiently clear at the beginning of what the judgment of taste covers. The nearest remark I find that might be taken to bear on this issue – and in context even this is rather strained – goes the other way round. "For from concepts there is no transition to the feeling of pleasure", which is a step in securing the element of universality (which of course is quite absent from the judgment of taste). But this is to suppose that we can be assured already that pleasure is already well established and what has to be justified is the universal extent that the concept *beauty* attributes to it.

Here the general supposition is that what we commonly take to be conveyed by a term may itself be sensitive to the way we are going to have to use it if what we take to be good evidence for its employment can hope to support a substantial claim that our assertions containing it may make. Why should one deny oneself such appeal to good sense?

"Apart from any concept". That the beautiful produces pleasure apart from any concept likewise iterates in the analysis something that appears in the specification of the judgment of taste itself. The same reasoning could be appealed to to explain its presence here. But it would be reasoning supplemented by the reflection that there is no discernible feature that objects possess on their own account which it is proper to think of as constitutive of their beauty. This is merely to deny that in saying that something is beautiful we convey that it possesses any particular property, independent of the way it strikes us, and we could say that Kant is doing no more here than to acknowledge what everyone realizes the moment they reflect on it, that to assert something is beautiful is to say nothing at all about what it is like, and to imply nothing at all about any observational properties it has in virtue of its beauty. There is nothing particularly puzzling or contestable about this claim, but because it is so frequently misunderstood, it is a good idea to mark a number of things that Kant is not committed to by adopting it.

(a) It is not to say that when something is judged beautiful it is not brought under any concept. Of course it is. In particular is it immediately brought under the concept *beauty*; less directly, where, as here, we are thinking of analysis in terms of what is conveyed by use of the expression, the object judged is also brought under those concepts employed in the analysis itself (though not, I think, under those that later appear in the more extended elucidation). (b) There is no reason to think that in judging that the rose is beautiful I am not bringing the object under the concept *rose*. Again, of course I am. Only that I am doing that is no part of what is conveyed by judging that the rose falls under the predicate ". . . is beautiful", which is all that Kant is analysing. (c) There is no cause to deny that in the particular case there may be a perfectly good cognitive answer to the question what it is about the thing that accounts for its beauty. Only that isn't what we are talking about when we say that it is beautiful. There just is no standing observable feature with which we might identify the aesthetic property or regard as being entailed by its possession.

Another matter will be of importance later on. It is that, whether Kant fully recognized it or not, there is no conflict between saying that beauty is explained apart from any concept and saying that what sort of thing an object is judged to be will play its part in determining if it is beautiful. We must remember that that involves commitment to universal pleasure in the contemplation of the object under some definite representation, and the representation will inevitably specify in its content what sort of thing the object is seen to be. Moreover, if it is true that what we judge a thing to be will determine how we see it as structured or ordered, and that, as Kant believes, beauty is a function of order or form, then it would be very natural for him to say that what form a thing has, and thence whether it is a beautiful one, will be in part determined by what sort of thing we see it as.

This idea is not at odds with the concept-free thesis, because the *whole* content of that is that a beautiful object is one for which we cannot identify a standing feature allowing us say in advance of experience just what it has to be like. This restriction is not infringed by taking the adjective "beautiful" to be attributive, as I believe we should, since that does no more than play a part in restricting the kind of order that can, in the particular case, make it true that an object is beautiful. However, in those (few?) cases in which the identification of the object brings with it the thought that we will judge it aesthetically accordingly as the thing looks well adapted to its function, there we can say in advance (maybe) what it will have to look like to be beautiful – and *there* Kant will say that we are concerned with a different kind of beauty (§16.1), adherent, or dependent, or impure, beauty. That is, if the attributivity thesis is taken to apply only in this very specific way, then conflict with conceptlessness can arise. It is as falling under this case that Kant sets aside the notion of dependent beauty. A question I shall leave undiscussed is how extensive he should take this category really to be.

Universal delight. The principal substantive feature of the analysis is that the pleasure that is taken in beautiful object be universal. Unlike the elements so far discussed, its appearance is not forced onto the analysis directly from the nature of the evidence on which we assert something to be beautiful. It is there partly as a reflection of what is in people's minds as they speak (§8.2), partly as a matter of proleptic sensitivity to what a transition from evidence to content might hope to achieve,[16] and partly to accommodate a distinction that we are all supposed to make between the beautiful and the merely agreeable. These considerations call for comment, but first I want to formulate Kant's claim more precisely and connect it with what has already been secured.

What Kant has in mind is straightforward enough. A beautiful object will provide pleasure to all who come to view it "apart from any interest". Although on occasion he runs together the thought that our pleasure is apart from all concepts and that it is apart from any interest, the two ideas are distinct. The former will have its place in a formulation of his analysis that merely specifies pleasure in the truth condition of *x is beautiful*, thus:

(x)Beautiful x iff (y)(Contemplates $<y,x>$, Pleases $<x,y>$),

since while it is left open by this formula that for any particular case the pleasure may have its basis in something about x that we are aware of in contemplation of it (in the 'representation'), no room is left for one such feature to be necessarily present across all cases. So as it appears here, the pleasure is apart from any concept. The other condition though is quite absent, since the analysans will evaluate an object as beautiful only if it pleases all perceivers, whereas Kant is concerned with a narrower class of them, namely with those whose satisfaction in the object that confronts them does not stem from its

[16] "Hope" is the key word. We cannot expect to tailor the analysis to what can actually be achieved, since we are not expected to know that yet. This would not preclude the analysis being recast at the later stage should it be necessary. But that might involve conceptual revision and not only transcendental legitimization of actual practice. On the other hand it might simply encourage us to see the analysis as representing our pretheoretical conception of the concept, which under the philosophical pressure of spanning the evidence–content divide may achieve greater accuracy to its real nature.

answering to their practical concerns, as would be the case say were I looking for a memento of my grandmother, and found myself pleased in the possession and contemplation of some gem just because it belonged to her.[17] Plainly, unless one were to impose some such restriction, it is most unlikely that one would ever come across items that would provide quite general pleasure. Kant's thought is that this pleasure must be one that is fully explained by reference to the nature of the representation (in the visual mode, say, by the look of the object as it is seen in a particular way) and that would not be so were I in the grip of any "interest". I shall mark that restriction without further comment in a revised version of the formula,

(x)Beautiful x iff (y)(Disinterestedly contemplates $<y,x>$, Pleases $<x,y>$)

Notice that the effect of the emendment is not to cut down the generality of the analysing pleasure. That is still expressed by a universal quantifier. But the class whose generality is in question is now narrower. Only those whose thought is for is the intrinsic character of their representations count towards evaluating the claim that something is beautiful one way or the other. Whether others falling outside that class agree with them or not, is neither here nor there. In consequence, that we do not find universal agreement in our assessment of a thing's aesthetic merit need not show straight off that on the Kantian conception it is not a beautiful one. Maybe the lack of consensus is explained by our consulting people who approach it with different interests in mind.

It may already have been remarked that writing the formula as I have done obscures something of importance to Kant, but

[17] Kant himself puts his point by saying that we are indifferent even to the *existence* of beautiful objects. Other than thinking that this is just his way of making the point that aesthetic satisfaction is quite distinct from the satisfaction of practical desire I am at a loss to know what to make of this way of talking. It is worth recalling that in the Introduction Kant asserts that the satisfaction of all desire brings pleasure with it, and that he might be running together the two distinct ideas (a), the tautology that a desire is satisfied when you have got what you wanted, and (b), the falsehood that when you get what you want you are pleased. Then it might (just) be comprehensible to think that aesthetic satisfaction does not require you to care about the existence of the object since it is a satisfaction that is not dependent on there being something that you have got. But still this is pretty far-fetched.

of which he makes insufficient mention. It is sure that the same object can be seen in a variety of ways (variably 'synthesized', in Kant's jargon) from person to person, or even at different times by the same person). And since it is the *representation* that is referred to the feeling of pleasure or displeasure, we must take it that the beautiful object is one that produces universal pleasure in respect of one and the same representation, one and the same way of synthesizing it. Because Kant never explicitly considers this entirely desirable feature of his talk about our representations, we do not know how he would express himself here, but the choices open to him seem reasonably clear. Either he might say that an object is beautiful if there is at least one representation to which everyone having it responds with pleasure. Alternatively he could insist that strictly speaking objects are not beautiful or ugly *tout court*, but, only as seen in a particular way or under a particular representation, and that for an object to be beautiful in some particular way will be for everyone who views it in that way to find pleasure in it. In my own view he would be advised to take the latter course, since in not needing to rely on a negative existential for the second half of the task it is better equipped than the former to allow us "to determine whether an object is beautiful *or not*" (§1.1, my emphasis). But whichever course he might choose, he will thereby open up a further notable source of merely apparent disagreement among aesthetic judges that does nothing to undermine the universality requirement. Diverse judgments are often made that set out from or implicitly assume different representations of the same object even when there is no question of any failure of disinterest on anyone's part.[18] Once universal agreement is tied to specific representations, such seeming divergencies are of no consequence.

So much for the content of the universality condition as it

---

[18] I think Kant shows some incipient awareness of this possibility at §16.8, where disagreement between critics is allowed to arise when one considers something as a free beauty and another as a dependent beauty. Kant regrettably articulates the difference between them by saying that "the one [judges] according to what he has present to his senses, the other according to what was present to his thoughts", but it could scarcely be claimed that he will be one to insist on this way of putting it. He is far too clearly aware of the role of thought in sensible representations for that.

appears in §§6–8. What of the grounds for its introduction? For the sake of what comes later I want now to suggest that none of them are utterly conclusive, and that we shall do well to be able to offer Kant a slightly less exigent option in due course. Two theoretical considerations of fairly low level operate in his view to convince people that their talk of beauty commits them essentially to universality of the pleasure it produces. One arises from the discussion of disinterest, the other from our need to distinguish what is beautiful from what is agreeable.

As to the former, Kant suggests in §6 that if our judgment of taste is to say anything more about the object than that I, the subject, am pleased by it, we could only suppose that it is one that pleases everybody. This turns on the recognition that my own pleasure is disinterested – "for where any one is conscious that his delight in an object is with him independent of interest, it is inevitable that he should look on the object as one containing a ground of delight for all men." (§6.1) He continues:

> For since the delight is not based on any inclination of the subject (or on any other deliberate interest), but the subject feels himself completely free in respect of the liking which he accords to the object, he can find as reason for his delight no personal conditions to which his own subjective self might alone be party. Hence he must regard it as resting on what he may presuppose in every other person; and therefore he must believe that he has reason for demanding a similar delight from everyone.

Here it is noticeable that the concern that fuels this argument is with what we might hope to be able to base on a judgment of taste – "a proleptic sensitivity", I called it before – but we should notice also that Kant is less than uneqivocal about the worth of the argument. It is put into the mouth of the unreflective theorist, and only dubiously endorsed by Kant when he says at the end of the quotation "therefore he must believe . . .". It would be quite open to him to say that he was doing little more in this passage than locating an assumption which explains why people are so ready to speak of the pleasure that beauty provides as being quite general,[19] but

---

[19] §8.2 introduces the universality condition directly as a reflection of what is at the forefront of people's minds as they speak: "this claim to universality is such an

without doing more than neutrally recording it. Were he to distance himself only a little from the common tendency of eighteenth century thinkers to assume an easily accessible universal human nature, he might think it rash to suppose that more could be expected from other disinterested spirits than a general tendency to share one's own pleasure in the things one contemplates. Contingencies of upbringing and training and self-understanding, he might feel, can not so easily be set aside.[20]

"As regards the agreeable everyone concedes that his judgment, which he bases on a private feeling, and in which he declares that an object pleases him, is restricted merely to himself personally . . . The beautiful stands on quite a different footing" (§7.1, 2). The proper expression of pleasure in the agreeable is "It is agreeable to me", while we express ourselves properly about the beautiful in a statement of subject-predicate form about the object: "The rose is beautiful."

If one were to think Kant believed one could only distinguish the beautiful from the agreeable by commitment to universality of the latter pleasure, that would be to attribute error to him. For if the agreeable is as he claims, purely private, then any essentially non-private pleasure would set the agreeable apart.[21] It would not need to be universal. But the agreeable is not just as Kant supposes – there is a difference between the wine being agreeable and its being merely found to be so by me, to which Kant seems insensitive where sensitivity, one might think, would provide him with a better ground for insisting on the universality of beauty's demand. Perhaps that is what he might be getting at when he contrasts the *general* nature of rules for producing pleasure at one's agreeable dinner

---

essential factor of a judgment by which we describe anything as *beautiful*, that were it not for its being present to the mind it would never enter into anyone's head to use this expression."

[20] It is of course true that he presents himself as investigating the possibility of beauty along lines that parallel those of the first *Critique* and that that can be seen as a doubling of the going stakes, not as a quit. I shall argue later on that there is more rhetoric to this than reality and that he is not unaware of these contingencies and of their importance for his argument.

[21] It is interesting to see him using the contrasting terms "egoistic" and "pluralistic" at §29 *ad finem* but in fact he never makes anything of the freedom this opens up.

parties with the *universal* ones that the judgment of taste claims to deal in (§7.3). But even if that were so, we should not be compelled to follow him, since it would be open to us to introduce for the purpose quantifiers of differing generality, neither of which were universal, and to restrict the narrower of the two to the agreeable, leaving the wider to pick up the beautiful. True, the resulting distinction might not be easy to deploy in every case, but if one were determined to draw the distinction in this way, then, unlike Kant, one might well think that vagueness is in the nature of the case.

It is in any case true that as far as Kant is concerned the distinction reveals itself in another way, which would, if correct, deprive him of any compelling motivation to rely on a distinction of quantifiers to draw it. It is that he believes that the pleasure of the agreeable is always "interested", it always arises out of the satisfaction of some prior desire and is not fully explained by the nature of one's representation or the intrinsic character of one's experience. To maintain this would allow Kant to say that the beautiful and the agreeable are distinguished in their pleasure quite apart from any difference in its extent, so it won't be that any thought about its extent is forced on us by a need to draw the distinction. The universal nature of that pleasure in the beautiful must recommend itself to us, if it does, on its own account.[22] Perhaps this reflection will do well enough as an *ad hominem* objection to Kant, but because the premiss from which it sets off, that pleasure in the agreeable is essentially "interested", is so unconvincing, it is not one to make too much of.

At the end of his initial discussion of the agreeable then, the dialectical position we find Kant in is that even though we shall acknowledge that the agreeable and the beautiful are distinct, he has not succeeded in persuading us either that we have to look to the disinterested nature of our delight in the beautiful to distinguish it from the agreeable, or even that the beautiful is anything more than the extensively (or, if the reader is generous, universally) agreeable. If this were where the matter

---

[22] And best so in the deduction itself with the other elucidating notions. The idea would be to put into the analysis only a dummy quantifier, recording a certain vagueness in our pretheoretical conception of matters, and one to be given a determinate content as we come to see what a transcendental deduction can achieve.

ended there would be ground for dissatisfaction, since whatever the proper range of the generality in question, no-one will allow beauty to be simply a species of the agreeable. And Kant himself must have felt some residual unease with the situation, since it is again to the need to distinguish the agreeable and the beautiful that he turns to introduce the rather more puzzling notion of the *necessity* of the delight to which the beautiful gives rise, a necessity from which the agreeable is exempt. Here I think we see this requirement for a contrast between them handled to rather better effect.[23]

Necessary delight. "The beautiful, Kant claims, is that which, apart from a concept is cognized as object of a necessary delight." The difficulty is to understand what he is getting at. If we take "necessity" as we ordinarily do, there are but two places for it in the schema last displayed, and neither of them is at all satisfactory. The first is to place it right outside the whole thing, encouraged perhaps by Kant saying at §18.1 that "what we have in mind in the case of the beautiful is a necessary reference on its part to delight", or again, later in the same paragraph, that "it is a necessity of the assent of *all* to a judgment regarded as exemplifying a universal rule incapable of formulation".[24] Then the analysis would read, abbreviated here and below in an obvious way:

$$\Box(x)(Bx \text{ iff } (y)(DC<y,x>, P<x,y>))$$

and would differ from the previous display only by explicitly announcing that the thought expressed is itself necessary. It is this harmless and quite comprehensible rewriting, I think, that encourages one commentator to suggest that there is nothing more to the moment of Modality than is already given us by that of Quantity.[25] Without qualification of the kind I offer

---

[23] In what follows I retain Kant's universal quantifier as faithful to his analysis and discuss some motivation to weaken it in the *Addendum* below.

[24] The "rule incapable of formulation" I have long found a puzzle. My inclination is to regard it as a pointer towards some thing unspecifiable in general – for it may not always be the same thing – that will account for the universal claim holding. Kant often talks of it as the supersensible substrate, but I think we can do much to shear this of unacceptable metaphysical implications. (See Chapter 6 below).

[25] K. Ameriks "Kant and the Objectivity of Taste", *British Journal of Aesthetics*, 23, 1983, 3–16.

below this must be seen as a defeatist interpretation, and all I can see speaking for it is that the only remotely plausible alternative placing of the necessity operator within the analysis leads to unacceptable falsehood. Thus we might try:

$$(x)(Bx \text{ iff } \Box(y)(DC{<}y,x{>}, P{<}x,y{>})$$

but then it would be hard to see how true claims that something is beautiful could be contingent at all. For if their truth depended on it having to be the case that all those who contemplated the chosen object with disinterest found pleasure in doing so, it would appear to be ruled out that the object in question should have been so conformed that it failed to produce this response. In that case we could only suppose that something that is beautiful just has to be so. That goes too hard against the grain.[26]

However, there is help to be had in the text for us to do better on Kant's behalf. First, the explicit motivation for talk about necessity lies again in the need to distinguish the beautiful from the agreeable. "Of what I call agreeable, I assert that it *actually* causes pleasure in me. But what we have in mind in the case of the *beautiful* is a *necessary* reference on its part to delight" (§18.1). So the necessity cannot simply be that of the analysis itself as expressed above. Further, Kant there denies that what he is concerned with is either a theoretical necessity, or a practical necessity. So it appears within the analysis it cannot do so in the form of the standard box operator just considered. He himself goes on to explain more positively that what he has in mind is an "exemplary necessity" but I believe that despite his willingness to make this move directly it has tended to prove

---

[26] The objection has to be made differently if the analysis is thought of as being of *x is beautiful under representation R* as I suggested it could be. Then we would have to suppose that people could not possible see *x* in that way without taking pleasure. Now providing that we don't beg the question by writing into the specification of *R* a pleasure-involving notion like harmony, elegance, delicacy, or concinnity etc, there is no apodeictic necessity here to be had. As long as we see Kant's motivation in introducing the necessity as restricted to distinguishing the beautiful and the agreeable there is no reason why he should dissent. *In fact*, though, I suspect that he believes empiricism can only be outflanked at this point by introducing a strong necessity of the apodictic kind here, and that goes to explain why he is so insistent that we are concerned with an a priori principle.

more of a hindrance to his cause than a help.[27] If we resist it for a moment, we shall see that another possibility presents itself, more in keeping with what the argument calls for, and quite neutral on the issue of whether others ought to share the pleasure in a beautiful object expressed by one who makes a judgment of taste about it. A later passage provides the hint we need.

At §57 Remark 2.3, in his comments on the resolution of the antinomy of taste, Kant notices that there can be chance convergence of taste as well as agreements explicable in terms of principles. He writes:

> It is open to us to deny that any *a priori* principle lies at the basis of the aesthetic judgment of taste, with the result that all claim to necessity of a universal consensus of opinion is an idle and empty delusion, and that a judgment of taste only deserves to be considered to this extent correct that *it so happens* that a number share the same opinion, and even this, not, in truth, because an *a priori* principle is *presumed* to lie at the back of this agreement, but rather (as with taste of the palate) because of the contingently resembling organization of individuals.

Here again we find him concerned with the agreeable, tastes of the palate being for Kant clear cases of that, and we can see him clearly envisaging that there might indeed be contingent agreement on a wide, even conceivably world wide, scale, where "contingent" is used synonymously with "accidental" or "fortuitous". And then, "contingently", we should be confronted with something universally pleasing but nonetheless not beautiful. This suggests that there is in Kant's idiolect a use of "necessity", meaning simply *non-accidental* or *non-fortuitous*, and one which he can happily draw on without appeal to any purported exemplary necessity to distinguish the beautiful and the agreeable within the framework of his analysis, and without getting into the position of identifying the beautiful

---

[27] Too often it encourages people to represent Kant as holding that to say *x* is beautiful is to say everyone ought to agree with me. True, he does occasionally express himself like that. But it isn't his best thought. It is better put by saying that that can be seen as a consequence of our making judgments of taste or as part of the elucidation of the concept – it is not part of the content of what is judged when I say that something is beautiful. I explore this option further in Chapter 6.

with the universally agreeable (or if we hesitate about universality, even with the extensively agreeable), as before §18 he seemed doomed to do. For what he may write is simply this:

$$(x)(Bx \text{ iff } N\text{-}F(y)DC<y,x>, P<x,y>),$$

where "N-F" renders the sentence operator "It is non-fortuitous that" or "It is no accident that".

To adopt this suggestion yields a reading of Kant's point that has a number of merits. (a) However implausibly, it effects a distinction between the beautiful and the agreeable in a way congenial to Kant by insisting of the former that whatever generality of pleasure turns up in the analysis be non-fortuitous, whereas in the other case such a condition need not be met. (b) It retains Kant's insistence that the necessity in question is identical neither with theoretical nor with practical necessity. (c) It paves the way for a later introduction of what in §18 goes under the name of "exemplary necessity" – the thought that the beautiful makes demands on people's responses that the agreeable does not – since it makes clear sense to say that and to look for an explanation why, when it's no accident that everyone (most people . . . or what one will) are agreed in some pleasure, others should be thought bound to follow them. This is a matter of the greatest importance in taking Kant's argument to its ultimate goal, and I shall postpone it for full treatment in Chapter 6. Last, (d), it gives us a reading of "necessity" that does nothing to move Kant away from holding that what is conveyed in the claim that something is beautiful is a content that can be assessed for contingent truth or falsity. In particular, it in no way resembles a command or an injuction or an exhortation, even though it is a content that could perfectly well be used with some such illocutionary force.[28]

Earlier on I said that we should not elide the issue of necessity and that of universality, at least not without very considerable qualification. What I had in mind was this: in §§6–8 Kant contrasts the universality of pleasure with a possible mere generality. On the reading that the text best supports, and which I have so far assumed, the contrast is

---

[28] *Pace* Mothersill, *Beauty Restored*, 211–218, who maintains that "Kant's concern about preserving the normative aspects of the judgment of taste leads him to construe it as an implied command".

between pleasure being enjoyed by many or most of those who come to my dinner parties and by all of those who actually come across the beautiful object, whatever it may be. Although I do not find Kant clearly addressing himself to the issue, it will not be long before the question arises whether such *de facto* universality is not too weak for his purposes. If we were to rely on that alone to distinguish between the agreeable and the beautiful, would not the private object that I allow very few to view, the beetle in my box, say, count as beautiful just as long as it pleases all of them? And are we to say that objects which no one actually views are beautiful, satisfying as they do the predicate ". . . pleases all who disinterestedly view them"?

This sort of objection is usually, and rightly, met by saying that we are concerned not with an indicative sentence, but with a subjunctive one, or that the analysing quantifier ranges over possible viewers of the beautiful thing as well as actual ones. Only in the early sections of the *Critique* there is little sign that Kant is aware of this move being open to him,[29] or that such a difficulty might be raised against him. However it is an instructive thought that the claim that it's no accident that all those who actually view something disinterestedly take pleasure in it can be backed up by saying that they all actually do so because anyone who were to view it with disinterest would do so, and the holding of the stronger conditional is what we are committed to if we are to rule out the rare cases of genuinely universal pleasure taken in the agreeable from being assimilated to cases of the truly beautiful. If the universality in the analysis were taken in this fashion, the appeal to necessity

---

[29] But not none. In the First Introduction. X.4 Kant writes: [I]f a judgment is represented as universally valid, and thus lays claim to the necessity of its assertion . . ." The only way I can understand this is as saying that if we take the universality to be quite unrestricted, we shall either be expressing a law (a necessity, an *a priori* principle) or a regularity that derives from some law (necessity, *a priori* principle). And perhaps also Kant may expect his readers to remember from the first Critique what he has to say about universality there. Recall for instance A 2 "[I]f we eliminate from our experience everything which belongs to the senses, there still remain certain original concepts and certain judgments derived from them, which must have arisen completely *a priori*, independently of experience, inasmuch as they enable us to say, or at least lead us to believe that we can say, in regard to the objects which appear to the senses, more than mere experience would teach – giving to assertions true universality and strict necessity, such as mere empirical knowledge cannot supply." Surely, one is inclined to say, in the *Critique of Judgment* Kant has nothing less in mind than "true universality".

would be largely superfluous.[30] I am not however saying that they are the same after all, for in the last schema displayed the generality concerned actual and not possible cases, and to say of all actual cases that they are non-fortuitously alike says something weaker than that all possible cases are alike or that any other case that might arise would be like in kind too. It would be a mistake therefore to treat the necessity of the fourth Moment as nothing more than the universality of the second. What is helpful in the connection that commentators have made between the universality condition and the necessity condition is that if we see it as central to our understanding of what is conveyed by saying that something is beautiful that all possible disinterested viewers would find pleasure in it, or that if anyone came to it in a disinterested frame of mind, they would do so (where explicit talk of "necessity" has fallen away), we shall be immediately curious to know what could underwrite such an assertion. That is, it straightway gives rise to a question we recognize as a real one. When that curiosity is expressed in Kant's language it takes the form of an inquiry after some "*a priori* principle presumed to lie at the back of our agreement" and which he is at pains to show we cannot hope to do without. The translation back into Kant's way of speaking will do nothing to deprive us of a sense of his quest's urgency.

III

Addendum. I have tried to avoid combining exposition of Kant's problem with criticism. But I did claim that his introduction of universality into his analysis is underdetermined. Looking forward to what claim we ourselves might think could be justified on the basis of a judgment of taste, I should also expect a modern reader to think that unrestricted universality

---

[30] It is not that it drops out entirely, since on the assumption that Kant is still concerned with actual generalities, and saying of them that they are non-fortuitous, a different thought is expressed. But once the move is made to the subjunctive there is no need to insist on writing the analysis in terms of an actual generality. The subjunctive formulation will be preferable anyway, because without it we are still liable to come up with unsustainable aesthetic judgments where no one actually views a given object for some principled reason. Say we consider something too small for the human view. Then it's no accident that it's true that everyone who actually views it takes pleasure. But we won't want to say it is beautiful on that account.

is too ambitious a goal. In due course we shall see how that turns out, but lest Kant fail to convince us otherwise, it is well to have something else that he might be content to fall back on. Earlier I suggested that different degrees of generality could play their part in keeping the beautiful and the agreeable apart – even if one thought to rely on nothing else – and it seems open to Kant to aim for a weaker claim than the one he actually makes, namely that the beautiful is that which provides *extensively many* with disinterested pleasure. The claim can be filled out with the same kind of necessity as has just been discussed, and we can certainly formulate it in subjunctive form. Such claims make a real demand on inter-subjectivity, as Kant requires of the beautiful, and seem to qualify as being genuinely true or false in particular cases. So as the Deduction is developed in the next two chapters, while I shall always consider the universal version of the claim that Kant himself propounds, should we find that it cannot be sustained it will do nothing but good for the Kantian conception of these issues to ask whether some such weakened version of the analysis could not be upheld without abandoning anything really central to his thought.

5

Cognition and Taste

Kant formulates the question that the Transcendental Deduction faces in two ways. He asks in terms of a *judgment*: How is the judgment of taste possible a priori?[1] He asks in terms of a *concept*: How is beauty possible? The last chapter should have served to give a sharp sense to both ways of putting it. The first is the question how the transition from paradigmatic evidence to content as already analysed can be legitimized. How is it possible that on the basis of a subject's own favourable response to something under a particular representation, he may legitimately assert that it's no accident that everyone similarly placed will take a like pleasure? The second is the consequential question: What, if anything, can we say that objects must be like in the way that they strike us if they are of a kind to legitimize the transition of the first question? I can put it like this: only a certain class of things will give me ground to think that everyone will subjectively (to use Kant's word) respond to them as I do. To say what these must be like will be to fill out what I called the elucidation of the concept *beauty*. The replete elucidation thus specifies how beauty is possible.

Lest it be felt that this second way of setting up Kant's problem must traduce his intentions by involving the prospect of bringing the beautiful "under a concept", recall that that prohibition stretches only to identifying the beautiful with

[1] The force of "a priori" in this question is no more than to emphasize that I look to nothing else than my own responses to assert my judgment. I do not "wait and see if other people will be of the same mind". (§36.3)

some observable feature of objects that they possess independently of us. It does not deny that we can say anything predicative at all about how they will seem to us to be if beautiful is what they truly are.[2] Kant's two questions are not separate though, nor shall I treat them as such. How beauty is possible is intimately intertwined with how the judgement of taste is possible. It will get its answer as we think about its fellow.

Continuing with this preliminary, it is well to emphasize here that we have to do with a transcendental question: How is something possible? What conditions need to be satisfied if we are able to think in this way or that? The question is not immediately how things must be if we are to do what we do do,[3] but if what we *take* ourselves to do is to be possible at all. Putting it like this is advisable, because there is the rather dismal sceptical possibility still before us, which we must not prejudge, that, like it or not, what we take to be something we do does not really live up to the conditions of its possibility. Then of course, while we will think we do it, we don't really – we merely make a shot, and fail.[4]

I

The deduction is conducted at various places in the *Critique*, at Intro VII, §9, §21, §38, and at §57; and in these various places,

---

[2] I am put in mind of Moore's observation in *Principia Ethica* (§121) that the naturalistic fallacy will arise in aesthetics as it does in ethics. Here we may see what Kant's attitude to this idea might have been.

[3] That would be a *metaphysical* question. Compare Intro V.1: "A transcendental principle is one through which we represent *a priori* the universal condition under which alone things can become objects of our cognition generally. A principle on the other hand, is called metaphysical, where it represents the *a priori* condition under which alone objects whose concept has to be given empirically may become further determined *a priori*".

[4] cf §38 Remark. ". . . the actual existence of beauties of nature is patent to experience". The evidence of experience is not in Kant's mind undermined by our coming to see that nature is not objectively final for our judgment (i.e. that it's not a genuine *purpose* of nature to provide us with aesthetic pleasure), because he thinks that there is another way of accounting for it – viz via its subjective finality, or, crudely, its seeming to us to be purposive in ways that we share with one another. But should the thought about how nature seems turn out not to be genuinely communicable, as the sceptic is inclined to fear, then what is for Kant "so patent to experience" would itself come under scrutiny. Experience may have the first word, even the second; it cannot have the only word.

in various ways. The fullest, and to me the most interesting, is the first of them occurring in the main body of the text, at §9 that is, and which Kant claims provides "the key to the critique of taste".[5] Here, at the end of the sections introducing universality of delight into the analysis, he immediately tries to show how our own pleasurable response to something could give us ground for thinking that others would respond in like manner. Given that the analysis of beauty does not get completed until §18, with the introduction of necessity, it might be thought that this is premature, but this need cause no worry as long as we see that the justification offered at §9 will eventually extend not only to all actual disinterested observers, but also to all possible ones.[6]

Everything important turns on a close similarity Kant discerns between ordinary cognitive judgments we make about the world and aesthetic ones. True, they are different in that only the former are aimed at knowledge under concepts. They and they alone teach us, that is, how things are independently of us; but each makes the claim it does universally, and each (surprisingly) involves universality of pleasure. Moreover, Kant believes they both do so on the basis of structurally analogous paradigmatic evidence. So given that we have no difficulty in accepting that theoretical knowledge is available to us, we have at the very least the beginning of reasoning to convince us that aesthetic judgments may be in no worse case than cognitive ones. This thought becomes particularly impressive for Kant once we observe that the very same intellectual capacities are drawn on in the one case as in the other.

How much more than a beginning it might be depends on which of two ways of reading the *Critique* comes closer to Kant's intentions, and how satisfying the more ambitious way of taking the official deduction turns out to be. For the sake of

[5] In Kant's vocabulary the world "critique" generally picks out discourse enquiring into the possibility of whatever it is a critique of by identifying what is conceptually internal to it. Hence "critique of taste", "critique of judgment" etc. The key is the insight that to mark the difference between the agreeable and the beautiful, pleasure in the latter must be provided with a proper internal object.

[6] The idea is simply that as long as the deduction supplies the basis of the subjunctive conditional in the analysis it will have accounted for the necessity that Kant introduces a little later on. As long as its reach is long enough, its location in the text will not matter.

what comes later, in Chapter 6, and before I look at any of the detail of the analogy with cognition just outlined, I sketch the two alternative paths he may be seen to follow. The one takes the argument just outlined to capture everything that could possibly be needed to secure the evidence to content transition; the other regards it as no more than a necessary foundation for a superstructure later to be developed. It is just a fact about the book that it can be understood in either of these two ways.[7] Which we ultimately prefer will depend on which we find intellectually more satisfying.

The ambitious interpretation is to hold that since the line of argument sketched two paragraphs back represents not just a beginning in the quest for a transition, but the end as well, since exactly the same faculties of mind are involved in inferences having the same form in both cognitive and aesthetic cases. We are invited to conclude directly from success in the cognitive case to the legitimacy of the evidence-content transition in the aesthetic one. Given that the possibility of experience itself prohibits scepticism being mounted in the cognitive domain,[8] aesthetic intersubjectivity is no less well assured than it – transcendentally.

More cautiously, and I think more subtly, Kant can also be read as saying that we know that using the same intellectual resources in the cognitive case as we do in the aesthetic one, we achieve the *cognitive* evidence-content transition without too much trouble. While this shows that transitions of this general sort are feasible for creatures having our mental capacities, it does not of itself show that it is something that we can be sure to achieve in the aesthetic realm, because similar though the two cases are, they are also importantly different. It merely shows that the transition is of a kind that lies within our intellectual competence legitimately to make. To take it further

---

[7] §38 fn provides the clearest commitment to the former. §22.2 and §57 embrace the latter. In this chapter and the next I try to develop a unified view that draws on both options. What moves me to do this is that Kant never explicitly chooses between them, though he must have seen that they are quite different in structure. If one declines this combination one will be left with the feeling that Kant was less clear sighted or just lazier than we like to think of him as being.

[8] A doctrine essential to the *Critique of Pure Reason*, and about which I shall say nothing here. See for instance B. Stroud, *The Significance of Philosophical Scepticism*, (O.U.P., 1984) Ch 4, for a development of Kant's reasoning.

and to assure ourselves that here too a transition of this kind legitimately made will depend on whether we can identify pressures on us that work to secure that our competence is properly exercised in the aesthetic case as it is cognitively. There, in cognition, we can perhaps see well enough what forces on us make for the achievement of intersubjective agreement; only if a parallel reflection is forthcoming for aesthetic thought shall we be able to take the argument further than the mere beginning that is constituted by the development of the cognitive analogy of which §9 makes so much.

The weaker of these two readings will of course not be forced on us if cognitive analogy is as strong as much of the time Kant is anxious to believe. So we have to inquire just what it is supposed to be and how impressive it is.

II

Knowledge that things are thus and so is expressed in judgments aspiring to truth. In the *Prolegomena to any Future Metaphysic* Kant calls these "judgments of experience" – the sun warms the stone, this event occurred after that one, and so on. But we assert such judgments on the basis of how things strike us, on the basis of "judgments of perception", its seeming to me that this event occurred after that one, the stone's feeling warm to me after the sun was felt to shine. Standardly, the best evidence for my (perceptual) claim that p is that it seems to me that p, just as the best evidence for my claim that x is beautiful is my experience of x. But what is it for p to be so, over and above my experiencing things as being p? How is the claim that it is so, made on this paradigmatic basis or some other, to be analysed?

In the Cartesian tradition against which Kant was reacting, that question would be answered by appeal to the obtaining of facts independently of the judging mind. For p to hold is for there to exist some fact $<p>$ created by God and quite independent of me, and evidenced by (but how so?) its seeming to me that p. That answer Kant eschewed, since he held that such an analysis would require an access to the noumenal world that we could not possibly enjoy. What after all would warrant us claiming such a [noumenal] fact existed except our having certain experiences? But these experiences can be fully expressed by a report on how things perceptually seem. So how can they possibly evidence or even express the existence of something beyond and independent of our seemings? Kant's positive proposal involves construing truth in terms of universal and necessary agreement in judgment, and abstracting from an explanatory ontology of facts altogether. Relying on the equivalence between "p" being true and p, we can say that in Kant's eyes the claim that p is nothing other than the claim that to anyone in my position it would seem as it does to me (universality),[9] and that this is no accidental matter (necessity).[10] Consequently, when we claim to know p, since its seeming to be the case that p is what we take as prime evidence for holding p itself, there needs to be a safe transition from my judgments of perception to regular judgments of experience, a proper warrant for the universal commitment on the restricted basis of my own individual experience. This we may note is precisely what needs to be provided in the aesthetic case as well.

Even someone who is sympathetic to some version of the thought that truth consists in (ultimate) agreement in judgment might not, as far as present purposes go, be very impressed by this line of attack. For he may think that even when we recognize that in the cognitive realm we do indeed have knowledge, and that therefore in the theoretical domain the transition from judgments of perception to judgments of experience must be assured, that will not be to point to a close analogy with the aesthetic case. After all, there we are not just hoping to pass from "it seems to me that p" to something like

---

[9] This is of course different from what Kant would think it was for p actually to be the case, since making the claims I do, I may nonetheless make many mistakes. To get to his view of that he would have to filter out possible sources of distortion in my position, and it is a difficult question to know whether that can be done in a non-question-begging way.

[10] In fact in the *Prolegomena*, he argues that necessity is imported via the categories. But we do not have to follow him here, since that would suppose that in mere judgments of perception the categories are not employed. And it would be imposssible to claim that simply by slapping on the qualification "it seems to me that . . ." in front of a proposition, we might somehow be subtracting the categorial component of the proposition that is not so flanked. After all, we have to do with the same proposition in both cases. We do better to say that the necessity of agreement is found in the thought that it is no accident that everyone agrees, which is just what we have done in the aesthetic case.

"it would seem to everyone that *p*", but from "*x* pleases me" to "*x* would please everyone similarly placed to myself". Once this difference is brought out the analogy between the two cases may appear too weak to bear any serious weight. Our pleasures, he will want to say, are too subjective to be assimilated to the cognitive case.

To this objection Kant has a reply. It is that pleasure and its projection to others is less alien to the cognitive case than we are apt to suppose. Indeed, on his view it is an essential ingredient of it. Thus at Intro VI.3 he writes, ". . . it is certain that the pleasure appeared in due course, *and only by reason of the most ordinary experience being impossible without it*, has it become so gradually fused with simple cognition, and no longer arrests particular attention" (my emphasis). When we understand this thought, we shall see that it can be presented as genuinely reinforcing the analogy Kant is intent on developing, but I should stress that this is one of those places where Kant is exasperatingly imprecise and any exegetical offering will be more a tentative reconstruction of his position than a straightforward report of what he himself unequivocally states.

On the picture I have drawn, in coming to acquire (perceptual) knowledge of things around me, I need to fashion a representation of a projectible kind, one such that, on achieving it, I can reasonably hold that everyone would similarly entertain it were they in my position.[11] Having or forming a representation is an active matter. It involves us in intellectual operations of a complex kind on what is given in sensibility, involving conceptualization (with the aid of under-standing) and mnemic and proleptic connections with the past and future (with the assistance of memory and imagination). Quite how these are carried out and quite what they are supposed to be need not here concern us. All that is important is that the representation we come to is of our making rather than blankly

---

[11] Being in my position must not be taken here as, for instance, now being confronted by this warm stone. That would be question-begging. Rather it must mean, given perceptual data of the same sort, where what identifies sameness of sort ranges rather wider than what I am actually aware of at the moment, taking in, say, what data I would receive if I were to move a little to the right or left. The claim is that if sensibility is common to *a* and *b* each will handle his data in imagination and understanding in similar ways, because the same "proportion", ratio, or mix of these will give them pleasure.

imposed on us by the world, though of course that plays its part through what it provides by way of sensory input. From this it should emerge that as we confront some new situation and set about making sense of it, we are constantly confronted by the epistemic problem of whether to stick with the representation of it that we have so far arrived at, or whether to exercise our understanding-cum-imagination further and elaborate some ameliorated view of the given situation. Theoretically, there is no clear limit to the possibility of elaboration of our representations, and it is always up to us to decide when we have a view of things that warrants acceptance and brings the perceptually based belief-forming process to a halt.

Now, the one thing that we must at all costs avoid thinking is that we might be able to select our halting place by comparing a representation fashioned up to a certain point with the world as it is independently of us, and decide then to stay with a view of it that matches up to that, and rejecting any representation that is inadequate by that standard. For to have such a view would itself be to have a representation, and then we should be comparing one representation with another, not matching one up against the world itself, as this unacceptable model understands it. So if that alternative is untenable, the problem presses: Why do we stop the synthesizing process where we do?

Kant's answer must be taken to be that we stop at a point that we find matches sensibility to imagination and under-standing *in a way that we find pleasing or satisfying*, and that were it not for the sense of pleasure or satisfaction that some syntheses give us, there would be no particular reason not to pursue matters further. There would then be no way in which we could express the thought that this representation that we now have strikes us as just right. Striking us as right just is finding a particular representation satisfying as a way of handling our perceptual data subject to the constraints that are imposed by our scanning them with a cognitive end in view.

In the snippet I quoted from the Introduction, Kant is telling us that we may be surprised to think that this is so and that we may be inclined to protest because we do not regularly notice any marked pleasure in our cognitive conquest of the world around us, certainly not in the everyday cases that we are first likely to think of. But, he says, that's because we so take it for granted, and the pleasure has come to be "fused with the cognition in our minds" as a result of habituation. When we reflect on it, we can see that failing such a satisfaction we should have no answer to the question why we should ever bring our fashioning of belief about a particular situation to a halt. And that is the same question as how we could ever come to form any particular (perceptual) beliefs at all, without which, obviously, knowledge itself would be impossible. In sum, we form the perceptual beliefs (and others) that we do because they strike us as satisfying in solving the equation posed by (a), our sensory data and (b), the constraints under which we exercise imagination and understanding in the search for (c), tenable belief.[12]

The analogy with the aesthetic case is now very close. For a belief of mine that constitutes cognition will, because it must be true, be one that everyone would hold too in the right circumstances, and thus would be one that I can see would be bound to please all others too (and not just as a matter of coincidence). So when I claim that this or that is the case, on the grounds that it strikes me as being so and constitutes a pleasing representation for me, I am committing myself to its being a representation that will be universally (and necessarily) pleasing. And in the cognitive case, just as in the aesthetic one, the question is bound to arise how we are to explain this ability we have to project our pleasures in certain representations to other people. How one might ask, in Kant's own language, may we deduce the communicability of our cognitive representations? This question, of obvious urgency, is not taken up head on in the third *Critique*, or, so far as I know, in the first, but for help with the deduction of taste we shall need to come back to it as soon as one objection about the analogy I have been developing has been got out of the way.

III

The usual reaction to Kant's analogy is to think it too absurd to be taken seriously. But once a fundamental ontology of facts

[12] It is interesting that Kant himself uses the language of equation solving when he talks of the importance of the role of geometrical regularity in cognitive perception at §22.6 in the General Remark.

and the accompanying correspondence theory of truth are abandoned, we see Kant facing a very hard problem in the cognitive domain which is given a perfectly real answer that cannot be dismissed out of hand. It certainly should not be our reaction to the strange-sounding comparison with what he calls the "subjective side" of cognition to feel embarrassment on his behalf. Yet having got this far one will undoubtedly begin to wonder whether the analogy with cognition does not become too close – for setting up the cognitive situation as I have, it looks almost as if it is going to be impossible to distinguish the aesthetic one from it. Why, if we consent to follow Kant this far, do we not find ourselves thinking that taste is a kind of cognition itself?

Kant's reply has two branches. The first, now familiar to us, is to say that aesthetic judgment is not interested to discern a property of the object. It does not record any particular feature entering into our representations themselves. By contrast, a cognition will (for Kant) record representational content, and hold it out as one that is universally and necessarily shared. It is no part of what is claimed by the maker of the cognitive judgment that p that I or anyone else will be pleased to represent the world as p, although in the vocabulary I have used before, and for reasons I have just outlined, it will constitute part of the elucidation of the cognitive claim that p that everyone will find satisfaction in representing the world in that manner. In the aesthetic judgment by contrast, we are, by reason of its very analysis, claiming nothing other of a representation, having the content that it does, than that it will please everyone. It is not cognitive for Kant precisely because saying that something is beautiful, it provides no particular specification of how [we will find it pleasing] adequately to represent it in our search for a true account of the world.

I do not suppose that this reminder of Kant's view will still the objection. Anyone whom it really worries will say that even so exactly the same mental constellation that makes true "The representation of x as F is beautiful" verifies the proposition that x is F; it's just that the same thing is being reported on from two different angles, in the aesthetic case from the side of the pleasure that is present in knowledge, in the cognitive one, from the standpoint of the content that is found pleasing.

Putting it this way may encourage one to reformulate the objection, but not to abandon it. Now the objector will not say that there is no difference between cognitive claims and aesthetic judgments – for he has just allowed that to be secured – but will contend instead that the analogy Kant is pressing for unacceptably entails that the objects of cognition will all be beautiful, and that everything we experience as beautiful can be represented as an object of cognition.

To parry this threat, we need to invoke the second branch of Kant's reply, which turns on the distinction he draws between judgments that are *determinant* and those that are *reflexive*. The explanation he himself gives of it at Intro IV.2 is rather unhelpful. Judgments of the former sort bring particulars judged under a *given* rule (are "subsumptive"), while the latter *seek* a rule to apply to the particulars judged. Now if, as I suppose, this is meant to help us distinguish cognitive and aesthetic discourse,[13] it won't do, for it often happens, particularly when we make dramatic advances in our understanding of the world that our knowledge moves forward not just by the application of concepts and regularities [rules/laws] that are already given, in the sense of being concepts that we already possess, but instead by our finding novel ways of thinking about our situation that effectively extend our conceptual repertoire. In default of some imaginative leap we sometimes should not manage to handle what the world delivers up to our investigative scrutiny.

To avoid this pitfall, let us simply align determinant judgment with thought about how the world is viewed as being independently of us, then it makes some sense to say that

---

[13] This is not quite right because teleological judgment in general as applied to the natural world is also seen by Kant as reflexive without being aesthetic. What is needed is an idea of how to understand a rule or a universal being given. It sounds as if it reflects one's actual conceptual repertoire, but it suggests that what once was not given might later have become so as a result of our having made "reflexive" judgments. Then of course the status of a judgment as determinant or reflexive might change over time, and I do not think Kant would be happy about that at all. On my alternative reading, "given" reflects merely the claim that is made about something, whether we are saying that the world gives us the object like this or that by possessing a certain property "on its own account". This is, for Kant, not true of aesthetic or teleological claims. Only once the distinction is explained like this it cannot have much leverage in the argument since it presupposes an understanding of what cognition is and so cannot help us to make it.

synthesis of our representations is *determinant* in so far as it is pursued with a certain interest in mind – roughly an interest in handling our data so as to yield objective knowledge. Then we can see that determinant judgment will be judgment conducted within the framework of certain regulative constraints such as are usually marked out by saying that we organize our data with a view to consistency, conservatism, simplicity, plausibility and so on. And the pleasure we take in cognitive representations stems in part from finding a way of accommodating what we are presented with within these methodological guidelines.

Not all judgment is so conducted. *Reflexive* judgment precisely is judgment not subject to these guidelines, and the pleasure we find here is therefore not pleasure that results from the operation of the cognitive faculties *under these determinant constraints*. Rather it is pleasure we find in representations that are arrived at *freely*,[14] where the synthesized representations we come to yield their satisfactions immediately.[15] So on my interpretation, judgments that we make are pursued either with a view to yielding cognition and then produce pleasure determinantly, or else for the sake of a pleasure we find in immediate confrontation with our representations and irrespective of the constraints being observed that we need to respect if cognition is our goal. Whether the representation does accord with these constraints or not is neither here nor there in determining the pleasure we take in the object's reflexive contemplation.

How does this help us? To me it suggests that the pleasure that is definitive of aesthetic judgment is different in kind from that involved in cognitive judgment, different in that aesthetic pleasure is not *essentially* satisfaction in a representation achieved against the background of determinant constraints. It is free pleasure. So, take a successful cognitive judgment that x is F. We recognize that we would only have formed the representation had it been pleasing as fitting into the body of

[14] The word picks up Kant's insistence that imagination and understanding must operate together *in free play*. My suggestion is intended to offer some idea about what their freedom should be thought to consist in.

[15] Again, a favourite word of Kant's for which faithful exposition (or reconstruction) needs to find a place. Cf §42.2. He would gloss it: "*that is beautiful which pleases in the mere estimate of it* (not in sensation or by means of a concept)." (§45.2)

beliefs we determinantly built up in the search for objective understanding of the world, but it is an entirely open question whether if we abstract from the constraints that guide our selection of representations for this purpose it would then have been freely pleasing. So it does not follow that all objects of cognition are beautiful. Of course it may be that something that pleases us cognitively is also the focus of a representation that is freely and universally pleasing. Then it will indeed be beautiful. But no one finds that objectionable. The threat was that absolutely anything we came to discover about the world should necessarily be universally and non-fortuitously pleasing *aesthetically*, and that danger is now out of the way.

If this is the correct Kantian solution to this problem, it ought to find its place in the analysis of the beautiful as offered in the last chapter at the point where mention is made of disinterested contemplation. The importance of contemplation is stressed in the text at §29 General Remark 6 and elsewhere. It is however never given any elucidation. My suggestion is that we see Kant thinking of contemplation as the exercise of the cognitive faculties of imagination and understanding non-determinately, in free play, and not bound to the constraints under which belief formation is guided in the theoretical, objective, understanding of the world. If that is accepted, the analysis offered does then ensure that only reflective pleasure is referred to in the definition of beauty that we are given. It is a consequence that simply falls out of its elucidation.

IV

I take up now the question left hanging at the end of Section II. How in the *cognitive* case is the transition from evidence to content to be accounted for? Although Kant does not go into it in the *Critique of Judgment* it is fruitful for our understanding of the aesthetic case to pursue it as far as we can. Knowing what to say about the cognitive case will guide us in thinking about the aesthetic one.

"If cognitions are to admit of communication, then our mental state, i.e. the way the cognitive powers are attuned for cognition generally, and in fact, the relative proportion suitable for a representation (by which an object is given to us) from which cognition is to result, must also admit of being universally communicated, as without this, which is the subjective condition of the act of knowing, knowledge, as effect, would not arise."

We have seen that what accounts for our forming the cognitive representations we do is pleasure of a certain sort. Here, at §21.1, Kant further describes that pleasure. It is, he thinks, a satisfaction we take in certain mental dispositions of our faculties, certain mixes of sensibility, imagination and understanding. The interplay of the three[16] provides us in cognition with a subjective, mental, pleasurable feeling, akin perhaps to the sort of bodily pleasure my journeyman might get from feeling his muscles working together as he scythes the long grass in the meadow beneath the house – a *mental* pleasure akin to the physical one in that what provides me with satisfaction in cognition is the feeling of the three mental "muscles" working together as they come to form a particular representation. And this pleasure, tied to this internal object, is what is causally important in getting me to stop with the representation that brings it about. This, I believe, is what Kant calls "the subjective condition of the act of knowing".

Now if such a pleasure explains why I end up in certain circumstances with a particular representation and it is true that others also have the same representation in those circumstances, as they must do if I am to count as acquiring knowledge through mine, then they must enjoy the same subjective mental pleasures as I do. That is, by §21.1, they must feel the same mixes of interaction between the faculties to be satisfying, and find that they are provoked by the same representations and not different ones. And Kant has a piece of vocabulary tailored to fit this requirement. It is that this communicability or sharing of mental pleasure must stem from *a common sense*.[17] That is, pleasure sharing is not just fortuitous, but occurs in a regular and principled way, rooted in a psychic disposition common to all. Thus he says at §21.1

---

[16] Different, he makes plain, for different representations. (§21.1)

[17] It is a mistake to think that the common sense is just Kant's name for the fact of universal agreement. That could explain nothing, certainly not the universal agreement it is meant to explain. The common sense is a disposition to agree that is responsible for such universal agreement as actually occurs.

"We assume a common sense as the necessary condition of the universal communicability of our knowledge, which is presupposed in every logic and every principle of knowledge that is not one of scepticism."[18]

In the case of cognition, our confidence that such a common subjective disposition exists is founded in (a) the undisputable fact that we have knowledge of the world around us and (b) the transcendental reflexion that this would only be possible if there existed a common sense of this sort. We do not need empirical investigation to be assured of its existence, since it is a priori guaranteed conditionally on our achieving cognitive success. Even so, it is admitted by Kant that there has to be some explanation for our possession of such a handy endowment. That it is something that humans actually possess cannot be passed off as a wild coincidence. I come back to this below. First though we may ask how these thoughts about cognition are exploited for the sake of the *aesthetic* deduction.

In essence Kant's line of argument is straightforward. In aesthetic judgment, just as in the formation of cognitive representations, we find pleasure in the workings of the mind.[19] This is secured by our needing to explain how we form or synthesize the representations that we do. As in the cognitive case, this can only be pleasure taken in the harmonious interplay of the representation-determining faculties. To come by and remain in contemplation of such a representation

[18] Recall that at §20.2 Kant is quite outspoken about the common sense in the aesthetic domain. "The judgment of taste, therefore depends on our presupposing the existence of a common sense. But this is not to be taken to mean some external sense, but the effect arising from the free play of our powers of cognition" (*die Wirkung aus dem freien Spiel unserer Erkenntniskräfte*). *Effect* must be the wrong idea, though it may be the translator's rather than Kant's. The *Wirkung aus dem . . .* construction is not received German for the relation of effect to cause. The common sense has to account for my judgment in the sense that it has to stem from this disposition that I share with others. In no way is it an effect of the play of the cognitive faculties; it is realized in their play.

[19] Cf e.g. §9.3 ". . . it is the universal capacity for being communicated incident to the mental state in the given representation which, as the subjective condition of the judgment of taste, must be fundamental, with the pleasure in the object as its consequent". And §9.4 "The cognitive powers brought into play by this representation are here engaged in a free play, since no definite concept restricts them to a particular rule of cognition. Hence the mental state in this representation must be one of a feeling of the free play of the powers of representation in a given representation for a cognition in general". I take it as essential that the feeling of free play has to be one we enjoy.

requires it to cause me such a mental pleasure. Now from our reflection about cognition, we know that the mental pleasures in the harmonious operation of the cognitive faculties that people enjoy are rooted in a common sense, so Kant thinks we can conclude that that is something we may rely on to secure communicability of our aesthetic, just as of our cognitive pleasures. That is why, on the basis of my own sense of mental harmony, I can be justified in claiming that everyone else will respond likewise. Thus is the transition from evidence to content supposedly secured.

Weak though it is, the argument is not without its virtue. First we should see that whatever is wrong with it, the story about cognition on which it rests is anything but risible. Anyone disenchanted with the metaphysics of a traditional correspondence theory of truth and belief acquisition can be expected to find some appeal to it. Then, it allows us to appreciate why Kant finds it natural to characterize beauty in terms of a sense of pleasure in the interplay of the cognitive faculties (e.g. §9.4, §20.2), which otherwise appears to step onto the stage in a rather mysterious and unmotivated way. That is a general consequence of his account of representation formation and retention.[20] Finally, it brings out something that will later be crucial for the development of the less ambitious argument, namely that there does exist a disposition to share our mental satisfactions, and that such agreements evidently lie within the intellectual repertoire of those who make aesthetic judgments, seeing as that ability can only be exercised by those who anyway display cognitive competence.

How sure can we be that Kant did accept the argument? Certainly some of the time he is sensitive to the need to say something else, as we shall see. But §38 fn is as explicit as anything could be. "In order to be justified in claiming universal agreement for an aesthetic judgment it is sufficient to assume: (1) that the subjective conditions of this faculty of

[20] I take it that we retain beliefs, for Kant, only in so far as a representation remains pleasing as we reflect on it. Aesthetically, we stay with a perceptual representation only as long as it continues to please us. "This pleasure . . . involves an inherent causality, that, namely, of preserving a continuance of the state of the representation itself and the active engagement with the cognitive powers without ulterior aim. We dwell on the contemplation of the beautiful because this contemplation strengthens and reproduces itself" (§12.1)

aesthetic judgment are identical with all men in what concerns the relation of the cognitive faculties there brought into action, with a view to a cognition in general. This must be true, as otherwise men would be incapable of communicating their representations or even their knowledge; (2) that the judgment has paid regard merely to this relation."

What really goes wrong with the argument is that under cover of his talk about harmony of the faculties Kant wants to assimilate the cognitive and the aesthetic cases, which he is in general at such pains to keep apart. This is very plain in this last passage, which repeats the formula of §9.4, where the harmony of the faculties in free play is said to aim at *a cognition in general*. However the fact that we have a common sense operating to account for the same cognitive representations of the world when we are guided by an interest in truth is insufficient basis for the claim that when I achieve a pleasing aesthetic representation in which my faculties are harmoniously operating, that same common sense will ensure that others will share my pleasure in the representation should they come to have it. For in the aesthetic case the harmonious operation of the faculties is not guided by, even if it may run side by side with, an interest in truth. They are thus not directed at anything that could be properly called "a cognition in general". As Kant repeatedly stresses, they are in free play, and we have no assurance at all once the identity with cognition is lost, that in free play they will provoke the feeling of mental well-being at the same point for everyone. One might say it could not be the same common sense at work in the two cases. But the only common sense we have any argued warrant for believing in is a cognitive one. To assume the existence of an *aesthetic* common sense on that basis is precisely to beg the very question at issue.[21]

The objection comes out more forcefully perhaps when Kant is encouraged to avoid the unnecessary detour through

---

[21] Often Kant stresses that we *presuppose* a common sense in making aesthetic judgments. Cf §20.2. But we must not think that this helps the argument along. It must be heard as acknowledging that only if there is a common sense can judgments of taste be warranted. Once we refuse to assimilate the aesthetic case to the cognitive one, grounds for believing that there is a common sense of the right sort remain to be provided.

the harmony of the cognitive faculties, as sometimes he manages to do. It may well be that since an instance of their harmonious operation cannot be identified except through the particular ways of perceiving things that we find pleasing, any logically distinct reference to the mind's working and to the feelings that it is purported to generate is otiose. The beautiful object, I suspect, is better thought of by Kant not as one whose representation occasions the feeling of the faculties in harmonious free play (however much he likes to stress this), but quite straightforwardly as one in the very representation of which there is a harmonious interplay of the two (cf §38 Remark), or whose representation, involving as it does the operation of imagination and understanding, is found pleasing on account of the way in which they are united in the image so formed, and independently of the way they might answer to or fail to answer to our cognitive concerns. Once it is put like this, we can see that the argument that assures us of communicable pleasure in cognitively formed representations, is unavailable, since what may make all the difference is that they and they alone are formed in response to constraints that anyone who seeks knowledge is bound to abide by. When these constraints are relaxed, and the mind operates freely, it is an open question whether the representations that I find harmoniously pleasing will be of equal appeal to you. Perhaps they will, but nothing in Kant's argument either deductive or inductive should yet persuade us that they are bound to be so.

V

As far as Kant's explicit statement of his argument goes, the direct and ambitious version of the deduction has now collapsed. We can still ask though whether there is not material available in the text to help him circumvent the objection over which it has stumbled. A passage in which Kant confronts the question of the existence of a common sense in a curiously tentative way is to my mind highly suggestive. At §22.2 he writes:

> This indeterminate norm of a common sense is, as a matter of fact presupposed by us; as is shown by our presuming to lay down judgments of taste. But does such a common sense in fact

exist as a constitutive principle of the possibility of experience, or is it formed for us as a regulative principle by a still higher principle of reason, that for higher ends first seeks to beget in us a common sense? Is taste in other words a natural and original faculty, or is it only the idea of one that is artificial and to be acquired by us . . . so that a judgment of taste, with its demand for universal assent, is but a requirement of reason for generating such a consensus . . . ?

We have seen above that a *cognitive* common sense is indeed a constitutive principle of the possibility of experience, but that we have found no grounds for thinking same to be true of an *aesthetic* common sense. But I said that Kant would be ready enough to admit that our possession of a cognitive common sense requires an explanation, for if nothing were on offer here the fact that the world contains creatures that find satisfaction in the same representations of their world might appear as a kind of unplumbable mystery. To say that they have to do so if they are to have experience and cognition – that this is a constitutive principle for the possibility of experience – is one thing, but that does nothing to resolve the mystery. That there is experience at all cries out for explanation too.

Later on in the work, in his discussion of the antinomy of taste in §57, Kant alludes to the supersensible in general as the substrate of nature (§57 Remark 2.4) and there identifies it ("this *same* supersensible") with the determining ground of the judgment of taste, somehow or other responsible for our sharing our aesthetic pleasures. The supersensible is here put forward as "the unique key to the riddle of this faculty" [viz. judgment] and Kant pessimistically avows that there is no means of making it any more intelligible.

It looks then as if Kant might think of arguing like this: that a *cognitive* common sense exists needs an explanation, and the only place to find one is in the to us necessarily inscrutable working of the supersensible. We notice also that there is widespread shared pleasure of an aesthetic kind – "the actual existence of beauties of nature is patent to experience" (§38 Remark) – and the question is whether we have reason to think that non-coincidental and, as such, universal. What could be more natural than to think that if the supersensible somehow – though in a way necessarily unintelligible to us – explains our agreement in cognitive satisfactions as being non-fortuitous and universal, the very same supersensible (there is after all only one) will in all likelihood account for our aesthetic satisfactions too, and account for them in the same way as in the cognitive case, through the operation of a common sense? If the supersensible has explanatory power for the cognitive case, then by a kind of eduction we may suppose it also to supply the aesthetic common sense that we are looking for reason to believe in. Developed to this limit, the cognitive analogy once again pretends to underpin the evidence-content transition for taste without moving far beyond the confines of reflection about cognition itself.

Now I am not offering this thought as one that Kant himself explicitly puts forward. He doesn't. Nor am I suggesting it as a good one. It isn't. But I do think that it is instructive in a number of ways and helps us to see how Kant is at least tempted to move at this delicate stage of his argument. In the first place, it is suggestive of a route to an aesthetic common sense that does not simply conflate the aesthetic and the cognitive cases as Kant appears to have done in the official deduction. Second, it moves as it does via recognition of the need for some explanation of observed facts in order that they should not seem just fortuitous, and third, it does this by helping itself to the idea of one and the same explanatory principle ("the same supersensible") operating in both domains.

Kant's high metaphysical explanation of the cognitive phenomenon could only have appealed (if in fact it did)[22] because a properly natural explanation did not come to mind. But if there is a key to "the riddle" of judgment, it has to be a natural key, and it has precisely not to be something that cannot be made intelligible.[23] Respecting this requirement, we

[22] The quoted passage suggests the natural and original/artificial and acquired distinction runs together with constitutive/regulative distinction. But we ought to note (a) that a common sense as constitutive of experience leaves something unexplained, something which, in accordance with the precept of the first *Critique* must as far as our understanding can reach have "empirically conditioned existence" (A561/B589) and (b) that "this principle does not in any way debar us from recognizing that the whole series may rest upon some intelligible being that is free from all empirical conditions and itself contains the ground of the possibility of all appearances."

[23] Wittgenstein is better here than Kant. cf *Tractatus* 6.5: "The *riddle* does not exist. If a question can be framed at all, it is also *possible* to answer it."

might say that our possession of a cognitive common sense serves a very clear function. It enables us to form representations of our world without which we could not come to adequate practical mastery of it. Unless we developed it, and developed it fairly early in life, natural pressures would soon enough select against us in competition with our better endowed peers and ecological rivals. So there is perhaps no reason to be surprised at the existence of the cognitive common sense and, at the end of the day, no reason to think of its existence as inscrutably mysterious.

Naturalizing the metaphysical thought in this way, as I think we need to if we are to make anything sensible of it at all, brings out the implausibility of trying to extend exactly the very same idea to the aesthetic case. For whereas there was only one supersensible to do the explanatory work when it was conceived of metaphysically, once some naturalized version supersedes it, there is no pressure on us to use the same explanation to legitimize our supposition of a common aesthetic sense. It is not going to carry conviction to claim *without further ado*[24] that agreement in aesthetic pleasure brings with it selective advantages prominent enough to ensure we are natively equipped with an aesthetic sense that is genuinely common – i.e universal, as Kant requires it to be.

Perhaps the most instructive thing about this excursion is that once we accept the naturalization of the demand for explanation we see it may make sense to look for an alternative explanation than that which works for cognition that might generate an aesthetic common sense, different from that which so quickly comes to mind for the cognitive one. Furthermore, and turning now to Kant himself, with this thought in mind we might hear the second alternative he alludes to in §22.2 as suggesting that he will be prepared to look for some suitably *non*-transcendent "higher ends" that we have and which are satisfiable only if we *acquire* a common sense that we exercise in aesthetic judgment. In the next

---

[24] The qualification is important. I dare say that the indirect route to his conclusion that we find Kant taking in the later sections of the work could be cast in this mould too, but it can only be done with a degree of filling in that forces us to explore beyond the limits of the cognitive analogy, which sets the boundary to my present ambition.

chapter, and setting out from this same passage. I shall argue that his reflections about the interest of the beautiful serve precisely this end, and that, whether this is how Kant steadily thinks of them or not, after the introduction of one crucial novelty it may lie within their power to take a revised version of the deduction of taste further than it can yet honestly hope to do.

The question does arise though, if we are leaving behind any thought of using one and the same explanatory principle for the two cases, whether Kant's reflections about knowledge do not now become totally idle. If that were the upshot of the adumbrated move forward, I think we should have to say that it could not be at all happily attributed to Kant simply because the reflections about cognition are so central to the overall argument. But we do not have to say this. In my preliminary remarks I said that we should remember that we were concerned with a transcendental question. Now the sceptic in these matters might well be one who thinks that there could be no reason at all for believing that *any* agreements in pleasure in our representations could be necessary and universal, and that once it is admitted that beauty has to be analysed in those terms we could have no grounds for thinking that true contingent claims that this or that is beautiful could ever be made.[25] The reflections on knowledge however are needed to show that such agreement is a *possibility*, by there, in the cognitive case, being actual. Further, they show that it is a possibility that draws on nothing more than powers of mind that are at work in the *aesthetic* judgments that we make. So even if the transcendental deduction as developed so far cannot get to the conclusion that the aesthetic judgments we make can rightfully claim legitimacy, we know that they pretend to a legitimacy that *is not beyond our intellectual competence to achieve*. The question that remains open is whether *as things actually are* the aesthetic judgments that we make exploit this possibility as we like to suppose they do. As far as the argument is set to continue, that will be shown affirmatively if Kant can persuade

[25] For contingency see Intro VII.5 ". . . one who feels pleasure in simple reflection on the form of an object, without having any concept of it in mind, rightly lays claim to the agreement of everyone, although this judgment is empirical and a singular judgment".

us that the aesthetic agreements that we notice flow from a disposition to share pleasures that is rooted in identifiable non-cognitive interests that are indisputably and ineliminably ours.

6

The Aesthetic *Ought* and the Acquisition of Taste

I

The reading of the deduction I have been exploring so far has followed Kant in attempting to treat taste as what he called "an original and natural faculty", depending essentially on our possession of a common sense "as a constitutive principle of the possibility of experience" (§22.2). Quite apart from the failures by which we have seen it beset, that programme is also clearly ill equipped to handle a thought we have about taste that Kant shows himself aware of in his discussion at §32.4 of the young poet and his mature and critical friends. The young, unpractised, poet is there portrayed as making a perfectly respectable judgment of taste about his own work – as disinterested and conscientious as may be – yet most certainly it is not a judgment that everyone else makes. His more experienced friends do not share his enthusiasm, and what's more Kant thinks of the situation as one in which the poet himself is *mistaken* in his judgment. His youthful enthusiastic view of his juvenilia is critically untenable. This throws up two related problems.

The first is to explain how a deduction of taste, the familiar evidence to content transition, can be rendered compatible with the plain fact that many judgments of taste are not widely, let alone universally, endorsed by other disinterested parties. As we have it so far, it must appear that if we have an explanation of why it is reasonable to infer from my own disinterested appreciation of something or other to everyone else's responding likewise, there really should be no breakdown of the connection if that really does stem from "an original and natural" faculty. One could of course surmise that breakdown should occasionally be in some way associated with interfering factors messing things up, but as the example of the young poet is set up this seems not to be envisaged. He is advised after all, not to abandon his own assessment of his verse in favour of his critics' view, but to wait until he learns to find himself responding as they do. There is nothing amiss with his natural endowment and nothing suspect about its functioning.

The second puzzle is this. It seems that it is just a contingent fact that the young poet has critics at all. He might just have had enthusiastic friends, an admiring *Jugendbund* say, whose aesthetic views all echoed his own. Since Kant evidently views the older critics as having a *correct* view of the matter, it would seem that even if, counterfactually, the young man's judgment of taste had been seconded by all disinterested parties, their universal agreement in taste would not in fact be sufficient to verify the claim that his poetry was beautiful. It would still be bad verse. Similarly, if we think of the mature critics' assessment of their friend's work as correct, we shall in no way be deterred by the reflection that its correctness would, on the "original and natural" faculty reading of the matter, seem to be impugned, falsified even, by failure of the *Jugendbund* to agree with them. Their aesthetic judgment is correct without being universal, and correct no matter how numerous the dissenting disinterested voices.

In §22.2, entertaining the failure of the "original and natural" understanding of the matter, Kant somewhat tentatively but, as I hear him, none the less favourably, adverts to an alternative view of the possession of a common sense involved in taste, this time as a merely regulative principle, and taste itself as "an artificial faculty yet to be acquired". If we put this idea to work, we can see how the two problems just raised can be resolved within the familiar framework that Kant offers his readers. What we shall say is that the young poet and his coevals make their judgments – and judgments that are unimpeachably judgments of taste – without having acquired critical sensitivity or taste proper, and that they get matters wrong because there is no inference to be had from their own untutored (though disinterested) responses to things to a universal response on the part of those who have acquired the "artificial" faculty Kant postulates. The first problem disappears because it rests on the false assumption that the deduction must embrace the task of warranting the claim that everyone would take delight here on the sole basis of a man's own disinterested delight, without any distinction between those individuals who have acquired taste and those who have not. More properly put, the deduction has to move from judgments of taste made by those who have acquired "the artificial faculty", and such is not the case of the young poet. Up until now this requirement has remained quite hidden.

The second problem also fades away. The universality of delight that constitutes beauty cannot just be the universality of disinterested parties. Rather it too is the universality of disinterested parties *who have acquired the faculty of taste*. Then the imagined situation in which everyone seconds the young poet's estimation of his work does not touch the supposition that they are all mistaken about its beauty. Similarly widespread disagreement with the mature critics may well be insufficiently well based to falsify their pondered and practised judgment.

The first question to ask about this new figure on the scene is whether the revision of the analysis of the beautiful that it involves is anywhere prepared for in the earlier sections of the text. When we reflect that the discussion of §32 does not even seem to present a shadow of perplexity to Kant's mind, it is only charitable to assume that he believed it posed no problem for him rather than that he had not seen the dangers it might lead to. When we further remember that the §22 passage lies at the end of Kant's discussion of the Moment of Modality we can perhaps see why this might have been.

The necessity involved in the concept of the beautiful was said in §18 to be not theoretical, nor practical, but *exemplary*. This, Kant says, commits us not to the view that others *will* agree with him but that they *ought* to do so (§19.1). A man who makes a judgment of taste exacts the agreement of others as a sort of duty (§40.7). So the beautiful object is not just one that every disinterested spirit would find pleasure in (given the right circumstances) but, in addition, is one that everyone *ought* to respond to with favour.[1]

When we came across it before, in Chapter 4, I simply said that this normative element in Kant's story was unmotivated. At least it was not forced onto us by the need to distinguish between the beautiful and the agreeable, which was how he presented it on its first occurrence. So I set it aside. Now however we may reflect that in Kant's mind it represents another element in the elucidation of the beautiful that will assist us not to misrepresent the proper relationship between poet and critic. In its absence the problems noted above would be inescapable. With it in place we avoid the threat they would otherwise pose.

I have suggested that the *ought* of §19 is connected to the acquisition of taste that is mentioned in §22. Textually this connection is made immediately after the rather convoluted passage cited from this section towards the end of the last chapter. It is one that is important enough to repeat here. I emphasize the crucial new clauses.

> This indeterminate norm of a common sense is, as a matter of fact presupposed by us; as is shown by our presuming to lay down judgments of taste. But does such a common sense in fact exist as a constitutive principle of the possibility of experience, or is it formed for us as a regulative principle by a still higher principle of reason, that for higher ends first seeks to beget in us a common sense? Is taste in other words a natural and original faculty, or is it only the idea of one that is artificial and to be acquired by us . . . so that a judgment of taste, with its demand for universal assent, is but a requirement of reason for generating such a consensus? *Does the ought*, i.e. the objective necessity of the confluence of the feeling of any one man with that of every other, *merely betoken the possibility of arriving at this accord, and the judgment of taste merely afford an example of the application of this principle*? – These questions we have neither the wish nor the power to investigate as yet; . . .

---

[1] We should not forget that once the deduction is complete, we shall want to say that everyone will (or would) take pleasure in the beautiful thing, only the generality is then restricted to those who have acquired taste. It quite abstracts from everyone else. The *ought* by contrast does apply to everyone, quite unrestrictedly, whether they have taste or not.

Here the faculty of taste and the aesthetic *ought* are quite explicitly brought together, though not perhaps in the way that might have been expected. What the *ought* here applies to is the acquisition of the faculty itself, and not directly to any delight in the individual beautiful object. What Kant is getting at is that if we could find a "higher purpose" for acquiring taste, then we ought to acquire it, and our doing so would make possible for us what otherwise we would not be able to do, namely regularly and predictably share our aesthetic pleasures with one another. Nonetheless we can see that on this reading of the primary *ought* it would still be fairly natural to say that "he who describes anything as beautiful claims that [one][2] ought to give his approval to the object in question" (§19.1), because if there genuinely were a significant rational requirement on us to acquire the faculty of taste, then it would scarcely be one that could be satisfied without that faculty being exercised. Hence it would be reasonable to say that beautiful objects are objects that people should take delight in, as objects on which they may properly exercise the faculty that they are rationally required to acquire.

If this is right we have an explanation of why previously it seemed so unnatural to try to make anything of the *ought* which now moves centre stage. If the possession of a common sense were as Kant puts it constitutive of experience and not a merely regulative idea, then there would be no *ought* about its acquisition; we should possess it willy nilly. We should have to have it as a condition of experience itself, and if we were to think of it as a capacity that (in reflexive judgment) we might or might not exercise quite automatically, there would be no parallel reasoning available to that I have just offered to explain why we ought to take delight in the individual beautiful object. Now however matters are different, and thinking of the faculty of taste as one we might acquire rather than come ready equipped with, it is quite in place to enquire whether it is not one that we ought to strive for. And to say that we should.

---

[2] The text here, as one might expect, has "everyone". My reason for making the change is only not to divert attention from the present issue of attaching the *ought* to the particular object. We shall attend to its range later on.

II

There is then some initial textual backing to support the alternative attempt on the deduction that I claim Kant is attracted to. What makes it significant is not just that it enables him to avoid the problems that the original version of the deduction would have been exposed to when it comes to discussing disagreements of taste, as between our poet and his critics, but that it makes the deduction itself far easier to carry through than before it was. Or so at least it seemed to Kant. The reason that this is so is that its crucial terms are no longer identified as they were before, and that this makes all the difference to securing an effective transition from one to the other.

Of course the problem itself is still the same: how to get from the judgment of taste that a man makes, to the truth of the claim that the object of his attention is beautiful. But the proper specification of each of the two terms, the judgment of taste itself and the analysis of the beauty have themselves undergone subtle alteration. In the first place, as I have said, not just any judgment of taste will warrant the inference that its object is a beautiful one. Only those will do so which are themselves exercises of the acquired faculty of taste, where the judgment that is made is sensitive to those considerations that the faculty itself is attuned to. On this score the young poet of §32 will not make a *paradigmatic* judgment of taste, though judgment of taste he will make nonetheless. When Kant tells him not to abandon his judgment of taste as a base for his assessment of his verse, not to prefer the opinion of his critics, even though he himself be in error in his estimation of the work, what he must have in mind is that while the poet should seek for a more sustainable response to his verses than he has, he should seek it by way of acquiring the right responses. It is not enough to make the correct assessment in any old way. He still has to make it on the basis of his own response. It is that which has to be improved on, not the basis of his assessment itself.

The term to which the inference of the deduction is aimed is now also significantly altered. For we no longer account something of beauty provided that it give pleasure to all (or most, or a significant number etc.) of conscientious and disinterested observers. Rather we are concerned with all (. . .) conscientious and disinterested observers *who have acquired the faculty of taste.* That is the elucidation of beauty itself now makes reference to those who are sensitive to the mooted rational requirements on them to share their pleasure in objects of certain kinds and not in others.[3] So the claim that has to be substantiated on the basis of the paradigmatic judgment of taste is that it is no accident that all those who have acquired taste should find pleasure in the disinterested contemplation of the object in question. Once we see Kant's train of thought developing in this way, as previously it was unable to do, it becomes apparent why he finds the deduction so straightforward a matter, at least as far as its formalities go.

Suppose I have acquired taste and judge this object to be a beautiful one by responding to it with pleasure. I shall, according to Kant, have come to find pleasure in it as I am required to "for some higher purpose", and shall reflect that everyone else is likewise rationally bound to share my pleasure in the thing if only they come across it in the right frame of mind. So if I assert the object to be beautiful and commit myself thereby to that holding true of it, I shall know that it will be true of it at least that others *ought* to find it pleasing. It is not a large step from here to the thought that I need, that others *would* in fact find it pleasing were they only to contemplate it. For we have seen already that Kant believes the acquisition of taste puts people in a position in which they *could* well enough share their taste and take pleasure in the object. Furthermore the supposition that they regard it disinterestedly and conscientiously will give me every reason to suppose that in those circumstances not only *could* they find pleasure in it, but also that they *would* do so.[4]

---

[3] One should not be scared of circularity here. The kind in question is not the beautiful.

[4] The transition from *could* to *would* here is one that Kant does not comment on. If what really matters to him is the universality of the analysing claim, then he would only secure this by giving a *would if* . . . account of the *could* here. We know however that such an attempt is bound to fail. Dispositions cannot be made fail safe, so there is no reason to think that even if everyone who has acquired taste could take pleasure in the designated object, that they would in fact all do so provided only they were disinterested and clearheaded and so on. Sometimes there will be failure. The right response seems to me to say that there is every good reason to think that in the

In the *Remark* appended to the official transcendental deduction of §38 Kant observes that it has been peculiarly easy to secure. We see now why this is so. He observes there, for the fourth time,[5] that the only real difficulty is to be sure one has correctly subsumed the particular case under the general principle. I think that what he has in mind, is that while we can in the abstract see why there is a good inference from the reformulated judgment of taste to the reformulated understanding – the proper understanding, we must now say – of the claim that something is beautiful, we are usually interested in making such an inference when we reflect on judgments that we ourselves make as we confront an object that strikes us as particularly fine. And then the problem is to be sure from within that situation that our response to it is indeed one that is tempered by our having acquired the faculty of taste. Sometimes we may be mistaken in thinking that our judgment is sound and that we are possessed of the faculty. On other occasions, while we may indeed have taste, our disinterested appreciation of the given object may not itself be responsive to our having acquired it, but somehow be deviant. In either case we are liable to be in error in our judgment that the object is a beautiful one, and not be able to deploy the deduction to provide insurance against the danger. But here there is no resource but to take care that we do not fall into these dangers. Evidently there can be no cast-iron assurance that protects us against them in all circumstances.

Now all this is, as Kant would put it, conditional.[6] That is, it all depends on our being able to make good the claim that men really ought to acquire taste, and hence on being able to argue that there are indeed higher reasons which we can rely on in the judgments that we make to ensure that our common ways of speaking about beauty and beautiful things are properly grounded. It is this that constitutes the more arduous task that Kant faces, not the deduction itself. Subject only to this

---

disinterested situation those who can now find the selected things delightful will normally do so, and that we should be content with a weaker generality than that insisted on by Kant.

[5] cf also §19.1, §22.1, §38 fn.

[6] cf §18 caption.

condition, that is now easy enough to secure. The real question is whether it is a kind of reasoning that we can rely on in our world, and in our world as things in fact are. Is the claim that we ought to acquire taste one that we are entitled to?

III

Someone might well want to deny that it is, on the ground that the only way in which it is proper to speak of what we all ought to find delight in will depend on our already having secured the notion of the beautiful, and that it could not be used to provide the foundations for it. This objection comes from the philosopher who thinks that the only way in which it makes sense to say that someone ought to share my taste is to use the "ought" as an expression of expectation and not, as Kant thinks, of (quasi-) duty. So, he will say, it can only function as we use it in sentences such as "your bath ought to be ready for you by now" or "you ought to make that train if you hurry", or "that wound ought to heal in a couple of days". And of course, he will say, if the analysis of *x is beautiful* gives us that everyone rightly disposed would find *x* pleasing, a man who judges *x* to be beautiful on account of the way it strikes him will indeed quite reasonably think that everyone ought to share his taste in just this way. Thinking that they will share it, he will expect them to do so. Only the source of his expectation stems entirely from his thought that *x* is beautiful, so he evidently cannot use the *ought* in any way to secure the warrantability of his judgment of taste. If it holds, it does so just because his judgment is already secure.

If there truly were no other *ought* in the offing, this objection would be cogent enough. But Kant is sure that there is; and he is right. Only he makes it difficult for us to recognize because of the connection he mistakenly perceives between *ought* and *duty*, and his idiosyncratic (and historically fateful) conception of duty as what is expressible by a categorical imperative. However if we set aside all thought about duty and moral obligation, it should strike us that by saying that a man ought to do something we often express the impersonal thought that there is a good reason for him to do it, and that this is a ground for him to do it whether he wants to or not. In the jargon of the trade "ought" may often express an external, or normative, reason for action. Putting it like this we can say that Kant apparently believes that external reasons extend to our affective responses, and that it is part of the notion of the beautiful that there is an external reason lying on everyone to find pleasure in it. This he signals in a phrase I have drawn on above by suggesting that there may be a "higher reason for producing a common sense in us for higher purposes" (§22.2). Whether we eventually agree with him or not, there is no reason to think that if such a way of speaking is in order and has this kind of foundation, it will itself need to be underwritten by the relevant object's beauty. Kant is explicit enough (at §40.7) that the ground of the *ought* is to be found elsewhere. What everything turns on is whether he has an adequate ground for thinking that some things do generate external reasons on us to find them sources of pleasure, that there is a genuine external reason lying on us to acquire the faculty of taste.

Remember that what has to be explained in the first instance is why we might think there is a reason to acquire a faculty that brings with it a common sense. Kant remarks at §40.7 "If we could assume that the mere universal communicability of a feeling must carry in itself an interest for us with it (which however, we are not justified in concluding from the character of a merely reflexive judgment), we should be able to explain why the feeling in the judgment of taste comes to be imputed to everyone, so to speak, as a duty". The search for an interest we might have in sharing our pleasures then is the same thing as a search for a higher purpose which might make it obligatory to cultivate a common sense. I take it that this is evidence enough that Kant would be happy to identify his *ought* with the existence of external reasons that bear on us. A corollary would be that he would naturally think the interest would have to be one that we all share, and that we could not sidestep. Only then would the *ought* that is to be generated be sufficiently akin to the categorical imperative that he thinks it must come close to expressing. Hence his demand at the end of §40 that we have a kind of *duty* to find pleasure in the beautiful, and the later developed theme that the exemplary necessity that is involved in the idea is analogous to that of moral obligation (like it, not being a practical, means-to-end, necessity).

The discussion starts off in §41 by setting aside a minor worry. How could there be an interest in our sharing pleasures that are by definition disinterested? Isn't there a contradiction here? If so, of course the enquiry would sink at launch, but Kant is swift to insist that while a pure judgment of taste can have no interest *as its determining ground*, that does not mean that no interest can be combined with it (§41.1). Thereby he means that our sharing our disinterested pleasures can perfectly well subserve some interest or need or concern. We could say it is one that we all have and whose satisfaction is of importance in our lives for our overall well-being, one which stems only from pleasures that are not themselves responses to the satisfactions of some specific practical desires we may have.

The first suggestion Kant considers is that sharing our pleasures furthers something empirical – "an inclination proper to human nature" (§41.2), he calls it – and that we are inclined to judge things in respect of how suitable they are for making it the case that we communicate our feelings to all other men (that is, I take it, that we share the same pleasures as one another). Our judgment of an object will be according as we think it able to produce pleasure in all, and our interest in the tendency to promote "what everyone's natural inclination desires", to wit, society, or social cohesiveness.

The idea is straightforward enough. We need to promote society against threats to disruption from within as much as from without. One way to achieve this is by fostering cohesiveness in our community, and this will surely be markedly assisted by the development of a capacity to share our pleasures. In particular it might be supposed that if we train ourselves to share our disinterested pleasures, we shall find ourselves emotionally knitted together, and not just utilitarianly in the way of business friendships or political or defensive alliances. Since it is this kind of cohesion that we set store by, we have the best of reasons to ensure that the disinterested pleasures we take in things around us are ones that others are likely to share.

As it happens, Kant himself rejects this suggestion as being unsuitable for his purposes, albeit not perhaps for the same reasons as we would. His objection is that while the cultivation of taste may provide for a need we all have, it is not a need of a kind that makes us say *you ought to develop taste* in anything like as stringent a way as would generate a categorical imperative. For this appears to be an *ought* that depends on our actually having a desire for social cohesiveness, and that, Kant thinks, is an empirical matter. It is something which it is at least theoretically possible for us to disclaim any interest in or concern for. On Kant's reckoning this could not give rise to an *ought* that might "be imputed to everyone, so to speak, as a duty". Even if the desire does in fact occur quite ubiquitously, the mere possibility of its not doing so unfits it in his eyes for its present dialectical role.

Quite apart from Kant's overheated conception of duty and obligation, the argument is patently a bad one. If the main question is whether, as we like to think, our best candidates for correct ascriptions of beauty have any legitimate claim to the term, it should be sufficient that *as we are* we have a fairly constant interest in belonging to pretty cohesive societies. Perhaps we might in far fetched circumstances encounter people who had a marginal interest in society and social cohesion. Then this empirical consideration would indeed provide no very good reason for *them* to develop a shared taste with us – or even a concept of good taste (if that is what Kant thinks of as identifying with what can regularly be found universally pleasing). In such a case, although there might be the formal possibility for people to share their taste, they would be unlikely to develop the faculty for its exercise, and if anyone in those circumstances should happen to develop a vocabulary of aesthetic judgment, it would have no grip on the world. But their case is not ours, and to provide the deduction he is looking for, tied as it is to *our* ways of speaking, Kant need consider no other case than our own. So his own reason for dismissing the social consideration "as of no importance for us here" (§41.3) in the underpinning of the aesthetic *ought* is not one with which we should sympathize. A more damaging objection to it will emerge after we have looked at the suggestion Kant prefers to put in its place in §42 under the title of "the intellectual interest in the beautiful".

IV

What §42 aims to do is to provide for Kant a more nearly a priori source of our universal obligation to cultivate a faculty of taste. Obscure though the reasoning of the section is, we can use the structure of the argument already in play to discern what is afoot.

To love natural beauty is, Kant says, a mark of a good soul. "When this interest is habitual, he goes on, it at least indicates a frame of mind favourable to moral feeling". Suppose that I find some natural object immediately pleasing to the extent of having a love for it. Then I shall have taken a step towards acquiring (or if already acquired made a useful move in reinforcing) a good character, in that I find myself disinterestedly attached to something that is entirely distinct from me and that I recognize to be quite self-sufficient.[7] If a man is extensively sensitive to natural beauty, then Kant thinks in his love of it the good soul will have found a natural expression of itself. He is sure that as rational beings we all have an indefeasible interest in acquiring a good soul, and, I submit, that we must believe that by the cultivation of what expresses such goodness and by habituation to the pleasure involved in that we may come to find ourselves on the path to becoming genuinely good men and women. So here we find another deep-lying interest in sharing our pleasures. Because it is one we cannot abjure, as we purportedly might the mere "natural inclination to society", Kant supposes it better able to ground his aesthetic *ought*. Consequently he thinks that as long as we restrict ourselves to judgments of taste about natural objects – our attachments to the beauties of art being less surely indicative or expressive of a developed moral sensibility – we may conclude that our own disinterested pleasures are universally projectible. In sum, there is indeed a higher purpose that allows us to treat the acquisition of taste as rationally

[7] It is interesting to compare this moralized thought with later, Kleinian, ideas, such as developed for instance by Adrian Stokes in "The Impact of Architecture", *The Critical Writings of Adrian Stokes III*, (London, 1978), esp. 195–6. Although his cases are artistic both he and Kant would agree in finding it important that we recognise objects that are distinct from us as whole and self-subsistent, and that we prize them as such. Here is a necessary basis in feeling for an eventual genuine concern for others.

required of us, and now that we are assured of that, we may put it together with the argument of the transcendental deduction to provide our common use of the aesthetic vocabulary with all the legitimacy we might desire for it.

This is, admittedly, a speculative reading of §42, because as he writes Kant seems rather to have lost interest in the question from which it really stems, and to have turned instead to an attempt to forge the link between the aesthetic and the moral that his general architectonic leads him to hope for, and which, at Intro IX, he represents as being the central role of the *Critique of Judgment* in his overall critical philosophy. Nevertheless, I surmise that only a reading along such lines as these can provide Kant's argument with the continuity that he must himself believe it both requires and enjoys. It purports to underpin the requirement for the acquisition of taste in an indefeasible way; it complements with something allegedly stiffer the weak and merely empirical interest in beauty that considerations about sociability and social cohesiveness provide; it connects the beautiful and the moral as Kant believes critical philosophy requires; and it fairly naturally paves the way for an understanding of how aesthetic judgments in the arts may be legitimized.[8] Yet despite these merits, something has evidently gone badly wrong.

The crucial mistake that has been made is to offer the considerations about the acquisition of a good soul as if they might plausibly secure the same conclusion as the previous reflections about sociability. For while Kant needs to show that we have an interest in developing a taste that ensures we find pleasures in the same things, all his reflections about good character could hope to achieve is that each of us should develop disinterested attachments *to some natural objects or other*, not that we all have an indefeasible interest in developing

---

[8] The point is that the legitimization of aesthetic judgment depends on our being able to argue that we ought to acquire a faculty of taste, and that this supposedly ultimately rests on the particular nature of our love of nature. Our love of art is far less easy to represent as the expression of a good soul. (It is perhaps too easy for us to be impressed by the fact that it is we human beings who have made the works that we find so appealing.) None the less once the faculty of taste is in place it can be deployed in the direction of the arts. It is just that Kant does not believe that we can look to any benefits with which they provide us to motivate in a sufficiently powerful way the rational requirement on the acquisition of taste in the first place.

such attachments to the very same ones. Yet it is only if this latter claim could be made out that the man of taste (he who has acquired this faculty) will be able to argue that when he finds something in nature pleasing, others are likely to do so too.

What prevents Kant from seeing this lacuna in his argument must be that when he introduces his thought about the connection between our pleasure in nature and the good character, he explicitly does so by saying that what we take as a mark of a good soul is a man's love for natural *beauty*, and in expounding his thought I have followed him by doing just the same. Only we must not forget that the love of nature is being introduced precisely to legitimize the notion of *beauty* itself, and consequently that this reference to beauty and the accompanying supposition that it be something that is found universally appealing must turn up only non-essentially. The moment that this is spotted, we are left without support for the one thing above all that Kant needs to demonstrate.[9]

This failure of the appeal to the intellectual interest in the beautiful then throws us back onto the empirical considerations that we saw Kant unduly suspicious of a couple of pages back. But while his own reason for rejecting our interest in society is ill founded, there is a much stronger reason for dissatisfaction with it than any he himself contemplates. This is that when he thinks of the reasons we have for acquiring taste they present themselves to him as no more than reasons lying on us to acquire a capacity to agree in our pleasures. The vaunted faculty of taste just is for Kant the ability to find pleasing what everyone else can find pleasing. Taste, as he usually regards it, just is a common sense (cf §40), and the interest that our need for social cohesiveness gives rise to is no more than an interest in finding something or other that we might all take pleasure in. If beautiful objects are those that fit this bill, then so far as I can see there is no way in which the mature critic who has worked so hard to motivate the introduction of the idea of sound taste

---

[9] I suppose it might be said that Kant is presuming only those attachments to nature that we all in fact share are marks of a good soul. But neither does he say so, nor is there any particular reason for believing it. I conclude that it has just escaped his notice that his reference to natural beauties here is question-begging.

in the first place could lay any more impressive claim to insight or judgment than that he has a better eye to what everyone might find pleasing than does his versifying friend. That consequence is quite unacceptable.

The lesson to be learnt is plain. It is that if Kant's general strategy adopted in thinking of taste as an acquired ability rather than a constitutive principle of experience is to work, he is going to be obliged to underwrite a more substantial notion of taste than he appears to believe he needs, one that represents our interest in acquiring it as something other than a mere interest in sharing our aesthetic pleasures with others around us. To this issue I shall turn in a minute, but first I want to suggest how Kant could have got into the uncomfortable situation in which we now find him.

In my exposition I have presented Kant as deriving the aesthetic *ought* as it applies to particular objects from a general reflection that we are rationally required to acquire taste as an ability to find pleasure in the same things as one another. I suspect that he takes this line because that is the reading that naturally presents itself to him of the thought that a beautiful object is one that everyone ought to find pleasure in. That is, I surmise that Kant was impressed by this adjunct to his definition of beauty:

$$(x) \text{ Beautiful } x \text{ only if Ought } (y)(\text{DC} <y,x>, \text{ P } <x,y>),$$

where the *ought* spans the whole of the right hand side. Then it would be understandable why he should set about looking for a reason lying on rational beings all to acquire an ability to take delight in the same objects. However, just because it has the unacceptable consequence just noticed, Kant should have seen that any *ought* that his analysis is to contain must lie somewhere else. In particular, since it needs to safeguard the integrity of the mature critic, it must apply *in the first instance*, and not derivatively, as I have represented Kant as presenting it, *to the individual object*. That is, the proper reading of Kant's idea, but one that up to the end of §42 apparently escapes even him, is not as just now displayed, but rather:

(x) Beautiful x only if (y)(DC $<y,x>$, Ought to take pleasure in $<y,x>$).[10]

To put it like this quite changes the nature of the rational requirement on us that Kant needs to identify when he explains why we are bound to acquire taste. Taste can no longer be thought of as an ability of everyone to take delight in the same things as one another, but, far more plausibly, is identified as a facility for finding pleasing some particular things, ones which we may think of as having an especial claim on our attention and to the attachment of each of us. If we all ought to share these pleasures, that is because the objects that give rise to them are of a kind to demand this quasi-categorical (and hence universal) response from us. What I find so extraordinary is that after the point at which Kant has at §40.7 not only misidentified what he needs to show, and then in §§41 and 42 gone on to misidentify the force of the arguments that he takes to show it, he should continue his work by discussing matters which are of *precisely the right sort* to satisfy the demands of the problem that he should have seen confronting him and which, as far as any explicit statement of his strategy goes, appears entirely to have eluded him.[11]

To this discussion we can now turn, thankful that the delusively attractive reasoning that has taken us from §22.2 through §40.7 to §§41 and 42 does not record Kant's last word bearing on the issue that faces him.

V

The place at which Kant introduces material that promises well to overcome this last difficulty is in his discussion of *aesthetic ideas*. Particularly in his treatment of their appearance in the

[10] I leave out explicit mention of necessity here. The analysis that Kant gives need make no mention of the ought. But it's only if the *ought* sentence holds that we can explain why the analysis holds, where that is adjusted in the way set out in Section II above. There necessity does turn up as before in the form of non-fortuitous agreement among those who have taste. What makes the agreement non-fortuitous is that their finding delight in the same things is something that arises in response to the acquisition of taste, to the demands that individual things of the right kind impose on everyone.

[11] Here is proof, if proof be needed, of the existence of philosophical nose, perhaps even nose of genius.

arts we find a different source of interest in objects of our aesthetic attention than anything – social or moral – we have yet come across and targetting on the universal need to form a faculty of taste conceived of merely as a common sense. Above all, it is a discussion that directs us not just to the acquisition of taste in general, but, independently of that, to engagement with the particular object that embodies this interest.[12] In some privileged cases, I contend, it can generate for Kant a highly focused *ought*, arguably akin to that which we have been concerned with in the last pages. In the next section I shall do what I can to connect this topic up with the deduction of the beautiful itself, but for the moment it will be helpful to leave that matter on one side and talk about the appeal that these aesthetic ideas, for short Ideas,[13] have for us. First, however, we want to know just what they are.

An *aesthetic idea* in Kant's most explicit account of it is "a representation of the imagination which occasions much thought, without however any definite thought, i.e. any concept, being capable of being adequate to it . . . [I]t is the counterpart of a *rational idea*, which conversely is a concept to which no intuition can be adequate" (§49.2). Later on in the same section (§49.9) he has another go: "In a word, the aesthetic idea is a representation of the imagination associated with a given concept, which is bound up with such a multiplicity of partial representations in its free employment that for it no expression marking a definite concept can be found, and such a representation therefore, adds to a concept much ineffable thought, the feeling of which quickens the cognitive faculties. . . .".

Neither of these two passages is terribly clear, but we can see well enough in outline what they are getting at. Generally Kant assumes that works of art treat of a subject matter or a theme, and that theme might either be something of a kind that we come across in our experience or something that outruns it.

---

[12] I would put it by saying that in the sections after §49 the faculty of taste is no longer an ability just to agree with others in one's pleasures, but an ability to take pleasure in those things that one ought to. We now move on to discuss why we ought to take pleasure in individual objects. Before this we were looking for some reason to think that we ought to agree with others in what we find pleasing.

[13] I capitalize here and below simply to mark a technical usage.

Examples of the latter sort that he mentions are "invisible beings, the kingdom of the blessed, hell, eternity, creation etc.", and of the former, "death, envy and all vices, also love, fame and the like" (§49.5). These themes I take it are what Kant calls *rational ideas*, and no intuition is adequate to them in that we can never say of any experience, concrete or imagined, in which such things might figure that it captures everything significant about them. Now, the single work of art that treats of such a rational idea presents to sense in a "representation of the imagination" *one* possible way of thinking about it, and may be said to be an expression or presentation of that idea or theme.[14] When a work does this through a representation that invites the spectator or reader to extensively explore the theme in his thought in the mode in which it is presented,[15] then that representation will be an *aesthetic idea*. On this account then, Ideas are identified as the concrete presentations of particular themes that are offered us by individual works of art. Consequently, whatever interest they have for us attaches to the particular work or object that embodies them.

The reason is plain enough. It is that if we are to explain just what this rich thought is that we come to as we read a fine poem or look at a great picture, we shall almost inevitably have to do so by reference to the particular way it is introduced and presented in the work itself; and if we attempt to say how we are brought to think through the theme (the rational idea) that the artist's work treats, and think it through in the mode in which the given Idea presents it, we shall not be able to do so without

---

[14] Kant does say at §51.1 that art *expresses* aesthetic ideas, rather than *presents* them, which is how he usually expresses himself. (cf Intro VIII.1 and §49.3). But this may be a slip. Properly speaking, what gets expressed is the *rational* idea (the concept that specifies the work's theme). It is expressed by the work, which Kant identifies as a representation or an intuition. Since an intuition is just what an aesthetic idea is introduced as being it must be that which does the expressing, not what gets expressed. It expresses the theme by presenting an intuition. An intuition is not the sort of thing that can be expressed anyway. The dubious transition from presentation to expression can be found taking place at §49.11 "Thirdly . . .", and is somehow connected with Kant's idea that in our elaboration of aesthetic ideas our imagination is free. I confess I do not properly understand the connection between the two.

[15] This is an important qualification. For only if we explore within the mode in which the theme is handled will we be acting under the artist's control, and only then will the fruit of our explorations be attributable to his work, as it needs to be if our appreciation of the value of this explorative thought of ours is relevant to our critical appreciation of the work from which it set out. This is to repeat claims defended in Chapter 3 above.

making reference back to the detailed embodiment that it is given in the work from which we set out. Consequently, we shall not be open to the objection that if a work of art encourages us to think in certain enriching ways about a particular theme, any other individual work that gets us to do that in just the same way would be equally attaching, and hence that the interest that the Idea has for us is general rather than particular. The specification of just what that enriching way is will itself require our making allusion to the Idea that engages us.

To the extent then that a work of art has an interest for us as a vehicle of an Idea, there is reason for us to engage with *it*. To the extent that there is room for an *ought* at all here, it is one that will be correctly expressed in Kant's mind by saying that this individual object or work is one that everyone ought to engage themselves with, understood in the way that the second displayed sentence at the end of Section IV put it. The only reason I can see that might encourage us to suppose otherwise depends on the ease with which we assume that the focus of our interest, Ideas, are universals rather than particulars. But to assume this would result only from a vagary of Kant's terminology: *ideas* (lower case and *rational*) *are* universals, but *Ideas* (upper case and *aesthetic*) are quite different. They are by definition intuitions and representations of the imagination. As such they are essentially particular.

I have claimed that Ideas have an interest for us, meaning that there often is good reason for us to engage ourselves with them. What Kant tells us is that they either "give to concepts of reason the appearance of objective reality" or else, with those themes that we encounter in our experience anyway, "go beyond the limits of experience and present them to sense with a completeness of which there is no example in nature" (§49.5). To put it in a nutshell, as we explore them in the work of the artist of genius we find them providing us with a deeper and more extensive comprehension (intellectual and surely affective too) of the (rational) ideas which he takes as his theme. There is, in addition, the further benefit Kant mentions, that feeling ourselves so enriched "quickens the cognitive faculties".

Now it certainly is true that Kant himself would hesitate to say in any particular case that we *ought* to engage ourselves with a given artistically presented Idea, however enriching of our mental life it might be to do so. Much as before he would doubtlessly balk at the "merely empirical" nature of the case. It would strike him that no particular theme that the artist might choose to handle in a certain mode (present via a particular Idea) is one that we are rationally required to occupy ourselves with. But we have already seen that this thought sets the standard for the application of an aesthetic *ought* too high anyway. A far more lifelike requirement to put in its place might be that in default of such engagement a person's mental life would in some notable respect be sadly lacking, or that the enrichment that doing so would provide is one that it would be an impoverishment to pass by. So for instance one might say to someone that they *ought* to read the *Recherche* or that they *ought* to work through the *48*, in that failing to do so they will miss out on some particularly enriching possibility for their mental and spiritual lives.[16]

To have got this far however is not to say that there are particular objects that we ought to take *pleasure* in, as needs to be the case if they are to be beautiful ones, for so far no mention of pleasure has been made at all. Nor is it to assert that we ought to engage ourselves with just any of the aesthetic ideas that genius might produce. Kant himself is at pains to stress that there may be Ideas that are dangerously unsettling for us and that very often genius needs, as he puts it, to have its wings clipped by taste . . . in order that its products be "cultured and polished". Taste, he thinks, as applied to the rougher artistic diamond, will "bring clearness and order into the multitude of the thoughts [of genius]; it makes the ideas susceptible of being permanently and at the same time universally assented to, and capable of being followed by others and of an ever progressive culture"(§50.2).

These ideas are suggestive, for what they point to is Kant's supposition that those Ideas that we have good reason to engage with are indeed beautiful ones, and that their beautiful handling will be what filters out or forestalls the possible

---

[16] I simply assume that Kant will want to extend talk of Ideas to music and the abstract arts. I do not claim to know how it might convincingly be done.

irruption of untoward effect. Only we have to be very careful here, because it is all too easy in presenting Kant's thought at this point to assume, as he himself undoubtedly does (and as we saw him also doing in §42), that the work of the transcendental deduction is already complete, and that therefore the concept of beauty is in sufficiently good order to enjoy powerful theoretical leverage.[17] In our reconstruction of Kant's deduction, though, this assumption has had to be abandoned. Consequently, we can not yet informatively say that it is their beauty that ensures that the Ideas we engage with will be fruitful, wholesome, socially beneficial or otherwise generative of 'interest'. But this should not worry us since neither is it to the point here to demarcate the fruitful Ideas from the untoward or harmful, nor is it likely that we should think to do so quite along Kantian lines. What is important, by contrast, is that in pursuing the deduction we manage to connect the intellectual and affective interest that the particular (fruitful) Idea has for us with the requirement that the beautiful object be one in which we ought to take delight.

The suggestion I shall make is that in his present dialectical position Kant should find it congenial to think that, on the assumption that we have an alternative way of identifying the fruitful (*ought*-generating) aesthetic Ideas than immediately by their beauty, there will be a regular enough connection between our engagement with them and our taking delight in them. If this were so, not only would we have an explanation in outline of why we ought to engage with them, but, with pardonable ellipsis, we should be able to say that they are individual objects in which we ought to take *pleasure*. Finally, since as we know men of taste are sensitive to aesthetic *oughts*, we could conclude that these particular works are indeed beautiful. The problem is to make good the mooted connection between the Ideas with which we have reason to engage ourselves and those in which we shall find delight.

---

[17] Witness his confident remark at §50.1 that what is most important in determining that art is beautiful art is judgment (taste), and not imagination (spirit or genius). The conclusion of the section (§50.3) does however insist that genius and spirit are *necessary* for beautiful art.

VI

The first thing to do is to set aside an objection that is rooted in §42 and which might seem to threaten the whole line of argument. It is that not only does Kant want to legitimize his account of the beautiful on the basis of natural cases rather than artistic ones – where after all the concept of a theme or rational idea that is more or less richly treated seems initially pretty much out of place – but, in addition, and more importantly, he seems there to propound such a dismal view of the arts as might positively forbid one thinking that their works could possibly generate an interest potent enough to give rise to anything remotely like an aesthetic *ought* directed at the particular case.

However, I surmise we may quite properly set this passage aside as dealing solely with art that is not expressive of aesthetic ideas at all, but only with that which flatters our vanity rather than nourishes the spirit (§42.4). Kant's animus there is surely directed more at the professional connoisseur than at the lover of art in general, and it occurs earlier in the text than does the first mention of genius.[18] Now, however, we are concerned not with art that is merely pretty or superficial, but with that which endeavours to present and elaborate for us the very deepest and most far reaching of rational ideas. There could not seriously be thought to be an identity between the two.

Suppose then, as I have suggested, that independently of their beauty we can identify Ideas with which there is good reason for us to engage. Can we go on to secure their beauty by saying that in engaging with them we satisfy clear spiritual needs that we all have, and by then applying Kant's general doctrine that the consciousness of the fulfilment of a need or a

---

[18] Cf §49.1: "We say of certain products of which they should at least in part appear as beautiful art that they are without spirit, although we find nothing to blame in them on the score of taste". I suspect that in seeking to contrast the powerful moral effect of sensitivity to natural beauty with that of sensitivity to artistic beauty he is making the frequent philosophical mistake of supporting a distinction with the help of a poorly chosen paradigm case. In §42 he isn't so much aiming to run down the cultivation of artistic sensitivity and taste in general as to gloss up sensitivity to natural beauty. If one wants a roughly contemporaneous sketch of the professional connoisseur one could do worse than to look at the art dealer in Oliver Goldsmith's *The Vicar of Wakefield*.

desire is pleasure?[19] If so it might seem reasonable to suppose that we *ought* to pursue such pleasures and to cultivate a taste for them. In that way those privileged works of art (those preferential Ideas) would qualify as beautiful, as they are required to, since they would provide all those who had acquired sensitivity to their beneficial force with pleasure as they came disinterestedly to contemplate them.

The trouble with this line of thought though is that the pleasure it alludes to can hardly be disinterested, as Kant defines it. We are thinking of ourselves as having certain spiritual needs, finding objects (Ideas) that satisfy them, and then finding pleasure in these objects. The pleasure has been introduced precisely as a response to the object's answering a need, and not immediately to the object itself. Kant would be the first to say that this unfits it for our present requirement and renders our pleasure and our consequent judgment impure. In this light, and reading Kant's talk of perfection as the answering of the work of art to our quest for enriching thought, we might perhaps recall the seemingly unequivocal passage from §48.4: "If the object is given as a product of art and as such is to be declared beautiful, then, because art always supposes a purpose in the cause (and its causality), there must be at bottom in the first instance a concept of what the thing is to be. And as the agreement of the manifold in a thing with its inner destination, its purpose, constitutes the perfection of the thing, it follows that in judging of artificial beauty the perfection of the thing must be taken into account . . ." The moral to draw would be that this pleasure is not the pleasure involved in beauty at all.

Could we, perhaps, alternatively, and better, say that some aesthetic Ideas of value are quite naturally found pleasing on their own account, and that what we have reason to do is to cultivate our natural sensitivity so that we find ourselves extensively pleased by the right cases? We might suppose that some of the Ideas that give expression to ways of thought we do well to engage with may be such that we can learn to find them and their likes pleasing in their own right, not on account of

---

[19] Cf e.g. §4.5 "To desire something and to take a satisfaction in its existence are identical".

their satisfying this need, but quite independently of it. Only here we run into a different worry. While the pleasures that are so come by need certainly not count as insufficiently disinterested, the apparently loose bond between the thought these privileged Ideas express and the pleasure they give us must flaw this idea. For if what we learn to do is to find pleasure in some Ideas as a development of a pleasure that is initially naturally given, there seems to be no clear reason why, once we move beyond our starting point, we should expect this developed capacity not soon enough to be found going hand in hand with art that is anarchic, that is dire or is the work of unpolished genius, the very art that is which on Kant's view we have good reason *not* to foster engagement with. So cultivation of pleasures that start off by being merely associated with objects which we ought to engage with may very well not generate pleasures of which the same could reliably be said. The objects that then gave rise to them would not be ones we ought to take delight in. Hence they would not be beautiful either.

There needs then to be a third way of forging a connection between the privileged aesthetic ideas and pleasure, distinct from either of these two, and one which can steer safely between the objections on which they have foundered. I suggest that this may be provided by saying, on Kant's behalf, that the exploration of the thoughts that we need, and engagement with the Ideas that embody them, is itself of its very nature pleasurable. That is, there is no way of taking them into ourselves as fruitful which we will fail to find providing us with pleasure in the object that presents them to us. The exploration and appreciation of the valuable beneficial Ideas involves us *ipso facto* in pleasurable response to them. Now it may of course also be that corrupt or harmful or otherwise dire Ideas are liable to generate pleasurable response, particularly when we erroneously experience them as enriching. But we know that it is for the former and not the latter that we need to acquire a taste, and as long as we remember that taste is thought of by Kant as something to be freely acquired, this is a requirement that can be fairly straightforwardly accommodated. Even though our pleasure in the individual objects is associated with the feeling for their value – and recall that Kant says the feeling of their expansion of our thought "quickens our cognitive faculties", which he clearly thinks of as a pleasurable matter – it does not arise here *in recognition of the fact that* the ideas are beneficial or meet a need. So our judgment of the object that expresses them escapes the charge that it is, in Kant's sense, impure and that it is illegitimately "interested". Nor does the cultivation of these pleasures as we gradually acquire taste look set to break loose from the connection with Ideas of a kind that allow us to say that the pleasure is one we ought to take in the objects that provide it. As soon as we come to discern them as deleterious, or perhaps even as suspect, they will cease to be apt to provide us with delight.

The distinctions between this last, and the first and the second, rejected, suggestions may seem to be fine ones. None the less, distinctions there are, and they are ones that Kant should be ready to rely on. In the first situation I was suggesting that the pleasure that we ought to find in valuable Ideas might come from recognizing that they satisfied a need that we take ourselves to have. It was straightforwardly a pleasure we took in an object that met a need *because it met that need*. Here, by contrast, we are concerned with pleasures in objects that do indeed meet supposed needs, only the pleasure is not a mere recognition that the need is met by the object: it is rather a pleasure in the object as it presents itself to us in meeting the need. What is so pleasing about it is the thought it offers us in meeting the need it does. The difference might be put as that between our being indifferent to the object itself and just being pleased that it meets a particular need we have on the one hand, and being pleased in the object as meeting a need we have on the other. The pleasure in the former case is indeed for Kant impure, but in the latter, §48.4 notwithstanding, there is no reason to think it is.

§48.4 is inert here because whereas our taking pleasure in an Idea on the first option depended on our assessing it as matching up to our intellectual requirement of it, on "comparing it with its concept", now our pleasure is in its "form" (as Kant would like us to say), only its form is one that carries spiritual value.[20] In assessing it, we do not, that is, "take its perfection

---

[20] Form, I take it, is whatever is left over when considerations of perfection (of "its concept") are set aside. The connection Kant sees between this and the primary qualities – as e.g. at §14 – is a separate matter that is best forgotten.

into account", even though its perfection is what gives it the pleasing form that it has. Putting this in terms of Ideas, what is so pleasing about the valuable Idea is the thoughts that are expressed through it; that our having these thoughts is of benefit to us though is not what we find so pleasing, merely the nature of the thoughts that the Idea embodies.

Nor will the objection to the second way of putting it arise. For the connection between what is of value in the Idea and our pleasure in it is now made internal to our perception and internalization of the Idea itself. It wouldn't be enriching unless it were pleasurable; but nor would it be pleasurable to the person of developed taste unless it were enriching. The two aspects are not just loosely associated, as before they were, but tightly intertwined. The cultivation of taste then will develop within the limits of what is perceived as valuable, and is conceived of as guided in its progress by that supposedly independent access we are allowing ourselves to have to the worth that particular Ideas have for us.

The time has come now to draw the various strands of the argument together. At the end of the last section but one I said that what Kant had failed to see was that even if he could show that we ought to acquire taste viewed just as a common sense, that would not convincingly yield the information that the individual beautiful object is one that we *ought* to take pleasure in. Hence it would not serve the inference to the claim that the beautiful object is one that all men of taste *would* take pleasure in were they to contemplate it conscientiously and disinterestedly. In this section, I have argued that Kant has material available that will allow him to assert that in the arts at least we find objects that do make extensive claims on us. They contain, at their best, objects with which we ought to engage ourselves and which we can colourably argue we ought to find delight in contemplating. Furthermore, if we are not impressed by the argument of §41 that urges us to acquire taste to secure our social needs, we can say that there is now available a derivative explanation of the need for taste in that only if we acquire it will we be able to enjoy the particular pleasures that the arts have it in their power to offer us. On this basis Kant is now well placed to put his official deduction to work. A beautiful object is, on account of the aesthetic Ideas it embodies, one that we ought to take pleasure in, and restricting ourselves to those who have acquired the capacity to identify these things and find them pleasurable, a beautiful object is also one that such persons *would* find pleasurable were they to come across it and regard it in the right light. Assuming that I am one such person as I encounter a given object with pleasure, then my judgment of taste will license me to judge that others who are similarly placed will do so too. The judgment that the chosen object is beautiful is thus legitimately assertible on the best evidence that we have for it. Similarly with other arbitrarily chosen objects that give rise to paradigmatic judgments of taste. Hence the concept *beauty* is legitimate, and our use of the notion in the judgments we make about the world around us augurs well to yield assertions in the aesthetic domain that can count for Kant as regularly true, notwithstanding their subjective and non-cognitive nature.

VII

As far as a reconstruction of the core of Kant's argument goes everything of substance is now done, but for two reasons at least we need to ask whether it can not be taken a little further. The first is to show that the text itself asks to be read in the manner I have been propounding, and the second is to show how Kant himself might want to handle what he would regard as two significant weaknesses in the line of thought I have extended to him. The first of these two is that he makes it quite plain that however valuable our engagement with the arts, the most extensive aesthetic *oughts* that we encounter are generated by natural objects and not by man-made ones. The other is that while I have said that works of genius that are handled with taste give us good enough reason to engage with them, I have in the last section been highly circumspect about asserting that they give us reason *all* to engage with them. Indeed it must be plain that any *ought* that the arts give rise to is most uncertainly universalizable, and even if he were willing to make some slight derogation from the demand for universality Kant would in all probability think that to suppose we might found the legitimization of aesthetic judgments on the back of thought concerning even the very richest art of genius would be to stretch credulity beyond breaking point.

As to the latter point it is certainly correct to think that when we say to someone that they ought to read the *Recherche* or work through the *48* we would not automatically expect to say the same to our neighbours on the bus or to their ageing parents. Our judgment is usually studiedly aimed at the particular ear to which it is addressed. Nevertheless this need not put it beyond the point at which deference can be paid to Kantian scruple, since despite its particular aim, the judgment will still enjoy a vague – though often pretty extensive – generality. To acknowledge this we just need to remember the wise observation of Hume's in *Of the Standard of Taste* that "at twenty, Ovid may be the favourite author, Horace at forty, and perhaps Tacitus at fifty". The point here is that if we set realistic parameters to our judgment and make explicit that we regard it as relativized to identifiable cultures, to particular times, to particular periods of life and their typical concerns, geared to the background of the possession of determinate skills and so on, we stand a good chance of saying that the *ought* we come out with runs widely within those set limits. Someone falling within them and who yet balked at the suggestion that he would do well to give his attention and find pleasure where we recommend him to do so could reasonably be asked to explain why he jibbed. If the suppositions of the last section are anywhere near correct, it would not be enough for him to say in reply that he is not sensitive to that kind of thing, that he has a blind spot or that he just does not enjoy it. So it is arguable that even within the arts the universalizability demand that Kant would assume to be a *sine qua non* of the availability of an authentic aesthetic *ought* is within reasonable hailing distance.

Whether it is or not, and whether for this reason or not, Kant firmly believes we have to concentrate our attention on the paradigm of natural beauty. Only if we can legitimize aesthetic judgments in its case does he think that the task of the deduction is fully executed. And here it may seem that the reconstructionist is under pressure, for what the development of our argument would require is that *Nature* offer us Ideas in the world around us just as the genius does in the art his talent fashions. For we have seen it is only with Ideas that the demands of taste can be brought together with the claim of the individual object to beauty, and only thus that the application of the term to the individual object of our aesthetic judgment be justified. Yet given that Nature is not judged as the work of genius,[21] it might seem that this crucial element is necessarily missing from it, and that in consequence judgments of natural beauty (and to Kant's mind *a fortiori* of artistic beauty) are unfounded and unfoundable. To the strict Kantian, here it must seem that the abyss is yawning before his feet, and if reconstruction is at this late stage in the day to make good the pretension that it is genuinely Kant's thought that we are still dealing with, it will be as well to reassure the purist that the text itself speaks in its favour here no worse than it does at the earlier stations along the way.

It is encouraging to notice first that at §51.1 Kant is willing enough to assert that "we may describe beauty in general (*whether natural or artificial*) as the expression of aesthetic ideas" (my emphasis), so if only we can find him offering a plausible account of what these *natural* Ideas may be there is a good prospect of conducting a version of his argument through in a way that he himself might approve of.

At this juncture, Kant is initially discreet in the extreme, since he continues the passage by telling us that "in beautiful art this Idea must be occasioned by a concept of the object,[22] while in beautiful nature the mere reflection upon a given intuition, without any concept of what the object is to be, is sufficient for awakening and communicating of the Idea of which that object is regarded as the expression."[23] But for all his discretion he does provide hint enough about the direction in which to look for what is needed.

[21] Or at least when it is it is not the subject of a *pure* judgment of taste (§48.4).

[22] Concept of the object that is represented I suppose, since whereas "a natural beauty is a *beautiful thing*, artificial beauty is a *beautiful representation* of a thing" (§48.3). Since Kant thinks that the artist will usually need to proceed by means of *attributes* or *emblems* (cf §49.7), the representation of a thing might be say Jupiter's eagle with the lightning in its claws, and the thing represented "the mighty king of heaven". The Idea occasioned by the concept of the object is the "approximate representation of the imagination" that the artist produces in his struggle with his theme.

[23] Note once again how the last occurrence of "Idea" here seems better fitted to designate a *rational* idea than an *aesthetic* idea.

We know from the Moment of Relation (§§10–17) that the natural objects that we single out for contemplation and description as beautiful please us on account of their form. They look as if they are designed, though we cannot say for what purpose, or indeed that there is any particular purpose for which they are designed. They are in Kant's technical terminology "final", but subjectively, not objectively so, (cf e.g. §15.4), and it may have struck readers that in my previous two chapters this notion of subjective finality has made absolutely no appearance although for Kant it is clearly of the greatest importance. Now is the moment for it to do so.

In the structure of the deduction of a common sense conceived of "as a constitutive principle of the possibility of experience" (§22.2), examined in Chapter 5, the subjective finality of our representations is on occasion supposed to be what guarantees their pleasing everybody. Kant is explicit about this both in the Introduction at VII.3 and in the corresponding body of the main text at §11.1. But just because there is absolutely no reason to think either that what I see as subjectively final everyone else will surely do so too, or (if that is not to the point)[24] to think that what pleases me on account of its subjective finality will also be bound to please others on that account – might it not inspire you with terror? and leave your more prosaic aunt indifferent? – this proposal was an evident non-starter. I therefore left it aside undiscussed.

Now however things may be different. For if natural objects that we see as if designed were to embody an Idea of value, then we might well have reason to learn to see things in this light and reason to take pleasure in them in parallel with the suggestions made about art in the last section. The crucial question is what this Idea is and whether it is one that we quite generally all have reason to engage ourselves with as Kant will want to insist.

At Introduction VIII.1 Kant is forthright about what the theme in question is to be: "*Natural beauty*", he there writes, "may be looked on as the *presentation* of the concept of formal, i.e. merely subjective finality . . .", and he makes it plain that to see

---

[24] If, that is, it were thought open to Kant to build some such specification of the way the object should strike us either into the definiendum or into the antecedent of the definiens.

an object in this light is indistinguishable from thinking of it as if it has been designed for the sake of our cognitive faculties. Now it does not make much sense to us to say that some objects strike us as if they had been designed to be cognized, but it does sound right to say that whatever this comes to it is certainly an instance of our seeing nature as if it were beneficently ordered *for our sake*. If we put these two things together we get the proposal that in seeing natural objects and scenes through the ordering of their parts as designed we find them presenting to us an Idea expressive of our relation to a benevolent and enveloping natural world in which we are unestranged and unalienated occupants. In the contemplation of natural objects that we learn to view in this light (assuming here that even in the natural cases we are going to have to regard taste and its common sense as a faculty to be acquired) we are encouraged to elaborate this theme as we elaborate the Ideas presented to us in art, namely "with such a wealth of thought as would never admit of comprehension in a definite concept, and as a consequence find ourselves giving aesthetically an unbounded expansion to the concept itself" (§49.6).[25]

So, for Nature to present us with Ideas, it does not have to be designed by a superhuman genius – even if sometimes it looks to us as if it had. Rather we need only develop a facility for seeing its products as if designed for us, and as we do that so we shall encourage ourselves to elaborate the thought that we are in Nature's care, or fundamentally at home in the world. It is perhaps one of those cases of which Kant would be happy to say that in this aesthetic activity we engender for ourselves "the

---

[25] Recall the wonderful opening lines of Keats's *Endymion*, written less than twenty years after the *Critique:*

A thing of beauty is a joy for ever;
Its loveliness increases; it will never
Pass into nothingness; but still will keep
A bower quiet for us, and a sleep
Full of sweet dreams, and health and quiet breathing.
Therefore, on every morrow, are we wreathing
A flowery band to bind us to the earth,
Spite of despondence, of the inhuman dearth
Of noble natures, of the gloomy days,
Of all the unhealthy and o'er-darkened ways
Made for our searching: yes, in spite of all,
Some shape of beauty moves away the pall
From our dark spirits . . . (ll. 1 – 13)

appearance of an objective reality" that we can never actually experience (cf §49.7 again). Furthermore he will expect it to be true that our having this thought amply developed, not just intellectually but in feeling as well, is something that we genuinely all have the best of reasons to cultivate. In this the Idea that we present ourselves with in nature has a quite universal appeal for us, and is in this respect superior to any Idea that the artist is capable of furnishing us with.

Kant himself says nothing that I can find to explain just why the Idea expressed by natural beauty has this unique status. But I surmise that two things will not be lightly challenged. The first is that it is hard to see how true human flourishing would be possible unless we felt ourselves unalienated from the natural world in which we live,[26] and the second, that as the human psyche is structured, to have this feeling is an important condition of our being able to develop a stable concern for things and people around us. Since this latter is something Kant thinks we are rationally required to do, he could hardly resist the thought that it is of the most urgent importance that we cultivate the feelings and thoughts that make it possible to do so.[27]

There are two questions outstanding about which something must be said. The first is whether as he builds his case around the natural world and the thought that its various beauties all express in different versions the same Idea, Kant can justifiably claim that we ought all to take pleasure in the *same* objects, rather than in any natural objects that the individual finds to have this expressive capacity for him. Unless the answer is 'yes' we shall be back with the difficulty that I said arose at the end of Section IV and which everything that has followed has sought to avoid. Second, we shall need to ask whether this last

---

[26] Think again of Keats's

> The passion poesy, glories infinite,
> Haunt us till they become a cheering light
> Unto our souls, and bound to us so fast,
> That, whether there be shine, or gloom o'ercast,
> They always must be with us, or we die. (*ibid.* ll 29–33)

[27] In Kant's conception of things we may be rationally required to do this, but it would be unrealistic to think that the intellectual conviction that something is our bounden duty is alone sufficient to secure its fulfilment. We need also to have built up the right dispositions of feeling and of character before our intellectual conviction can hope to ensure corresponding action.

defence of the concept of beauty rooted in the natural world can be defended against a charge of irrationality. If the answer is 'no', precipitation into the abyss will only have been briefly deferred, not definitively avoided.

VIII

Although I have said that in the arts each work that handles a given theme presents its own Idea of the theme, when we turn to the natural cases this is harder to make out. Of course if I see both the splendid sunset and the mist rising off the winter fields as presentations of the natural world being designed for our sake, then I shall find this "theme" presented by each in a different way. But for this notion of difference to carry any weight, it really should depend on something more than the difference between the sunset and the rising mist. It should, that is, depend on a notable difference between the way in which the sunset gives rise to amplification of the thought that we are integrated in nature and the way in which the rising mist does so, and that these significantly different ways of elaborating the thought are closely tied to the two individual cases. Only then could we say, in strict parallel to the artistic cases of the last section but one, that the aesthetic *ought* they give rise to binds people to the very same objects.

This ideal seems unrealistic though. We do not in fact think that for each natural beauty there is some so to speak specific essence that it would be a serious loss for someone to miss out on. One fine sunset can be much like another, and mountain views in the Alps may not be significantly differently rewarding than in the Pyrenees. We also feel perhaps that as long as we have the sunsets, the loss of the mountain views might not perhaps be too great to bear, and that from the standpoint of the elaboration of our thought about our relation to the natural world there is a degree of commensurability between many distinct beauties.[28] Does this really threaten Kant's line of thought?

---

[28]
    . . . .Such the sun, such the moon,
Trees old, and young sprouting a shady boon
For simple sheep; and such are daffodils . . . (ll. 13 – 15)

The answer, I believe, is no. For the Idea in question which Kant must believe it so important for us to explore and anchor in our minds is one that needs to be sustained, and cannot be expected to take firm hold as the result of a few brief exposures to objects are its vehicle. It is thought of a kind that needs to be borne in on us repeatedly and reinforced over the course of a life time.[29] So in the natural case, more evidently than in the artistic one, we should welcome any occasions that come our way to foster it. So when we say of a given natural object that it is beautiful, we shall think that everyone has good reason to take delight in it, in that for anyone who were to be in the vicinity and who were at liberty to do so, there would be something on offer that would be of value for them and which it would be a loss to miss. That they might well find a commensurable good round the next corner too, would not diminish this truth. It could thus still be said of them that *this* is a scene or a sight that they ought to take delight in, even though the Idea it offers is one very like that which another natural object might provide.

The other prospective worry I mentioned was that of irrationality. In explaining the force of aesthetic Ideas we saw Kant urging that they present with the appearance of objective reality what we can not meet with in experience. And he puts the same thought directly about beauty in nature in a fine passage at §58.3:

> The beautiful forms displayed in the organic world all plead eloquently on the side of the realism of the aesthetic finality of nature in support of the plausible assumption that beneath the production of the beautiful there must lie a preconceived idea in the producing cause – that is to say an end acting in the interest of our imagination. Flowers, blossoms, even the shapes of plants as a whole . . . seem to be planned entirely with a view to outward appearance: all these lend great weight to the mode of explanation which assumes actual ends of nature in favour of our aesthetic judgment.

However, in §58, Kant is anxious above all to *deny* the

Nor do we merely feel these essences
For one short hour: . . . (ll. 25/6)

realism of aesthetic finality, not to advance it, so he must believe that the truly rational man must not only cultivate the idea that gives the appearance of nature being organized for our sake, but at the same time remain firmly aware that this thought is not one we can have any reason to believe.

This in itself may not be a matter of concern, but what must surely be so is the thought that "the appearance of objective reality" of nature's benevolence in our regard provided by our engagement with natural beauty is ultimately important for Kant because of the way in which it impinges on our behaviour and on our attitudes to those around us, and on the way in which we view our own lives. Yet how can this thought be fully effective in these ways unless we do come to *believe* that this apparent benevolence on nature's part is real? To the philosopher convinced that "the *idealism* of the finality alike of nature and of art [is] the sole principle of aesthetic judgment" (§58 caption) this can not be tolerated; but unless it is embraced, it seems, we shall miss the underpinning that is required for the introduction of the crucial aesthetic *ought*. Beauty is then immediately under threat.

I myself believe that Kant has some room for manoeuvre here, and to end with I shall sketch a possibility that might be open to him. The reader who finds himself unable to sympathize should not however conclude that the Kantian endeavour is irremediably flawed. He should instead return to the possibility of treating the arts as basic, and view our aesthetic judgments about nature as extensions of a vocabulary to an area beyond that in which it finds its only possible original legitimization. It is only the Kantian purist who will have to work harder.

To meet the danger then, what we need to capitalize on is the capacity we have to entertain thoughts which we have no reason to believe true, and which yet have affective precipitation by virtue of our entertaining them. In literature we naturally think here of feelings we have as we read works which we are clear in our minds are nothing more than fictional. Yet our feelings are not feelings we think of ourselves as imagining ourselves having, but strike us as genuine enough but with the fictional characters as their internal objects. Outside fiction proper, but still within the realm of pretence, I may frighten myself by imagining and dwelling on possibilities that I have no reason to think will come about and which I would deny that I believed real, but which because of their propositional content and the way I entertain them have the grim effect on me that they do. Beyond the realm of pretence, we might think of the arachnophobe whose attitudes and actions are the expression of thoughts about the nature of spiders, but who may be perfectly prepared to admit that they have a grip on him which is not that of belief. Analogously, we might think it open to Kant to say that the pleasure we take in natural beauty cannot be divorced from the forcefully entertained thought of nature's benevolence, yet for all that need not involve belief. *A fortiori* it does not commit us to irrational belief.

But what is it that makes the thought forcefully entertained? It would seem that that has to be answered in terms of the affective attitudes and resulting dispositions to action that come with it – the way in which a feeling of confidence in our surroundings or willingness to regard them as objects of love and admiration eventually spills over into our subsequent action and not simply a feeling I can introspect at the time. These attitudes then have real effects, and it is important from Kant's point of view that they should not be inhibited – as are so many of the affective attitudes we have to characters of fiction and as the arachnophobe would probably wish his own to be. So we will need to know what it is that might prevent us from saying in that case that they are indeed believed. After all, is it not that these are just the attitudes we might expect to have if we *did* believe the thoughts we forcefully entertain? Must not the rootedness of the attitudes to nature that holds Kant's argument in place already have crossed the threshold of belief if they are to be as effective and sustained as he requires them to be?

Kant's best reply might be that if we really did believe the thoughts that our aesthetic contemplation of nature gives rise to, we would find ourselves ready to make assertions about nature that in fact we decline to make. We do refuse to assert that nature has a benevolent attitude to us; we refuse also to accept the consequences of this thought such as that nature possesses a mind or that it can reflect about what our interests really are. Nor are all our actions consistent with belief, since full-blooded belief would surely encourage us to pan-psychic research and so on. So, clearly there are many tests for not believing the thoughts that are forcefully entertained that we shall all pass. Maybe this alone will provide Kant with scope to say that the "as-if" attitude he endorses can allow a forceful entertaining of the thoughts not amounting to belief, but nonetheless having sufficient guiding role in determining our attitudes and responses to the world around us – without which "understanding would not find itself [at home] in nature" (Intro VIII.3). If that is so, the challenge that the aesthetic only has a real place in the structure of the world if constructed upon an irrational base can be met without giving up anything that is genuinely close to Kant's heart.

If that is so . . . The reason I said before that I was uncertain about the force of this last move is that reticences of the kind just mentioned could be urged as evidence less for our *not* believing that nature has our interests in mind than for our more specifically believing nature has *not* got our interests in mind, which is after all what we do most certainly hold. But that would not exclude our *also* believing that it does do so, a belief the holding of which is indeed evidenced by the continuing affective force of the thoughts we entertain. Holding contradictory beliefs is not impossible, but it certainly is inconvenient, and the moral for the fully rational theorist might in the end be that to avoid the inconvenience he should do his best to expunge precisely those beliefs that the legitimization of beauty would then be supposed to rest on. The upshot here is of course quite inimical to Kant and not at all happy for the aesthete. Whether it can surely be resisted is a question I can do no better now than pass on to others.

Appendix: The Unity of the Critique

At the start of Chapter 4 and the end of Chapter 5 I looked forward to an integrated account of the main line of Kant's argument. Whether or not Kant actually presents his thought in that light, I have suggested that we might find a place for the reflections about taste and cognition and those about the acquisition of taste in a way that would absolve the *Critique* from the charge of being broken-backed. That was to say that in the earlier passages – in particular in §9 – Kant could be represented as being concerned with our universal possession of the *capacity* to exercise taste, viz to all share our pleasures, whereas in the official deduction of §38 he is concerned with the question of its exercise, the question whether we have grounds to think that this capacity is one that we actually exercise in making the aesthetic judgments that we do.

Now it may seem that I have been somewhat disingenuous here. For it will be said that with the distinct changes imported in this chapter into the two terms of the evidence–content transition by the normative notion of taste, all semblance of an unified argument leading from §9 to §38 must vanish. Indeed, if we accept as more promising Kant's deduction cast in terms of taste as a faculty to be acquired, then it may even seem that the earlier reflections about cognition, and which considered the universal sharing of subjective pleasure as partly constitutive of experience are quite beside the point and should, in an ideal rewriting of the work, be quietly omitted. Thinking like this, it will be inevitable that we see Kant first as trying out one solution of his problem, failing, then recasting his problem and finally trying out a different and more hopeful solution to it.

Maybe this does give the best reading of the text as it stands. But the pathway I have taken through it does not have to be seen in quite so disjointed a way as this map would have it. To appreciate this we must notice the distinction we customarily make between our having a *capacity* to do something and having an *ability* to do it.[30] Thus I am born with a capacity to swim, even though I don't acquire the ability until I am taught to swim in my early years Then later on maybe I exercise my ability, or maybe I don't. Again, when I was much younger I suppose I had a capacity to speak perfect Chinese. I never acquired the ability to do so, and probably now have lost even the capacity and so can't acquire the ability, let alone exercise it. With this distinction in mind, we might think of Kant concerned in the §9 passage and its like to be concerned with our *capacity* to take universal subjective pleasure in things, and in §22 onwards with our *ability* to do so.

---

[30] A distinction remarked by Aristotle in his discussion of potentiality at *De Anima* III, 4, 429 b6–10.

Taking this hint, we might say that our making judgments of taste will be legitimate only in those cases in which we can be right to think that others who have acquired the ability to find pleasure where they should would all do so, but that a fully worked out deduction of the concept of beauty (demonstration of its legitimacy) would need to show that such an ability is one that we all have a capacity to exercise. Since the justification of claims that something is beautiful depend essentially on arguing that there are things that all men ought to take pleasure in, this comes to a demand for Kant that we can show that this is an *ought* that lies within the range of a relevant *can*, here a *capacity* to share our pleasures in things, and *a fortiori* in things we ought to find pleasing. And this, we might think, is what he demonstrates as he argues in the earlier passage that the sharing of our subjective pleasures is a precondition of our having cognitive experience of the world at all. So to the extent that our willingness to make aesthetic judgments presupposes the acquisition of an *ability* to take pleasure in the same things as one another, this presupposition is not open to the sceptical reflection that it is merely the *idea* of an ability that we would have to have if judgments of taste were to be possible. To that reflection, and relying on §9, Kant can respond that it is an ability that we know we have a capacity to acquire – for we see that without such a capacity we would not have the sort of cognitive experience that is so singularly ours.

FRIEDRICH SCHILLER:

ON THE AESTHETIC EDUCATION OF MAN

7

Beauty and the Ideal of Man

The grand sweep of Schiller's *Letters*, the determination with which they yoke together the political, the moral and the aesthetic, and their confident optimism in the perfectibility of man easily enough explain the honoured place they hold in the canon. Their author would hardly think this place justly occupied though unless the intricacies of his reasoning could withstand scrutiny; and here, sadly, confidence is apt to falter. Students' common experience of the work is to find the argument unimpressive; sometimes even, worse, it is not to find the argument at all. Both perceptions are misplaced. The *Letters* have a coherent and unified structure filled out with a wealth of apposite detail; only it is a clumsily presented structure, whose understanding is impossible without piercing through the dark 'night of Kantianism', as Carlyle called it, that tends to baffle even the most tenacious. Here it is that we must start; and in the first of these two chapters on Schiller's aesthetics I shall restrict my attention entirely to an elucidation of the extraordinarily challenging conception that he offers of beauty as "a necessary condition of man's existence" (X.7).[1]

[1] Following E.M. Wilkinson and L.A. Willoughby (OUP, 1957) I cite Letter number with Roman numerals and paragraph number with Arabic. Their translation is used throughout with occasional minor adjustment. References take the reader to a paragraph of Schiller's text that should support the interpretation offered. The kind of support however varies; sometimes my exposition is a simple paraphrase of the indicated passage, sometimes the indication merely illustrates Schiller's use of a certain word or concept.

To see this as the keystone of the whole is to be well positioned later on to appreciate the rest of this admired, but curiously neglected, philosophical work.

I

The stage is set in the diagnostic and programmatic Letters I–IX that make up the first third of the book. Schiller looks around him at societies existing at the close of the eighteenth century and finds little evidence in them of any authentic political freedom. Growing up under regimes preoccupied with the satisfaction of need and the pursuit of utility (II.3) rather than with the enthronement of reason (III.2), men have more or less inevitably succumbed to two crippling ills – on the one hand, tyranny of sense, which makes for violence and savagery (V.4); on the other, tyranny of thought, which fosters pleasing illusion at the expense of truth (V.5). It is hopeless to look to the State itself to cure these banes, for it is in the (actual) State that they are enshrined and whose (actual) ends they serve (VII.1). Reason's natural ally, philosophy, is itself too weak and too insecurely anchored in men's minds to root them out (VIII.2). What is needed, Schiller claims, is a force that will act directly on men's characters, making whole what is broken, unformed or incomplete (IX.1). That force, he contends, is beauty, and in particular the beauty that the artist of talent has to offer us (IX.2). By it, and it alone, man may hope eventually (VII.3) to win through to a liberal social existence adequate to the inalienable freedom with which his rational nature endows him (II.5).

Having announced it as the role of beautiful art to bring back a lost wholeness to man's character, Schiller pauses at the start of the central part of his work, that is, Letters X–XVI, to consider a fundamental challenge to this ambitious programme. An imagined opponent is given to speak. He points out how frequently despite their concern with beautiful form and beautiful appearance the arts have encouraged neglect of reality and truth rather than their pursuit (X.4). So surely there can be nothing in the nature of beauty itself that might preclude it from having detrimental, even corrupting, effect – quite the opposite of what Schiller himself supposes its proper end to be.

Disconcertingly, in the very same paragraph and in the two following, and speaking now in his own voice, Schiller endorses these thoughts and acknowledges that wherever the arts have attained a high degree of excellence and historically wherever good taste has reigned, humanity itself has tended to fall to low estate. We are, he admits, hard pressed to discover even a single case in which high aesthetic culture has coexisted with political freedom and bourgeois virtue.[2] How then, one wants to ask, can he make these admissions and yet persist in his course?

The answer must be that we are here to take Schiller as allowing this challenge to his programme to be incontestable only on the supposition of a conception of beauty that his opponent mistakenly believes to be shared by both parties, legitimized by usage and by common experience. It is, it turns out (XV fn 1, XVIII fn), a view of beauty as identical either with what produces mere gratifying response, or else with pleasing form taken in isolation from all consideration of content. It is, Schiller thinks, attachment to the empiricist aesthetic of Burke, Shaftesbury or Hume that encourages the former reading of our experience of art and attachment to that of Kant which promotes the latter. In either case and the accuracy of his perception of these theorists apart, what Schiller is acutely pointing to is the ease with which disputable claims in philosophy or aesthetic theory are liable to determine the interpretation of experience offered by those who are guided by them. He sees sharply that what is needed before experience can be properly understood is well-fashioned theory that can avoid deforming it. Thus it is that he announces a search for a novel account of beauty, answerable not to experience for its credentials, but to be derived transcendentally, as a "pure concept of the understanding", deduced in such a way as to establish it as "a necessary condition of the existence of man" (X.7). With this securely in hand, the sceptical objections of the "estimable voices" of X.4 will eventually fall, and Schiller's ambitious path forward be unimpeded. That at

[2] In the light of the suggestion made below it is open to us to question just how seriously Schiller wants his admissions to be understood. Perhaps as we read on we are expected to read back a measure of irony into the expressions "high aesthetic value", "good taste".

least is what he hopes. The difficulty for the reader is to see what he is being offered in this heavily brocaded Kantian dress.[3]

II

Leaving for later all speculation about the way in which a transcendental derivation of the concept is going to help us replace established conceptions of beauty by a better, and taking that for the moment on trust, we have first to ask how Schiller's deduction is supposed to be carried through. Knowing that we shall be better placed than we are at the end of Letter X to see what it is that it derives.

The startling expression "this pure concept of the understanding" (*Dieser reine Verstandesbegriff der Schönheit*)(X.7), taken together with the earlier announced allegiance to Kantian principles (I.3), inevitably sets up the expectation that Schiller has it in mind to deduce the concept *beauty* as a worthy companion to the twelve categories that figure in the *Critique of Pure Reason*. Pure concepts of the understanding are nothing if they are not that. In fact however he does nothing of the sort. No attempt is ever made, or even hinted at, to show that we have to employ this concept if we are to make genuinely true or false judgments about an objective world. However central he thinks the aesthetic is in our experience, it is not along these lines that he is tempted to move, and the use of this resonant

[3] To avoid confusion I should stress that what Schiller admires in Kant is more his method than the concrete conclusions that he draws from it once he leaves the area of transcendental metaphysics. In particular he thinks Kant's account of beauty in the *Critique of Judgment* is seriously mistaken in being insufficiently objective, in not recognising that considerations of content as well as those of form determine whether something is beautiful and in denying that any concept is involved in judgments of taste. Schiller himself believes that strict application of Kantian method will eliminate these errors and show that one concept in particular is indissolubly united with that of beauty, viz the concept *freedom*. The details will emerge as we go along, only here I insist in a preliminary way that there is no inconsistency between Schiller's endorsement of Kantian procedure at I.3 and the persistent, if often inexplicit, rejection of Kantian formalism that permeates the work. It should go without saying that Schiller's rejection of Kantian thought is rejection of Kantian thought as Schiller understood it, and that that frequently diverges from what Kant himself would have taken it to be. What I would take these divergencies to be should be apparent from the representation of Kant's aesthetic I have offered in earlier chapters. I shall not comment on them further here at all.

expression must be written off as simply misleading or just rhetorical.

By contrast, it is clear that beauty as "a necessary condition of man's existence" (*eine notwendige Bedingung der Menschheit*) (ibid.) is what Schiller really wants to put to work, and he makes it plain that his own positive conclusions are to be seen as flowing from the metaphysical principles concerning man that are developed in Letter XI. Fruitful understanding of his strategy must focus on them. At their core stands the doctrine that in man two essential elements are to be distinguished, Person and Condition, or the Self and its Determinations (XI.2). Each implies the other: were there no Determinations there could be no Self; without Self, there would be nothing for Determinations to be Determinations of (XI.5, XIII.5). On this basis all Schiller's substantive aesthetic conclusions are to rest. How we understand them to do so will depend on just what we take the matter of this core to be.

First instinct is to see Schiller just alluding here to those Aristotelian considerations of substance and accident that Kant incorporated into his own metaphysic. Indeed, the thought is given encouragement by Schiller's illustrating the interdependence of Person and Condition with the sentence "The flower blooms and fades", and commenting on it in terms of a persisting substance and its changing states (XI.5). Only this should not be taken to represent his ultimate intention, since out of this traditional machinery alone no conclusions follow about the nature of man's *experience*, nor, *a fortiori*, about the place of the aesthetic within his experience. This must be so because even if it is an a priori truth that men, being substances, have various states or properties, that does not warrant any conclusion about the nature of those properties; hence it does not justify treating them as experiential states. No transition from *Condition* or *Determination* to experience is forthcoming from the Aristotelian base.

Close behind this first suggestion though comes another, nearer to the forefront of Schiller's mind. At the end of XI.5 he tells us that "only in the succession of its representations does the persisting self become an object for itself", and that remark (of a kind pervasive in these central letters) must incline us to identify the metaphysical Person not just with a persisting thing, but with a self-conscious subject, and its Condition not just with any old states of such a substance, but with its experiences. If this is the metaphysical datum from which Schiller's argument more sympathetically understood sets off, it can no longer be ruled out from the start that beauty should be derivable as an essential constituent of man's experience, and hence, a little elliptically maybe, but still in Kantian language, of man's very existence.

Schiller, I think, just assumes it to be a necessary truth about man that he is a subject of experience, and he certainly does not spend time arguing for it.[4] That we are necessarily self-conscious subjects of experience is perhaps something that he regards as too obvious to spend time over, and there is no reason for us here to do other than accept it as so. What is difficult is to see how he might think his transcendental argument can be moved on from here. At this point, and indeed from this point on, exegesis and speculation are not to be entirely divorced. Certainly, unambiguous direction from the text is not to be had, but there is one point at which leverage for an argument wholly Kantian in style can, if only dimly, be discerned.

At XIII.4 Schiller tells us that man is endowed with a drive, the drive to form, whose internal object it is to bring him to freedom, "to bring *harmony* [my emphasis] to the variety of his appearances and to affirm his Person amid all change of his Condition". This remark is obviously not offered in the spirit of empirical observation, or generalization of observation; it is no commonplace of experimentally established or even plain commonsensical developmental psychology: rather it is an a priori assertion about what is required if the self-consciousness with which men are necessarily equipped is to arise. And the signalled Kantian path might perhaps be made to meet up with Schiller's aesthetic preoccupations if we hear him as pointing out in this passage that the affirmation or construction of self can only take place through our finding harmony among our "appearances" (*Erscheinungen*), or experiential states. The introduction of the fundamentally aesthetic idea of harmony is

---

[4] We may assume tht Schiller thought the reader could find that work done by Kant. The transcending unity of apperception is frequently, if mistakenly, seen as securing the necessary self-consciousness of experience.

otherwise quite unprepared for, and only along such a tentative line as this will we succeed in finding anything like a genuinely transcendental deduction of the concept.[5]

It would be a mistake to judge this idea dud simply on the ground that the experiences that I am to find harmonious must already be thought of as mine and that they therefore presuppose self-consciousness rather than pave the way for it. Perhaps that is true, but if it is, it in no way impugns the thought that what self I come to recognize as mine, how I come to think of myself, will depend on the view I have of the world, and therefore on which of my experiential states I take to be objective representations of it, and which not. Now that is a matter that I, not being God, can only judge from the inside, and working, as I must, from the inside, the only tools I have to make these judgments are those that rely on considerations of harmony, good fit, simplicity, plausibility, comprehensiveness and the rest of the aesthetic or quasi-aesthetic panoply. Hence, it might be said, the existence of, or construction of, Self, and thus of man, presupposes harmony; beauty (or something within discernible distance of it) is a necessary condition of man's existence.

Following the idea of looking to Kant for the detailed complementary argument that Schiller neglects to provide, we might be struck by the way in which such a reading of Schiller's thought tallies with the notorious passage at §9.3 of the *Critique of Judgment*, which Kant called "the key to the critique of taste", and which Schiller certainly knew. I have argued in Chapter 5 above that Kant there overoptimistically hopes to show that in order to explain the ineluctably public aspect of cognitive judgments, their inter-personal communicability, we are bound to look to agreements in our subjective feelings of pleasure (in the harmony of our faculties). The only marked difference between that Kantian idea and the one offered here to Schiller is that for Kant the emphasis is on the inter-subjectivity of the pleasure in question whereas for Schiller

[5] It is no objection that the concept Beauty and the concept Harmony are distinct and that a derivation of the one is not a derivation of the other. Neither Kant nor Schiller would find the distinction compelling. Kant explains beauty in terms of a harmony between the imagination (sensibility) and the understanding, Schiller in terms of harmony between matter and form.

only its intra-subjective aspect is in point. In either case aesthetic considerations would enter essentially into the notion of experience and into the construction of the self that is dependent upon it.

None the less, there are overriding counterweights to set against these tenuous and speculative pointers. The most compelling of them must surely be that the argument just sketched does not lead us, even in prospect, to expect to find any aesthetic content *within* our experience. It merely employs aesthetic notions in determining which experiences to count as objective, but does not involve them with the substance of our objective experience itself. This objection may be reinforced by observing that under these assumptions any experience of the world that is accorded objectivity will turn out to be harmonized to the transcendentally requisite degree, and that result could not possibly provide a basis for an account of beauty[6] selective enough in its application to detach it from those works of art which, judged as nicely as may be, we reckon to be corrupting. Whatever the other constraints on Schiller's preferred analysis, it cannot abandon the obligation to allow for the possibility that some of the things we come across should fail to be beautiful, works of art as well as natural things.

Lastly, and turning finally to Schiller's text, there is no place in this would-be Kantian interpretation for the idea that the full aestheticization of experience is an *ideal* that we might set ourselves to attain in the course of our lives, but from which we may nevertheless fall far short. This theme in Schiller's thinking is so central a topic in the *Letters* that no reading of them that failed to accommodate it could possibly do justice to them (cf XVI.4, XVII.1/2). Consequently, we are bound to cast around for some other way to take the argument even if, in doing so, we find that we abandon much semblance of strict adherence to Kantian models.

III

An alternative conception of Schiller's strategy which is open

---

[6] More generally "aesthetically excellent", since Schiller claims to be using the term "beauty" in the most extended sense (XV.2).

to none of these complaints and which still retains a tinge of Kantian colour, is this. While it is no longer advanced as a constitutive truth about human experience that it is imbued with the aesthetic, it may still be regulative of experience that it be so. As rational beings, we are bound to adopt an ideal for our lives in which beauty has a central role to play. If this can be made out, there is some hope for Schiller to use the result in forcing his opponent of X.5 to make significant readjustments in his particular identifications of individual works of art as beautiful. In particular he may no longer find it so easy to think in that way of art he judges to be corrupting.

All detail aside, it is easy to see what is Kantian about such a plan of attack. Working out from the same metaphysical assumptions about man as before, Schiller will argue that they impose on us an a priori ideal of life from which we can not rationally resile. It is one that is eventually to lead us to a conception of beauty that is in no way directly derivable from everyday experience. In such a scheme as this there is material enough to warrant calling the path to be taken a transcendental one (X.7), though it is not one whose twists and turns can be found worked out or, as far as I know, even hinted at, in the critical writings of Kant.

The thought that everything of importance is to hinge on the notion of an a priori ideal for life is prompted by a leading passage that occurs just after Schiller's discussion of the metaphysical constituents of man touched on above. From those principles, he says (XI.9),

> follow two opposed demands on man, which constitute the two fundamental laws of his sensible-rational nature. The first strives for absolute reality. It has to make into World everything that is merely Form, and to make manifest all [man's] natural aptitudes. The second strives for absolute Form. Its task is to destroy everything in [man] that is merely World, and to bring harmony to all his changing states. In other words, man has to externalize all that is inner, and bring form to all that is outer.

This passage makes it plain enough that Schiller believes a quite specific ideal to be derivable from our nature as Person and Condition, or, as I have cast it, from our being essentially self-conscious subjects of experience. At this point, someone who mistrusts Schiller's ambitions may immediately want to raise an objection without considering the minutiae of his proposal. It is that Schiller gives his reader no reason to think that men are bound to embrace an ideal at all. Maybe they often do so in fact, and maybe it is true that the ideal that Schiller lights on is a good enough candidate for rational acceptance; only, if it is eventually to force the sceptic of X.4 out of business by would-be transcendental means, what is indispensably required to start with is a demonstration that men are rationally bound to concern themselves with ideals at all. Otherwise the a priori standing of the particular instance that fascinates Schiller will be contingent both on the truth and on the modality of the more general claim. It is not only the cynic, the objector might say, who sees three quarters of mankind as too busy getting on with life to bother themselves overmuch with how to live it.

As must already be apparent, it is not Schiller's style to defend theses that he believes to be self-evident, and whether this very general thought about ideals crossed his mind or not, he would certainly have held it impossible to deny. Men, we know, are of necessity persisting, self-conscious subjects of experience. Within the natural limits, he might say, it lies within their power to determine what sort of experience comes their way, and it also lies within their power, again within limits, to determine what to make of the experience that is theirs. These powers men have in virtue of the freedom that their rational nature confers on them, and the way in which these powers are exercised will do much to determine what personality or character the individual comes to have. For Schiller, to determine his personality is to fix the self that a man acquires and of which he is necessarily self-conscious. So he will not hesitate to conclude that it necessarily lies within men's power to decide who to become in response to their own reflective deliberation. Since such deliberation can only be brought to any practical conclusion in the light of a conception of the good, the worthy and the valuable, men must have the power to fashion their lives and their Self in accordance with some conception of what their good consists in, in short in accordance with an Ideal of Man.

Perhaps the objector will not find too much to protest about here.[7] What may irk him rather more is the suspicion that Schiller is assuming not just that men necessarily have this power, but also that it is a power they necessarily exercise. It is, after all, the denial of its exercise, rather than the denial of its potential possession, that prompted the gloomy reflection about three quarters of humanity. Only this protest will not disturb Schiller, since he is as likely as anyone to make just such gloomy observations himself (IV.6, V.3–5). His claim is, and it is important to be clear about this, that men cannot *rationally* abjure concern for an ideal in their lives; it is not that men cannot *in practice* abjure that concern. Too often they do; but in doing so they fail of rationality. The connection between the nature of man and the possession of an ideal is thus not a matter of pure theoretical reason; it is rather an a priori truth of practical reason that the Self should be formed under some concept of the good.[8] For, Schiller might reason, suppose a man failed to be guided by some such concern. He might do that either in response to some reflection of principle – as for example the reflection that the best sort of life was one uncluttered by futile considerations of rationality, or the good – or else he might just fortuitously fail to bring to bear on his life the power of rational reflection that is necessarily his. There could be nothing to say in favour of the second of these alternatives that did not straightway turn it into a case of the first; so anyone who found that his life was entirely fortuitously following such a path would be powerless before the accusation that he had abandoned concern for rationality. If, on the other hand, his life of laid back Californian spontaneity was adopted by some *principled* choice, choice, that is, of the first sort, then what he would have done would not be to have abjured concern for rationality, but to have made an irrational choice in the name of rationality itself. Against that sort of person

---

[7] Though he should point out that the argument relies on man having a richer essential nature than is derivable from the ideal of self-consciousness alone. Freedom and rationality are obviously being taken for granted.

[8] Putting such an argument in Schiller's mouth is not entirely fanciful. Apart from the sense it makes of the whole, he expresses clear insight about the distinction between pure theoretical and pure practical reason in *Kallias*, and connects aesthetic matters there unequivocally with the latter. See the letter to Körner of 8 Feb 1793 (Reclam, 1971, 15).

Schiller has no need to bring transcendental argument to bear, but just the ordinary kinds of reflection to which his opponent's willingness to make a choice of principle shows him to be open anyway. There is no guarantee that he could be brought to see the error of his ways; but then neither does there need to be, nor would Schiller suppose there was.

So let us allow that Schiller could defend himself against the objection that his chosen ideal is at best only conditionally necessary. A more urgent worry than that must be whether it is necessary at all, for even if we are rationally bound to pursue some ideal or other for our lives, it does not follow from that that there is any particular ideal which we must pursue on pains of irrationality. We pressingly want to know, that is, on what grounds we are to accept the claim on us of an ideal according to which we are to internalize the outer and to externalize the inner.

The last paragraphs suggest that the a priori standing of Schiller's designated ideal, like that of the possession of ideals in general, is one of pure practical rationality. Letter XIII can be seen to hold the key to its demonstration. In the broadest outline, I suggest, Schiller seems to think first that any rational creatures, men, . . . , angels, gods or whatever, could not cry off from the ideal of their perfection without irrationality, and then second, that what their perfection turns out to be in each case is a function of their metaphysical constitution. It is from the last of these two thoughts that we shall ultimately have to move to the material of Letter XI about internalization and externalization.

The first of these claims I arrive at from Schiller's eagerness to employ the notion of perfection immediately he comes to specifying what our ideal consists in. He even speaks explicitly of "the ideal of perfection" at XIII fn 2 in warning us against certain abuses that the ideal man is open to.[9] Since there is nowhere any suggestion that man is in any way special here I assume that he would take it to be a quite general truth that any

---

[9] The idea is perhaps first adumbrated at IV.2. "It is man's great task to bring his manifold changes into harmony with the unity of his ideal". What would link this claim with the *Kallias* passage I allude to is that the ideal is explained in terms of the perfection of man's essence (i.e. his concept). Schiller refers the reader to Fichte's *Vorlesungen über die Bestimmung des Gelehrten* here.

creature seeking its a priori ideal should look to its perfection to find it. Hence my anthropocentrically neutral formulation of the idea in the last paragraph.

The second thought is not explicitly offered in the *Letters* as a doctrinal claim, but in the *Kallias* (the letters on beauty he wrote to his friend Körner a couple of years beforehand, in 1793) Schiller states in quite general terms that "an object is perfect when its manifold states coincide with the unity of its concept".[10] It is application of this rather obscure thought to the case that interests us, to man, that we find at XIII.3:

> Since the world is extension in time, that to say change, the perfection of that faculty which connects man to the world must be the greatest possible degree of alteration and extensity. Since Person is what persists through time, the perfection of that faculty which opposes change must be the greatest possible autonomy (*Selbständigkeit*) and intensity.

Putting these two gobbets together yields the idea that a thing's perfection consists in what an earlier century would have called the maximization of its essence; its manifold disposition to behaviour coincides with its concept in that everything it does or is disposed to do is geared to bringing about an increase in some dimension of its F-ness, where 'F' stands for the set of properties essential to things of that sort. Applied to man, the doctrine requires that what be maximized are Person and Condition, and, in accordance with the thesis of pure practical rationality, it will consequently be held irrational for us imperfect men to conduct our lives except under the guidance of an ideal that spurs us to maximal consciousness of self and maximal variety in experience. Furthermore, reverting to Schiller's claim that beauty is a necessary condition of humanity, we can now see how that is to be understood. In as much as attainment of the ideal can not be envisaged without engagement with the beautiful, men's ideal existence depends on beauty. While humanity may perfectly well actually exist with no concern for beauty, only with a concern for it operating as an element of our behavioural dispositions may humanity exist perfectly.

[10] Cf *Kallias* letter to Körner 23 Feb 1793 (Reclam, p. 47).

These last matters will occupy us later on. For the moment though we still need to ask how Schiller is to connect his doctrine of perfection with the material in XI.9 about internalization and externalization. After all, there are no ready links to hand that obviously relate maximal persistence and autonomy of Person with internalization (of the surrounding world (?)), nor that relate maximal variety of experience or Condition with externalization (of the inner life (?)).

For the puzzlement this hiatus causes there is some remedy to be found perhaps in recalling how, when he allows "abstraction to rise up as high as it can" (XI.1), Schiller is inclined to think in the traditional vocabulary of substance and accident. That, I suspect, is what is guiding him at XIII.3, and what leads him to identify our perfection with autonomy (of substance) and variety (of accident). Only, as we saw in §4, what he is more concerned with when he reflects on the a priori ideal of man, is his nature as self-conscious subject of experience. Once we start from there, the abstract doctrine of XIII and suggestive concrete claims of XI.9 may not be impossible to tie together.

The suggestion is, then, that the ideal of man will consist in his pursuing to the maximum his essential metaphysical constitution, and that this somehow involves the maximization of self-consciousness and the maximization of variety in experience. Only, if the idea is taken absolutely literally, it will occasion hilarity and disappointment; hilarity, because, what it might appear to recommend is a life of total sleeplessness (to preserve self-consciousness) and intolerable length (to amass experience); disappointment, because these things are no less distant from the activities of internalization and externalization than anything suggested by the rejected Aristotelian reading of XIII.3. Fortunately, Schiller is neither obliged nor inclined to such excess.

It would be silly to take the injunction to maximise consciousness of self as leading to a search for more and more moments in life during which one is aware of oneself as something or other, as this or that. For *consciousness* is not what is at the centre of Schiller's attention. It is *Self*; and consciousness he takes to tag along with that automatically. We increase Self in his view by pursuing a life in which what we are conscious of ourselves as yields greater and greater reflective internal satisfaction. Hence I suggest in brief, to seek the greatest possible autonomy (*Selbständigkeit*) and intensity is to find oneself concerned with making the most of one's life, finding the greatest possible meaning for it, judged by criteria of which, after all deliberation, discussion and argument, we ourselves must be the ultimate arbiters.[11]

Read in this way Schiller's idea can immediately be connected with his concern for the internalization of the external, for what that comes to is now something both familiar and natural. As we find significance in our lives, so we are able to bring the things and events that we come upon within the ambit of our mind. We see them in a certain way, and in consequence, find that they have a sense for us. And as more and more of our experience acquires a sense and is thus 'internalized', so we come to possess a more determinate and fully formed Self. With consciousness of increased Self, well-being is increased. So too is Freedom, for with the formation of Self comes command of the direction of a man's life. He is, according to Schiller, less at the mercy of external and internal forces (XIV.6), and harnesses them to goods that are of his choosing (XXIII.5).

Thus are linked together, as Schiller wants, the ideal of man, the maximization of his essence, the idea of man's perfection, the affirmation and formation of Self, the internalization of the external, man's freedom and the meaning of his life. The last of these is not explicitly mentioned by Schiller – that expression and its German equivalent were not current at the end of the eighteenth century – but it is an idea we are pretty much bound to use to put his views across to a modern audience. In these terms the ideal of man that Schiller is telling us we cannot rationally abandon is in large part that of finding the fullest possible significance for our lives.

About the element in the ideal that derives from Condition,

---

[11] There is much to be said, by someone else somewhere else, about "ultimately". What has to be remembered here is that Schiller will reject the standard of *Glückseligkeit* being imposed externally in the name of objectivity (cf XXIV.8). Equally he will reject the idea that internally determined choice brings with it capriciousness or subjectivity. For him it is a matter of reason, something autonomous and internal to man (XXIII.8, XXIV.8). I signal this in the text by referring to *reflective* internal satisfaction.

little need perhaps be said. One maximizes that side of one's nature by seeking "the greatest possible degree of alteration and extensity" (XIII.3), by acquiring the greatest variety of experience that one can, and this, one may suppose, by extending one's direct (and through the arts, one's imaginative) acquaintance with the world's contents. But while this is most certainly part of what Schiller had in mind to complement the development of Self, it does not immediately lead us fully to understand what he intended in speaking of the requirement of XI.9 that we should externalize what is inner. To get there a missing element has to be supplied.

As I have presented his conception of the ideal of man I have followed Schiller in engaging in a certain pretence. I have tried to make it look, at least in abstract terms, as if we could say what the perfection of Person came to without reference to Condition, and also what the perfection of Condition comes to without reference to Person. In the latter case that may seem relatively easy, for there is nothing very much that prevents us accumulating meaningless experience. On the other hand there can be no such thing as experienceless meaning, and in my discussion of the maximization of Self I was forced to speak of finding a sense *for one's experience*, even though in doing so I was preparing the way for an apparent asymmetry in my treatment of man's two essential elements.

However, Schiller will say, and surely rightly, that this distinction is merely nominal, not real. As he puts it (XIII.5), "once you take away Person, so you remove Condition, because they are mutually dependent concepts (*Wechselbegriffe*) – because change requires something persisting . . .", so, when it comes to stating an ideal for man that rests on the maximization of these two nominally distinct elements, we can not simply sum two independently specifiable qualities. Instead, we specify a maximum that results from their joint operation, from a dual demand on our mixed sensible-cum-rational nature (XI.9). And it is in relation to this dual nature that we get not only the requirement that we internalize what is outer, but also externalize what is inner. For the world that we endow with significance in bringing what we encounter within the ambit of the mind is also a world within which we act and on whose materiality we set our stamp. We are both receptive and productive (cf XIII.3) in the construction of our world, and the variety of experience that is ours will be increased not just by extensive acquaintance with what the world contains as we dumbly confront it, but rather by our extensively forming and fashioning what it contains in the development of ourselves, whose world it is. In the end, Schiller will want to say, knowledge of the world and self-knowledge are of a piece; likewise the formation of the self and our formation of the world. Thus is symmetry regained, and asymmetry merely apparent.

Because so much is left unsaid by Schiller in the development of his thought, a substantial proportion of my exposition here has been somewhat speculative; but that we have now arrived at a reasonably fair and accurate understanding of the content of Schiller's ideal of man may, I hope, be confirmed by the moving picture of his vision of human well-being that completes XIII.3. It is a picture I leave to speak for itself:

> The more man's receptivity is developed, the more labile it is, and the greater surface it offers to appearances, so much more of the world does man grasp and so many more capacities does he develop in himself. The greater power and depth of person and freedom of reason he acquires, the more of the world does he understand and so much more form does he create outside himself. . . . [Cultivating both activity and receptivity] . . . man will combine the greatest fullness of existence with the greatest independence and freedom, and instead of losing himself to the world, will take it and the infinity of its appearances within him and subject it to the unifying power of his reason.

IV

In Schiller's exposition everything that follows, and in particular the major contentions about beauty, is made to hinge on an irreducible conflict within the ideal I have presented him as setting up, a conflict he perceives to arise between the demands it makes on Person and those it makes on Condition. Now although he does speak of a "pure and rigorous opposition" between feeling (=Condition) and thought (=Person) (XVIII.4), he is acute enough to see that there is no straightforward formal opposition between them. Even if we say that Person demands stability and Condition demands change, they do not demand these for the same objects, and as he puts it, "where there is no meeting, there is no collision either" (XIII.2).

Nevertheless, there is a constant tension between these demands which comes out particularly clearly at the limit when we envisage trying to maximize both breadth of experience and its depth or its significance. For to pursue variety of experience singlemindedly, I must, given the contingent facts about the world, sacrifice significance; likewise, I can only achieve maximal significance if I abandon all attempt to make my life a maximally varied one as well (XIV.1). Schiller goes on, we cannot hope to overcome this conflict through finding some third term (XVIII.2) in which all the desirable aspects of the two conflicting ones may be subsumed and realised. There is no such mean, nor could there be. Rather our task must be to find an optimal combination of the two: "Man must not strive for Form (=Self) at the cost of Reality (=experience), nor for Reality at the cost of Form" (XIV.2). The two principles must work at the same time in harmony and as mutual subordinates (XVI fn I). And it is at this point in the development of his thought that for the first time we find mention of beauty. For it is precisely the task of beauty to resolve the tension between the conflicting elements in the a priori ideal that Schiller offers us and to find an optimal mix in a whole life of those elements of 'sense and form', or Person and Condition, or as I have put it, of breadth and depth that ideally demand their due.

When we look at the way in which talk of beauty is introduced in Letter XV, however, what is so striking is the very lack of elucidation that Schiller gives it and the utter silence in which he passes over the question of how it might be called on to resolve the conflict to which he sees men as being inevitably exposed. In fact all he does to identify and secure an optimal, tension-reducing, mix of Person and Condition is simply to locate it as what is aimed at by a drive that seeks to overcome conflict between the drive to form and the drive to sense. This new third drive, mediating between the other two, as between the psychological motors of our two metaphysically posited constitutive elements, is the famous "play drive". What it aims at, its formal object, Schiller calls "living form", and from the exposition I have offered it is plain that that must evidently be identical with the Ideal we are rationally bound to pursue. Then having got here, Schiller at once goes on to say (XV.2) that it, living form, is "a concept that serves to designate all the aesthetic characteristics of appearance, and, in a word, everything that in its broadest sense we call 'beauty' ". And that, abruptly, is how he leaves it.

Now at this point the reader understandably suffers his greatest let down, even experiences a measure of outrage, for after all the wearisome metaphysical toil it looks as if the transcendental derivation of beauty just takes the form of an arbitrary and empty association between that notion and a final highly abstract specification of the ideal of man. Could anything be more fraudulent? What on earth, one wonders, could be intended by such an identity? And how could Schiller possibly believe that anything so purely stipulatory as this might move his opponent of X.4 away from the experientially formed conception of beauty on which he claims to rely?

It has to be admitted that in the *Letters* Schiller does nothing at all to help his reader here. He talks as if everything that needs be said about the concept of beauty is now said and as if the passage from that to the importance of natural and artistic beauty in our lives was self-evident. However, when we remember the tenor of the earlier *Kallias* doctrines and step back a bit from the usual eighteenth century assumptions about the way our understanding of the aesthetic should proceed, we can, I believe, see rather more in Schiller's mind than his text itself readily divulges.

Looking at the way in which the issue of beauty is discussed by Schiller's contemporaries, we see all parties to the debate fixing attention on the question of what it is for an object (or work of art) to be beautiful, and answering in terms of some effect the object produces in the perceiver or else some standardly observed features that regularly produce pleasure in those who give the work their attention. In reading the *Letters* we are primed by the discussion in Letter X with the knowledge that Schiller rejects the going answers whether they be empiricist or Kantian in style. What we are not led to expect is that he is dissatisfied also with the way in which the analysis is itself is conducted, so we naturally expect him to offer us a modification of the traditional story which leaves its main lines intact while introducing some novel variant. Naturally enough we feel cheated not to find it. Thus it is that the commentator is inclined to complain that Schiller does not keep his promise to provide a transcendental account of beauty, on the supposition that that will follow from his failing to provide any familiar kind of account at all.

Help however is to be had by recalling the earlier doctrine of beauty given in *Kallias*, which Schiller never abandoned, and by keeping in mind also his main preoccupation in the intervening essay *On Grace and Dignity* (*Über Anmut und Würde*). *Kallias* proposes that beauty should be generally understood as freedom in appearance, *Anmut und Würde* is centrally occupied with the question of what it is for man to be beautiful. Now at XV.2, in his talk of "living form", Schiller is still obviously concerned with the perfection of man, and in the sentence I quoted from that paragraph speaks of the aesthetic features of appearance. Now I suggest that if we allow ourselves to be guided by considerations of continuity with the earlier work, the proposal we may hear Schiller to be making in Letter XV is that *beauty in man* is nothing other than the way in which the ideally harmonious balance of his metaphysical constituents (his maximization of essence, or under our revision, his fulfilment) is manifested in appearance. Schiller is not, that is, immediately making any suggestion at all about beauty in art, or, beyond man himself, in nature either. Nor is he making any suggestion about men's sensitivity to beauty at all and its importance in an ideal life. His only concern is for what it is for men themselves to be beautiful.

What is more, and again continuously with the *Kallias* doctrine, the beauty of man remains freedom in appearance here because when the forces of sense and reason are in balance, all tension between them is resolved and they cease to exercise any constraint on man. He is then freely self-determining (cf XX.2/3, *Kallias*, Reclam 36/7). Only there is now an advance on the *Kallias* analysis. For whereas there the theoretical base for the identification of beauty as freedom in appearance was furnished by reference to inspection of significant cases, in the *Letters* the base has become the perfect harmony between conflicting forces in man's metaphysically determined make up. That then provides the understanding Schiller offers of freedom, and which, when manifest in appearance (behaviour), is straightway identified as beauty. Beauty, which is a feature of appearance, is of necessity identified in terms of what the relevant appearance is appearance of, to wit, the realized human ideal. It is tht with which Letters XI–XV have been concerned, as at heart the *Kallias* was not.

To relocate the centre of Schiller's reflection as the beauty of man rather than the beauty of natural objects or of works of art that men produce and contemplate, as ingrained habit leads the reader to expect, is not to forget that we are still owed an explanation of how the term applies to these other natural things and to the arts. Nor is it to suggest that anything more has yet been done than assign the word "beautiful" by way of quick stipulation to men under given conditions. All we have so far in Letter XV is a linguistic proposal, and with that alone Schiller can get nowhere. But there is, I think, no reason for him to dissent; his way forward from here is, at least in outline, pretty clear.

V

To resume: The ideal state of man, wherein we maximize our essence, or find fulfilment, is schematically identified as one of harmony between the potentially conflicting demands of Person and Condition, effectively a challengingly satisfying mix between breadth and depth of experience. For Schiller that is one a priori truth. Another is that men are rationally bound in life to strive to attain that ideal. Should they succeed in doing so, they will be free, and this freedom cannot but display itself in their bearing and behaviour. Our freedom and its manifestation are thus among the most important goals in life we could possibly have, and we are in consequence liable to assess things that directly bear on our achieving or missing this goal in the light of how they do so.

We have seen in Letter X that both Schiller and his opponent are impressed by the arts' causal powers. Both agree that the arts may prove harmful to men, and we can see that for Schiller this will come to their taking men away from the realisation of that ideal which they are rationally bound to realize. On the other hand it is plain from his exhortations to the young artist of talent at the end of Letter IX that he hopes the arts may, by working on our character, promote the attainment of that ideal or at least a recognisably close approximation to it.[12] He might add that given that the attainment of our ideal is the organizing goal of men's lives (or at least ought rationally to be its organizing goal), any activity that bore on the likelihood of attaining it or failing to attain it would only merit our concern and protection if its best instances did not militate against our attaining of this central goal.

Now Schiller's extended metaphysical argument is supposed to persuade the sceptic of the centrality to our lives of the goal of maximizing our essence. Suppose that he has been successful in that, and that his opponent is brought to recognise that we are rationally bound to pursue our ideal, our freedom, and that success will manifest itself in our being what Schiller calls "beautiful". Once he sees that the art that is usually thought of as being beautiful tends to inhibit our attaining this goal, he must either recommend that we abandon all close concern with the arts, or else readjust his way of speaking. Of the two alternatives the latter will be strongly preferable as soon as he comes to think that the arts *also* have it theoretically in their power to bring us nearer to the realization of our a priori ideal. It could not be a rational proposal to abandon concern with anything that might help us to achieve that.

There is a missing premiss here. But it is not one that either party would reject. It is that whatever else beauty may be, it is also and essentially the prime quality at which the artist aims. That is a quality his work will enjoy if and only if it is fully successful. That they may have been in agreement about all along. Only the sceptic was inclined not to think that the deepest canons of excellence in art would have anything to do with the achievement of the ideal of man, but only with what is gratifying or formally satisfying. It is this stronger contention

---

[12] The artist cannot of course select for us a specific realization of the ideal that we then set out and live. Rather we have a view about how the ideal might look and the internalization of that helps us to develop a character that makes it natural for us to aim for (one or another) form of the ideal in our lives. The artist is not didactic (XXII.5).

that Schiller's Kantian argument has tried to establish.

I shall not add to this chapter by commenting on the argument. My aim is purely expository, and anyway I aim not to bury Schiller, but to praise him. There are just two unrelated observations however that I want to finish with. The first is that the interpretation I have offered of his argument may be thought defective on the grounds that it commits Schiller to advocacy of tendentious or didactic art, which in Letter XXII he explicitly denies. How else, one might ask, could he believe that beauty in art might bring us close to our a priori ideal? His full answer to this accusation is given at XXII.3 where he says that the true criterion of excellence in arts is that it puts us in an "indifferent, equilibrated state", in which all sides of our nature are in balance and that it is not didactic work that does this. About this piece of theory I shall have more to say in the next chapter. For the present though it should be enough to note that Schiller does not think that we can be moved to the ideal by exhortation; rather it is by being *shown* some version of the ideal in a pleasing light, one that precisely appeals to us aesthetically, that our characters are moulded and opened up to achieving the ideal in life itself. The very importance of the arts lies here. It is in our moments of disinterested contemplation that we are most likely to be effectively touched by visions of the good (IX.7).

The other is this. I have advanced an interpretation of Schiller that claims as a matter of necessity that beauty in art is what makes men "beautiful". A frequently occurring thought in aesthetic theory is even stronger; namely that beauty in art makes men beautiful; a claim that we find for example Lessing ascribing to the Greeks at *Laocoon* II, 15 and there apparently endorsing. This, it curiously happens, is a contention that Schiller might perhaps subscribe to as well, though now as a contingent, rather than as a conceptual, truth. For he does think that "beautiful" men have the quality of promoting the satisfaction of the ideal of man in others. As we encounter men who manifest freedom in their behaviour and dispositions so we become attached to what we see in them and are encouraged to emulate them in our own persons. As we attempt to become like them on account of their "beauty", so we come to have the power to affect others likewise. Then we will be like beautiful works of art, beautiful. Hence it is an empirical truth, predicated on this broad psychological generalization, that beautiful art makes men not just "beautiful", but beautiful as well.

8

Aesthetic Education and Social Character

The prime concern of the central section of the *Letters*, Letters X–XVI, that is, is to arrive at a more satisfactory conception of beauty than Schiller believed either eighteenth century empiricism or Kant's own transcendental formalism was able to attain. The upshot of his investigation there is that beauty is to be identified neither with what produces mere gratification, nor with empty form (however satisfying); instead it is essentially what makes men beautiful. The beauty of man is identified as the visible manifestation of perfect harmony between opposed forces that express his metaphysical essence, to wit, the drive to sense and the drive to form. I contended in the last chapter that it is no travesty of Schiller's thought to spell out this a priori ideal of human life in terms of an optimal combination of variety and significance in experience, the best possible balance to be found in life of breadth and depth. In consequence, the burden of Schiller's contention is that beauty in art, or in nature, will be whatever has the power to bring this ideal to fruition.

Such is the reading I have offered of the heart of Schiller's argument. It is, admittedly, a disputable reading, but one consideration that will count in its favour is its ability to lend an overall unity to the *Letters*, which they are so often thought not to possess. Exactly what, students ask, has "the pure rational concept of beauty" (X.7) got to do with the edification of the ideal State, that perfectly rational polity that is prefigured in Letters I–IX? And what has it to do with the a priori psychogenetic tale of man's development that occupies such a large portion of Letters XVII–XXVII? These questions will find their answer here. In answering them it will, I hope, become possible to understand and assess Schiller's most ambitious a priori claim, namely that only through mankind's aesthetic education can his social and political freedom be won (II.5, XXVII.10).

I

To have identified the beautiful in terms of what makes for true harmony of the soul (XX fn) is to leave open the question whether there is, or even could be, any such thing. There is nothing in the foregoing analysis that will guarantee that the idea is not internally incoherent or, if unexceptionable on that score, guarantee that it can actually have instances. And this point has to be taken if the transcendental reasoning of Letters XI–XV is not to misfire. Certainly Schiller is anxious to maintain that "ideal beauty" can never exist in this world, and that it must remain an idea of reason (XVI.1,2);[1] by contrast he does believe that *approximations* to the ideal are possible, although he leaves it vague how close to it we should take them to come. The best extant examples, he thinks, are furnished by works of Greek art (IX.4); closer to our own day we have been less successful in our efforts (X.4). Nevertheless, there is no call for despondency about the future, provided only it can be shown that even if we have not in fact succeeded, we might well do so. Once we know what it is that we are looking for, and know that its existence is a real possibility, rationally underpinned desire for it combined with active search may surely expect to bring it forth. The most urgent matter is therefore to enquire whether approximation to the proposed ideal is indeed a real possibility. It is in terms of this question that Schiller's story concerning man's spiritual development must be understood.

[1] The phrase is, of course, Kant's, and designates concepts that can have no adequate instances in experience. Cf *Critique of Pure Reason* A 310/11, B 367/68, *Critique of Judgment* §49.

When we ask whether there can possibly be approximations to Schiller's ideal beauty, we are asking whether our characters can be so affected by the things we encounter that our dispositions to thought and action can be significantly altered for the better (X.1).[2] If beauty is what makes us more nearly ideal, approximations to ideal beauty cannot fail to bear well on thought and deed. Further, if the connection is to be a genuinely causal one, it needs to be mediated through some stable structure of the mind (III.5, IV.1).

With one additional constraint, these considerations set up Schiller's problem and indicate in general terms what sort of model would provide its resolution. This last requirement is the demand that we should be able to give a reasonably naturalistic account of whatever causal mechanisms we rely on to do the work, naturalistic in that their operation must be such as can be seen to be triggered entirely by forces that bear on men in the phenomenal world (IV, XX). For the moment it will suffice to note. this requirement. Its point will become plain as we go along.

A description of a mechanism that Schiller sees operating within the mind, yielding changes in the mental constitution on which it works in response to mental inputs, is this. In nature, or in art, we can be presented with something, or a representation of something, that appears to us in an attractive light. In consequence we come to think well of it and of things perceived as relevantly like it – something which, in the normal run of things, we should not otherwise do. Thinking well of them, we are disposed to modify our responses to them in ways we also would not otherwise do. Thereby we manifest a changed disposition, or in the case of a change that becomes stably anchored, a change of character. Here art and nature are on a par, the only difference between them being that whereas in nature we come to see things themselves in a certain light, in the case of art we see things in the light in which they are presented to us by the artist.

Several features of this mechanism suit it well to Schiller's purposes. In the first place, this model makes it easy to see what

[2] The whole content of "better" is given by the nature of the ideal for man. It is not in itself an essentially moralized idea, though the connection with morality comes to assume a dominant place in Letters XIX–XXVII. See especially Section IV below.

Schiller means when, at XXII.6, he observes that for a beautiful work of art to be properly effective there needs to be form in both the work and in the perceiver. Not only, we might say, does the artist have to find a suitable light in which to present attaching material in order to render it attaching to the perceiver, but the perceiver must also be sensitive to what is presented to him as attaching. However well devised the inputs to the model are they can only be effective if the mechanism on which they work is adapted to them.[3]

Second, it is happily neutral between the good and the bad, or between what Schiller would identify as the beautiful and its opposite, being just as well able to explain how the arts can corrupt as how they might in theory improve and edify.[4] To give a simplistic illustration, it might happen that the light in which Court life is presented in some Renaissance painting should give rise in a man to an attachment to sumptuary display that he would not otherwise have had. In consequence, and in the worst of cases, he might come to find a place for such display in his life that distorts his ordering of other more pressing concerns, even entirely displaces them. Should the effect become widespread, and not depend just on the idiosyncracies of the stray individual, should it also come widely to dominate people's character, then Schiller would say that the artist had a share of responsibility and that his work had proved corrupting. There is then no systematic connection to be had between what appears attaching (what is generally thought of as beautiful), and what is good. Hence the danger of aesthetic corruption to which men are exposed (cf X.5). Fortunately, though, neither is there any impediment of principle to such a beneficent connection holding, and for Schiller, it will be the task of the genuinely talented artist to make that beneficent connection a regular one. Should he succeed, and succeed on a sufficiently wide scale, his work will be worthy of the appellation "beautiful".

Third, this model is one that Schiller can call on in constructing, as he must eventually hope to do, a convincing

---

[3] At X.3 Schiller describes the man without form as one who suspects all grace in art of being corrupting. There is no call to think that insensitivity to the good that the artist can offer need invariably manifest itself as starkly as this.

[4] For Schiller's certainty that the arts can corrupt see X.4.

picture of the way in which our aesthetic tastes mature. It would after all be little use if all it could achieve were an understanding of how aesthetic attachments are made first of all and then had no role to play in explaining how we may from that be taken on towards a stopping place which, given the right inputs, will coincide with the realization of our a priori human ideal. All we have observed so far is that in response to a suitably chosen input a change may be effected in men's character or dispositions. This change in character, we can now go on, may sensitize a man to new inputs with which he may be presented, which then play their part in further changes in his mental life and his behaviour. Once the initial step is taken and the process has got under way, the receptive mind comes to be furnished with beliefs, desires and values that were not originally part of its make up at all. Equipped with such adjustments to an old established stock, we are liable to find attaching ways of thinking about things to which previously we were unresponsive or even inured, and liable to modify our dispositions still further in response to further new inputs. This picture of continual, or at least recurrent, feedback cannot of course account for an eventual maturity of taste all alone. That can not be achieved without reference to the content of the inputs to which we successively respond and to the consequential modifications to the ways of thought and dispositions to behaviour that make up character. However these things will not appear in any specification of the general model by which maturity can come about. All we demand of that is that it should enable us to understand how with the right additional material it comes about if and when it does. The feedback potential of the model achieves just this.[5]

Finally, on this conception of how the aesthetic works it becomes clear why Schiller wants to insist that the proper response to beauty is that of love.[6] So far I have spoken rather

[5] It is interesting to note that Schiller seems to have discovered the germ of an explanation of why art must have a history, and why its products have to be historically understood.

[6] "[The sentiment of respect is inseparable from the dignified.] On the other hand, with grace (Anmut) as generally in the case of beauty, reason can see its demands sensibly realized, and unexpectedly comes across one manifestation of its own Ideas [viz. freedom, A.S.] in appearance. This surprising coincidence of the contingent in

blandly of our finding a way in which things are seen or presented as attaching, and that idea will do well enough when we think of what is aesthetically engaging as neutrally effecting a wide range of changes in our dispositions. But once the beautiful is elucidated in terms of inputs to the mind that bring us close to the ideal of human existence, it has to be thought of as modifying our characters in ways that ensure the resulting dispositions are firmly lodged in the structure of the person. The natural way for Schiller to write this into the process that he takes to operate is through the particular quality of attachment that it can provoke in the man of form. Calling it "love" in the central cases, rather than just "pleasure" or "enjoyment" or, even worse, "approval", correctly marks out the kind of response to inputs to the mind that is liable to have the right sort of enduring structural effect.

I have pointed to no portion of the *Letters* in which Schiller discusses this matter. Certainly it is not an aspect of his general inquiry that he finds demands much discussion. It is, I suspect, self-evident to him how aesthetic matter works on us, and he is anxious to devote his fullest concentration to a different, though intimately related, topic that he finds more urgently pressing. None the less, in one noteworthy passage he does reveal very clearly the part of our psychology to which he thinks the artist can appeal to secure his effect. At IX.7, at the end of the programmatic section of the *Letters*, the young man of talent is instructed how to fulfil his desire to change men's nature. Schiller exhorts him:

> Live with your century without being its creature: give your contemporaries what they need, rather than what they want. Think what they ought to be when you have to work upon them, but think how they are when you are tempted to act on their behalf. Seek their approbation by appealing to their dignity, but measure their happiness by reference to their insignificance. Thus your own nobility will awaken theirs and

---

nature with the necessity of reason awakens a response of joyous approval (Beifall), which acts realisingly on the senses, but works vitally and actively on the mind inevitably producing an attraction towards this sensible object. We call this attraction benevolence – love; a feeling that is inseparable from grace and beauty." *Anmut und Würde* (Reclam 1971) 128.

your endeavours not be brought to nought by their unworthiness. The severity of your principles will make them flee you, but in play they will still bear with them; their taste is chaster than their hearts, and it is here that you must seize the timorous fugitive. You will rage against their maxims in vain, in vain berate them for their deeds, but you may try your shaping hand on them in their leisure. Chase caprice, frivolity and coarseness from their pleasures, and you will eventually and unremarked banish them from their actions and their dispositions. Wherever you find them, surround them with noble, grand and challenging (*geistreich*) forms, surround them with emblems of the outstanding, until appearance triumph over reality and art over nature.

Comment should be superfluous. It will not be missed that the artist is here assumed to make the unquestionably right choice of input to the available standing causal pathways; he clearly is supposed to operate by finding something which in moments of reflection and contemplation men can find attaching; and the effect of his work is in the end to alter for the better the dispositions to thought, feeling and behaviour of those who give it their attention through the changes that it brings about in their taste.

II

The issue I alluded to that occupies the greatest part of Schiller's attention and presents what he takes to be the severest challenge for aesthetics (XVIII.3), is that of realistically characterizing the sort of mechanism that the last section has so sketchily described.[7] How is it that men, who all grow up in a world that starts out for them as sense and matter, and is initially conceptualized only to a minimal degree, can ever come to offer a soil in which these processes can work themselves out? This question must be crucial for the success of Schiller's

---

[7] What Schiller actually says in XVIII is that the whole problem of beauty lies in finding a way to reconcile the conflict between thought and feeling in the absence of any middle term between them; but the continuation of the Letters makes it plain that the question 'How is it possible for beauty to do this?' is answered by describing a path by which it can come to have this effect. It would be a mistake to think that we should be looking at an analysis of the concept to effect the reconciliation.

overall argument, since if all that he were able to say in the end was that he had identified a psychic mechanism whereby men might possibly be brought to internal harmony and wholeness, given the right mental development, we should still be right to wonder whether the idea of beauty was well founded. In theory, we should say, it may be delineated well enough, but in the absence of a demonstration that is properly adapted to the way in which men do in fact have to develop, its ability to function at the higher stages of growth, when the powers of the mind are already advanced, would not provide the assurance that Schiller thinks is needed. How, we would want to ask, does it get off the ground in the first place?

For two reasons it would be easy to think that Schiller is needlessly agitated about this point. If he is in any doubt, why should he not appeal here to other, non-aesthetic, considerations if he wants to bring men to the point at which the described mechanism can be brought into play? And then given that we can look to our experience to see that the proposed mechanism does work, why should we not simply infer backwards and argue from that to its evident adaptation to the human mind, even at the very start? Why concern ourselves at all, that is, with the details of how it actually takes root?

These suggestions do Schiller injustice. We saw before how wary he is of the interpretation of experience in the absence of sound theory (cf XVII.3), and that in part may explain his persistence at this troublesome point. Since he also thinks that nothing other than application of the aesthetic machinery could serve to get the process of development started, and that there truly is an explanation available of how it does so, we need not be surprised to find him setting the matter out at considerable length. If he is successful in his psychogenetic speculations he will not only have cleared some ground in the territory of psychology that needed clearing, but also have laid the foundation for his contention that aesthetic education is necessary for the social development of man (XXVII.10).

It must be evident, Schiller thinks, that it cannot be considerations of reason, be they conceived of in terms of pure practical reason or in more austerely moral terms, that could provide men with a motive to first engage themselves with beauty and the arts. At this stage in the argument (XVII.2) we have, he remarks, left the domain of pure thought and of the ideal man to descend into the arena of reality, where far too few can be relied on to act as reason commands. Openness to the claims of reason ("truth") and morality ("duty") (XXIV.6) is what application of the aesthetic machinery is ultimately to bring about. We cannot therefore sensibly look in their direction to explain its initial appeal (XVIII.4). As he puts it later on (XXVI.1), "the aesthetic moment of the mind . . . must be a gift of Nature – only by the operation of chance (good fortune) can the bonds of the physical state be released".[8]

The most fully articulated resolution of the problem is offered at XXIII.7 in the context of a discussion of self-conscious action rather than of our accessibility to the aesthetic itself, but since the issues are so intimately related, not much can hinge on the shift in context.[9] The story Schiller tells is that men have to develop through an initial "physical" stage in which thought and feeling are, if not entirely absent, at least fairly rudimentary and relatively unstructured. At this stage, men's actions, as well as the course their reflections take, are determined by natural forces. Only Schiller contends here that we should distinguish between what men do and how they do it, between the content of their action, and, so to speak, its form; and he qualifies the deterministic thesis that he espouses[10] by insisting that natural forces can touch only the content of what is done, not its form, or the manner of its doing. Thus (ibid.), "the exigencies that nature imposes concern no more than what man does, the content of his actions; it follows that as to how he acts, as to the form of his deeds, Nature has nothing to say".

It is simple enough to transpose this thought from concern with action to our contemplation of the natural objects around us, to artifacts and even to works of art, though it would of course be unrealistic to suppose these last to play much part at

[8] The same thought is announced earlier at IV.1.

[9] The shift in context is far smaller than might appear, for the sort of self-conscious action Schiller would naturally have in mind is that in which the self is expressed, and that he believes is initially in the decoration of our weapons, our choice of clothing, the organisation of our homes (cf XXVII), all matters in which aesthetic considerations easily take hold.

[10] Very probably I suspect in line with Kant's own causal determinism of the phenomenal world as developed in the first *Critique*.

the earliest stage of psychic development. We shall then hear Schiller saying that the kind of things that we are initially liable to respond to with attachment may be fixed by our physical nature, but as far as the light in which they are seen is concerned, or the way in which they are shown or handled, that is something that nature has no power to fix. There it is up to us to decide, and hence up to us to temper the character of primary attachments by considerations that escape the purely natural constraints under which our inner development originally takes place. He continues (ibid.):

> It thus depends entirely on man's free choice whether he carries out his physical avocation simply as a sensible being and a force of nature, or whether at the same time he acts as absolute power and as a reasoning creature. It is doubtlessly superfluous to ask which of these two ways of acting correspond better to his dignity as a man. Rather, just as it lowers and degrades him to do what morality demands out of purely physical motives, so it honours and ennobles him to strive for lawlikeness, harmony and unconstrainedness, where the common man merely satisfies his permitted desires. In a word, in the realm of truth and morality sensation has no place of command; but in the realm of happiness [eudaimonia(?)] (*Glückseligkeit*) there may be form, and the drive to play may rule.

Now doctrine though this is, it plainly cannot do what Schiller wants. It is not just that appeal is made to an unreliable contrast between form and content with a view to minimizing the rule of a determinism that Schiller pretends to take fully seriously at the early stages of our development (III.1, XIX.11, 12). Nor that no ground is given to think that the light in which things appeal to us (cf "the manner of our actions") is not as much naturally fixed as is purportedly the appeal for us that those things have (cf "what we do"). The really crippling objection here is that Schiller allows himself to appeal to a thought that is itself highly moralized in order to ensure the injection into the causal pathways of the mind of the kind of attachments that will alter men's dispositions and character in the direction of the harmonious life-ideal. Yet that is exactly what he has been at pains to warn his reader against in the earlier paragraphs of the very same Letter. Considerations of honour, nobility and dignity are products of the causal pathway, so they cannot, on Schiller's way of thinking, originally motivate us to look to the aesthetic machinery to initiate the search for our well-being. That is a power they can obtain only later on, when man is advanced to the point of having recognized and internalized his *a priori* ideal. This particular move is clearly not one that Schiller should regard as open to him.

However, reference to the play drive in the last quoted sentence of XXIII.7 points in a direction in which he may be better advised to move. It is happily also the way in which, at XIV.2,3, he does move; only because the topic of man's development has not by then been properly introduced, it is very easy to overlook the relevance of this earlier passage when we are immersed in the later Letters. Since it makes the inappropriately moralized argument of XXIII quite superfluous, speculation suggests that Schiller may even have overlooked it himself.

To men's fundamental metaphysical constituents, their Person and their Condition, correspond two psychological drives whose function it is to affirm these constituents in life. These drives are indispensable to man, and original in him in that their existence and functioning are not explained by reference to any other bits of psychological machinery. Now we saw in the last chapter that Schiller holds that men are also potentially equipped with a third drive, the play drive, which comes into action quite fortuitously, though we are to suppose, pretty ubiquitously. We might say that the potential for our character and for our lives being formed by the play drive is innate, but that their actually being so formed depends on the triggering occurrence of experience of a kind that we nearly all have fairly early on in life, though it is always a contingent matter of fact that we do. The experience in question is spoken of in hypothetical terms only, at XIV.2. It is one in which both original drives are suppositionally for a moment at work quite harmoniously and in which man is aware of himself both as free (qua Person) and as embodied existence in time (qua Condition). If only such an experience were to occur, Schiller remarks (XIV.3), that would give rise to a new drive whose function it would be "to annul time within time, and to combine becoming with absolute being and change with identity".

What Schiller is getting at is somewhat obscured by the rhetoric of its presentation. Remembering that we have already identified Person with the element of significance in man's experience and Condition with the concrete sorts of experience we have, I gloss his thought thus: If only we should find ourselves on some occasion with a concrete sort of experience that presents itself as having rich significance, a new sort of drive will arise, one that aims both at repeating and at increasing the scope of that kind of experience in our lives, so that the lives we lead become more frequently and more fully illuminated with meaning. The original harmonious experience is a gift of nature (cf IV.1, XXVI.1),[11] and not to be explained (XV.4), but fortunately it comes to practically all of us in due course and sets us on the path towards the consummation of our humanity (XIV.2, XV.5).

It will be said that what is quite missing here is any explanation of why it is that the occurrence of this original experience should give rise to the third drive, the play drive. About that Schiller is silent. It must be apparent that he could not suppose that the explanation is given in the later passage from XXIII in which appeal to dignity, honour and nobility are made. What we are looking for, I stress, is what in the last section I called a 'naturalistic' explanation, and that will not be supplied by these moralized ideas.

Happily, the thought that Schiller needs is not far away, and maybe once again he passes it over because he takes it to be so obvious. It is simply that the supposed original experience is so notably pleasurable. That is a feature that it naturally has, and the possession of which is a brute fact not to be explained. Pleasure, being something we all desire, there is ready to hand the insight that once the primary aesthetic experience has come our way we shall naturally seek further examples of it, and then, in consequence, more pleasurable experiences of the

---

[11] Schiller's claim is that we cannot explain the genesis of beauty – how it is possible – and it may seem that this is indeed just what I have represented him as doing. This is true enough, but since the story about the play drive is his story, we are bound to take his remarks about what is unexplainable as fixing on why we should find the particular elements of the original experience so happily joined. (He does not of course consider whether teleological considerations would yield explanations of that.)

same sort throughout the rest of our lives. The play drive thus arises in response to originally fortuitously occurring pleasurable significant experience, and has as its goal the occurrence of other significant experience that we will find equally, or more, pleasurable.

Here we have it then. The question of the origination of the aesthetic[12] mechanism in a world in which mental and moral growth are to arise out of material that is subject only to natural forces, is answered by alluding to a capacity men have to take pleasure in certain combinations of sense and form, combinations in which, we must suppose, they feel themselves to be at one with the world. Taking pleasure in some such combination, they are engaged in a process that results in the formation of strong attachments to things as seen in certain lights, which (spell themselves out) in life as dispositions to thought and action that, through the feedback mechanism already described, are liable to modify the combinations of sense and form that we can come to find deeply satisfying. Once the mechanism is primed by the fortuitously occurring original experience, development commences and then generates an impetus of its own.

I said before that the mechanism described here is in itself quite neutral between the formation of attachments to the "beautiful" (= man's ideal harmony) and to its opposite. So the combinations of form and sense to which the play drive leads us to take satisfaction in may, or may not, be those that pure practical reason would recommend. Consequently, one thing is still importantly missing if we are to be persuaded that beauty is a really possible idea, and that is the conviction that there exists a regular route by which men may be encouraged to find what promotes the good and the objectively harmonious more deeply attaching than the kind of degraded things they allegedly find themselves more instinctively drawn to in their non-ideal, sense-dominated or thought-dominated states (V.3). And it is here, for the first time in the structure of the argument, that the arts make an essential appearance, for it is their peculiar role, Schiller believes, to direct man's attachments to

[12] What justifies the appelation "aesthetic" is supposedly the disinterested appeal of what it presents to the mind. Schiller briefly elucidates his use of the term at XX fn 1.

the ideal and wean them from the non-ideal. For although it has been programmatically announced in Letter IX that it is through art that men are to be rescued from the perversities and deformations to which their nature is subject, and systematically assumed that the inputs to the "aesthetics" machinery are artistic ones, everything of importance up to the present has been concerned with the nature and possibility of an a priori ideal of man that consists in the maximization of significant experience in a harmoniously conducted life. In that argument the arts have had no particularly privileged part to play. The connection between what helps man to that ideal and art cannot simply be left in this entirely unexamined state.

III

As far as Schiller is concerned it is not in dispute that the artist has a theoretical power to place before men's eyes and minds a vision of the ideal that appears deeply attaching.[13] Objectively speaking it *is* deeply attaching, and there is nothing amiss with the thought that an ideal might theoretically be represented (XXVII) as being just as attaching as objectively it is. So any hesitation that might be felt at the reliance on the artist at this point will be concerned with the difficulty in placing much practical trust in the artist of the future to do any better than his predecessors. To underline this doubt though, it may be recalled that on Schiller's reckoning the only clear examples of art that has been properly speaking beautiful is the art of Greek antiquity. Only that art, Schiller allows, has now served its turn, and if his admissions at X.4 are to be taken seriously, he would judge most "great" art of later date as missing its true vocation.

However, Schiller would reply that we are not here concerned to make predictions about the future on the sole basis of knowledge about the past. Rather the final conviction that true beauty is a real possibility will be won once we see that

---

[13] So far I have been careful to say only that the artist produces what promotes man's ideal. That leaves it open whether he does so by offering visions of the ideal or not. It is quite silent on that. Since Schiller speaks of the artist as surrounding us with noble, great and challenging (*geistreich*) forms (IX.7), it is very likely that they will take the shape of representations of the ideal under some aspect or other, and that is what I assume here.

there is no serious practical obstacle to man's attaining (a reasonable approximation to) his ideal through commerce with the arts once their theoretical power has been acknowledged. Now IX.7 makes clear that there are really only two things that might seriously hamper men in forming strong attachments to the ideal. One is a lack of imagination in our perception on their part of what that ideal really is, and the other is the difficulty posed by the likelihood of reinforcement of misdirected attachments through unreflective habit. It lies within the power of art, Schiller is sure, to overcome each of these two barriers to our progress.

In the first place the artist can present to men's imagination what we are not able to imagine for ourselves. That precisely is the power of attaching "semblance" (*Schein*). Then as to his effectiveness, he presents his work to men *aesthetically*, "in their leisure" (IX.7), when the reflective and contemplative resources are at their most active and potent (XX fn). So if there is any serious practical obstacle to men achieving or approximating to their ideal through the arts it must rest on some block within the artist, not on some block in those on whom his work is liable to exert its influence.

Setting aside the individual artist's lack of genius, his laziness or even maybe, on occasion, his deeper psychic infirmities, all of which are without systematic import, there is nothing else that could present a regular block to the artist exercising the power that is in principle his than the block of ignorance. For if he is ignorant about what true beauty consists in then he may in all good faith naturally[14] prefer to present to men what in fact corrupts them rather than what leads to their ideal. Hence, I suggest, for Schiller the untoward episodes in art's history on which both he and the sceptic are agreed at X.4.

Only Schiller will now confidently say that once the artist understands the correct, transcendentally imposed, conception of beauty, the threat of ignorance should be disarmed, and that nothing remains to prevent him from engaging others with true beauty through his art, and hence from realizing beauty in

[14] "Naturally" because for Schiller the likely form that ignorance will take is unreflective espousal of and accommodation to the aesthetic doctrines of Burke, Shaftesbury, or those of Kant, and we know from the historical excursus of Letter IX that both lead firmly away from the attainment of our ideal.

them. Thus shall "semblance triumph over reality, and art over nature" (IX.7). To do this, of course, the artist may need not just wisdom and talent but, in addition, the philosophy of *On the Aesthetic Education of Man*. But with that before him, what reason could there be to doubt that the last piece is provided in the proof that beauty is a genuine possibility? For *living proof*, (XV.5), and not just in Hellenic climes, we might perhaps suspect we could do worse than look to the dramatic and poetic work of Schiller himself. If Schiller does not say so, that will for once not be because he takes it to be self-evident. Modesty forbids.

Beauty, then, we may conclude, is a really possible idea. We have described a mechanism whereby powerfully affecting stimuli may move us equally towards or away from the ideal for man; it is argued to be a mechanism that can be fired in a world governed by natural forces; and in the best art we see scope for the production of work that may counteract those nefarious forces that act on us in our non-ideal state and threaten to make our development follow the course of barbarism or savagery.

To have got here is certainly not to have got nowhere, but it is at most a preliminary step in the direction of Schiller's principal goal. That is not the proof that men can be helped by art to realize their ideal, but, more ambitiously, it is the effective demonstration that through aesthetic education and involvement with the arts men may hope to win an authentic political liberty that otherwise they would be unlikely to come by. Nothing that has been said so far suggests that the approximation to the ideal of humanity that we can be helped to by the artist does anything at all to secure our citizenship of the ideal State, or anything to make for the social harmony and liberty that we so ardently desire. We have to enquire how Schiller proposes to move on.

IV

It cannot be denied that the delineation that Schiller offers of the Ideal State, the State of Reason as he calls it, is underdrawn. He has no concern for its constitution and nothing of substance to say about its constitutive institutions. We gather that it is a

State that respects men's subjectivity (IV.3), that it serves the individual rather than sees him as its creature (IV.2), and that it excludes a hierarchy of classes and privileges (XXVII.11). That is about all we glean. A fair guess[15] would be that Schiller envisages his ideal State to be one that answers to the aspirations of the French Revolution (as he saw it), and that any social organization which serves the achievement of men's freedom, understood in terms of the imposition of no obstacles to its citizens' pursuit of the fullest rational self-realization would qualify.

However underdrawn the picture of Schiller's ideal polity may be, it is apparent that the socially harmonious organization that it has to display is to arise out of a familiar kind of moral character in the individual in which citizens are not inspired by self-interest, as they purportedly are in the State of Nature (XXIV.7). In the State of Reason what moves them are the social virtues of love, benevolence, honour and chivalry (XXVII.7). This suggests that the route Schiller's discussion needs to take is one that connects the pursuit and engagement of true beauty with a certain kind of moral character and which leaves the generation and development of the appropriate political institutions to follow more or less routinely from such a character once it is deep rooted and sufficiently widespread. "The aesthetic state, he says, makes society possible because it satisfies the will of all through the nature of the individual" (XXVII.10). So what we shall have to be persuaded is that as engagement with the beautiful in art develops dispositions in which we come closer to achieving a life in which breadth of experience and significance are harmoniously maximized, so we shall also come to develop a character of a kind that is fundamentally other-regarding. This thought is one for which argument is both needed and given.

Before turning to the details we may note how Schiller avoids two traps which might easily have seemed alluring. The first is posed by the apparently uniform statement of the ideal for men on which he so heavily relies, the maximization of Person and of Condition. If that is the goal that all men are

[15] See Wilkinson and Willoughby's Introduction to their translation of the *Letters* at p xv.

rationally bound to set themselves, it might appear that when it is widely realized, men's fundamental desires, those that social organization helps them to satisfy, will be the same and not in the end seriously conflict. Hence achievement of the ideal for man might be thought naturally to bring social harmony with it.

Now Schiller does in fact sometimes speak as though in attaining our ideal we somehow cease to be individual and become universal or species (cf XXIV.3), but whatever he may mean by that,[16] it can scarcely negate his acknowledgement of the *plurality* of ways in which men seek to realize their ideal (IV.3. XI.9). Nor does he show the slightest inclination to suppose that the satisfaction of our individual ideals will in practice lead to anything else than a plurality of potentially conflicting concerns and aims. As I said before the prime political task for Schiller is precisely to ensure the reconciliation and harmonious realization of competing ends (IV.2). He can not fairly be represented as trying for an easy solution by ignoring this problem or denying its existence.

The second temptation he resists is to secure his social goal by simple stipulation or to argue in such a way as to make his conclusion vacuous. This would have been easy enough to do by writing in to the ideal of man from the start (say under the rubric of "perfection") the possession of positive virtues such as benevolence and magnanimity, and then defining beauty in their terms. It would then too quickly follow that engagement with the beautiful would bring about a moral character from which a politically liberal state might emerge. But even though Schiller does use the notion of perfection in his specification of the ideal for man it is not one that for him generally carries moralistic connotations.[17] In his use "perfection" is taken to

---

[16] I suspect that Schiller employs this way of talking to indicate a sensitivity to whatever concerns he may have. Certainly he is anxious to see men's subjectivity preserved and not dissolved in some characterless universal amalgam (IV.3). Sometimes it is simply his way of talking about the realisation of the ideal (cf IV.5), understandable enough when we remember his inclination to think of that in terms of the maximization of essence (XIII.3).

[17] XIV.6 provides an exception to this, where perfection is assigned to *Person* and happiness (*Glückseligkeit*) to *Condition*. There there is a clear assumption that maximization of Person will yield moral perfection, but elsewhere this is never assumed. Recall note 1 above.

denote no more than an optimal (= the richest possible) combination of the drive to form and the drive to sense, and moral considerations are formally speaking irrelevant in determining what this optimum in fact is, even if they should eventually (and ineluctably) turn up within anything like a full specification of its content.

At this point it might easily seem that Schiller's aspiration to make the aesthetic a bridge between the natural and the moral world is no more than a pious echo of a similar endeavour of Kant's. In the critical architectonic the aesthetic material of the *Critique of Judgment* was primarily intended to serve (however obscurely) as a proof that in the phenomenal world noumenally based morality is no impossibility (*Critique* Intro IX) and beauty's main role there was as symbol of the Good (*Critique* §59). It is certainly true that there are clear echoes of this Kantian thought in the *Letters* (XXV.6/7), and at IX.7 Schiller even speaks of the artist's finest efforts as symbols of moral excellence. Only what Kant leaves as a shadowy mystery Schiller attempts to work out in some detail, setting out between Letters XIX and XXV a formal model of the growth of mind towards morality as necessarily passing through the aesthetic. Later on, in Letter XXVII, he supplements this by offering a rather more empirical and detailed rendering of a kindred thought, based on a conception of one possible course he believes the development of aesthetic sensibility itself may naturally be expected to take. For the moment I leave the precise relationship between these two passages quite open and treat them separately, as in fact they are treated in Schiller's text.

The model of psychic development offered in XIX onwards is fairly straightforward. At origin the mind is vacant, touched neither by sense nor by form. With growth it is naturally dominated in the earliest stages by sense or matter – we might almost say by incoming experience as traditional empiricism views it – but steadily, as self-consciousness grows, matter is given form, and the world of raw experience becomes more and more a world of the mind. With the progress of civilization the tendency is even for form to dominate over matter, rather than matter over form. Growth can theoretically tend therefore to any one of three possible positions: dominance by thought, dominance by sense, or equilibrium between the two. In equilibrium we have arrived at what Schiller calls the "aesthetic state" and there have left the "natural state" behind us.

Now, he importantly claims, it is only by passing through the aesthetic state that we can reach the moral state. The reason given is that the moral state supposedly requires a Will that is perfectly free, and that only comes about when the mind is dominated neither by sense nor by reason. When it is so free, morality follows almost automatically. So, given that beauty is, as we have seen, a really possible idea and the transition from the aesthetic to the moral relatively unproblematic (XXIII.5), engagement with beauty should be sufficient for morality. Since morality is, to Schiller's mind, both necessary and (so far as I can tell) sufficient, for the realization of our political ideals, effective engagement with the aesthetic should itself be both necessary and sufficient for the achievement of that desired state.

Here in a nutshell is the structure of the thought that is to take Schiller's argument to its close. It is easy to scoff at the simplistic nature of this proto-Hegelian tale and the faith it displays in the power of a priori psychic mechanics. But before dismissing the whole machinery to the waste bin of the history of ideas we should have a clear view of what the model is meant to be a model of, for understanding that we may be able to detach something important from the implausible mechanism that is meant to drive it.

Evidently the new and quite obscure element on the scene is the Will. What, we must ask, is its connection with morality supposed to be? Schiller's diachronic, three-stage, model of growth (XXIV.1) very much encourages the idea that it must be the function of the Will to select a moral character that is manifest in particular practical choices that men make, as say a benevolent character or an egotistic one. And then it might further be supposed that Schiller believed that if the mind comes to be tyranically dominated in the earlier stages of our development (the proto-aesthetic stage) either by sense (matter) or by thought (form), the character that the Will eventually selects is unlikely reliably to promote morally desirable behaviour; we shall, that is, get our choice of character wrong.

But this would be a nonsense; not only in itself, but also

because it ignores too much of what Schiller actually says. It is nonsensical very largely because the development of a benevolent, loving, altruistic character is not something that could possibly be the output of reasoned choice. That a man might develop his personality in a harmonious way and only *then* find he was free to decide rationally what sort of character to acquire (not, note, "adopt", as one might want to say) is a travesty of the way in which moral character is, or could be, formed. From what motivational standpoint, one might ask, would any such choice as that between egotism and altruism supposedly be made? What could reason possibly appeal to in finding one alternative attractive rather than the other?

Regarded textually, also, such interpretation makes nonsense of Schiller's saying that the transition to the moral stage from the balanced, aesthetic one is straightforward (XXIII.5), and that "the aesthetic man will act morally as soon as he should desire to". He evidently foresees no such question of choice arising; the matter is envisaged as a purely conceptual one. It also overlooks his saying that "To lead the aesthetic man to insight and noble feeling, he needs no more than the right occasion, but to get the same result from the natural man he must first change his nature" (ibid.), that is, that all the work in acquiring a character must *already* have taken place. It further ignores his earlier assertion (IV.1) in the same vein that "if we are to reckon on moral behaviour *as a matter of course* (my italics) [man's] various drives must lead him to act as only a moral character would". These remarks all indicate quite a different function for the Will, and getting that right will make particularly clear the intellectual challenge that Schiller faces in taking his thought through to its conclusion.

To do this requires abandoning all thought of the relation between the "aesthetic stage" and the "moral stage" of growth as being best presented as one of development over time. Instead we must think of them as conceptually related, and of the moral somehow presupposing the aesthetic. Just what this presupposition amounts to emerges from asking what sort of a morality it is that Schiller thinks of as flowing from a Will that is dominated neither by sense nor by thought, and what the italicized expression *"as a matter of course"* is directing us to look for.

Not taking the Will to be concerned with the formation of a moral character, we can only see its object to be the making of practical choices about what to do in specific circumstances, acting well or acting badly as the occasion arises. Now, Schiller will say, there are all sorts of different reasons for which a man may come to perform apparently virtuous and laudable (*pflichtgemäss*) actions which would not encourage us to rely on him unhesitatingly to do so in the future if only we knew what those reasons were. A man might for instance perform well on account of some mistake, or on the advice of friends, or out of fear (XXIV.8). Further, Schiller will add to these that he might act (a), because it was useful to do so, or (b), just as a response to feeling, or (c), Kantianly, out of a sense of duty. None of these various spurs to proper action encourage unhesitating reliance because it is so easy to see why on future occasions they might not operate. I might discover my mistake, my friend's advice might change, I might give up belief in retribution at the Day of Judgment, my ends might be reassessed, my sensibilities may change, and despite my sense of duty who knows whether I shan't succumb to temptations which this time did not present themselves or, if they did, did not present themselves in as attractive light as in future they might. In other words I might not act well *as a matter of course*.

From the snippets I cited from XXIII it must be apparent that the one thing that Schiller believes can secure constancy in the Will is making it responsive not primarily to the sort of considerations just mentioned, but to a character that is *already* formed. Then mistakes will be stray, advice will often not be needed, and above all, if character is of the right sort, the prospect of weakness of will that makes a Kantian sense of duty so shaky a thing to rely on need not present a problem.

Now as Schiller sees it, if our character should happen to be one in which contending forces are equally balanced, there is no ground left from which adverse pressure on the Will might be exerted. This thought is confirmed and made clear at XIX.10 by his giving two examples of the Will responding to an *un*balanced character, one unbalanced in favour of the worse, the other in favour of the better. "A violent man", he writes, "is not turned away from injustice through even the most powerful desire to be just, which he need by no means lack; nor need the most powerful temptation to pleasure prevent a steadfast man from sticking to his principles".

The first of these two examples is unproblematic; less so the second, and to understand it will enable us to dispense entirely with the unsatisfying psychic mechanics in terms of which Schiller's position is cast. In the first case, the passionate man gives way to his violence, and we can assume suffers remorse thereafter. Although attached to justice, his will is dominated by the overgrowth of sense in his character, and in consequence he cannot be counted on to make the just practical choices that will be required of him in the situations that confront him. The other man, by contrast, is one in whose character thought or reason is dominant. He has temptations, but they are not "cancelled out", and it is only his intellectual principles that enable him to resist the temptation.[18] What, one wonders, can be wrong with that?

Schiller's view can only be that a morality that is governed by principle risks being unseated or undermined, and while it is as well that a man should have principles and that they be strong, it would be far better if his was a balanced nature in which temptation is "cancelled out" (is absent) and does not need to be stifled by thought of principle or duty. The man of principle in Schiller's eyes is one who sees the attractions of worse courses of action: consequently he has a flank exposed on which the Devil may work.[19]

[18] Someone might want to say that what Schiller finds so dangerous about dominance of thought or principle is set out differently in XIII fn 2. There he objects to principle that is not adequately fed by feeling. But the trouble is that in those cases 'duty' is misidentified. Here we are to suppose that it is correctly identified all right, but that something else is wrong. See also next footnote.

[19] I certainly would not have understood Schiller here without the help of John McDowell's 'Are moral requirements hypothetical imperatives?' *PASS* 1978. However, this is no indication of anachronism in my interpretation of Schiller's views. Even if the theme has never been prominent in moral philosophy, literature has shown a fascination with it both before Schiller's time and after it. We have only to think of the legend of the pure fool in Chrétien de Troyes' *Percival* and in von Eschenbach's *Parzival*. Dostoyevski's *The Idiot* provides a later example that is independent of the Grail Legend. The most immediate example that must have been before Schiller's eyes would be that of Christ. See *Matthew* 4, 1–11. Further confirmation that this is a vision of the truly good man Schiller works with is provided by his version of the parable of the good Samaritan offered to Körner in his letter of 18 Feb. 1793; (*Kallias*, Reclam 29–31). Many who pass by the wounded man are willing to do the right thing by him, but the truly estimable man is not he who helps out of a sense of duty, or merely

Contrast him with the man whose nature is so formed that he is motivated to the good anyway – he sees that, and that alone, as attractive, and is disposed only to benevolence and good-heartedness towards others. Out of such a character as this decisions that are morally required can be reliably expected from the Will; not just decisions and actions that are morally proper, but also ones that can be counted on in the future and are minimally subject to the sorts of vicissitudes listed above. And this kind of Will, one rooted in fixed good character, is the sort of Will that Schiller takes to be necessary for the attainment of an ideal and genuinely liberal political regime. That, I suggest, is why he says at XXIII.2 that there is no other way to make the man of sense into a man of reason except he become "aesthetic". So, for the ultimate political goal to be achieved, the kind of Will that is needed is one that leads to what in *Kallias* Schiller called "moral beauty", and which is the kind of will he there described a man as having when "duty has become a matter of nature to him".[20]

If I am right, what these reflections go to show is that Schiller firmly believes that the so-called moral character itself is formed as we approach the terminus of the aesthetic stage of

---

because he sees what is needed, or acts out of feeling (he hates the sight of blood), but he "who acts as if duty has become part of his nature" (19 Feb. 1793, Reclam 32). I cannot resist illustrating the thought by reminding the reader of J.S. Mill's moving tribute to Harriet Taylor. "Her intellectual gifts did minister to a moral character at once the noblest and best balanced, which I ever met with in life. Her unselfishness was not that of a taught system of duties, but of a heart which thoroughly identified itself with the feelings of others, and often went to excess in consideration of them by imaginatively investing their feelings with the intensity of her own." (*Autobiography*, OUP, 1951, 159). Reliance on the mechanical model is entirely accountable for Schiller declaring at XXII.3 that the touchstone of true artistic excellence is the tendency of the work to set us in a state of high "indifference". Once we abandon the model we are free to replace this critical principle with something more plausible, and without thereby diverging seriously from Schillerian aesthetic. Schiller uses this thought to rebut the suggestion that he should welcome didactic or tendentious art (neither set us in an 'indifferent' state) XXII.5. What he should say is that the reliable route to moral character lies not through exhortation or propaganda – but through the pleasurable and lasting appeal of the noble and excellent. He expresses his resistance to the didactic by saying that in the truly beautiful work of art content should do naught and form all, "only from form is true aesthetic freedom to be expected" (ibid.). But once we remember his detachment from (Kantian) formalism it will be difficult to see this as anything more than a clumsy piece of bluster, or else a curious way of talking about the way that the beautiful must take hold of us – through the splendidly described mechanism of IX.7.

[20] Letter to Körner: 19 Feb. 1793, Reclam, 32.

growth, and that the attainment of man's ideal in life will *at one and the same time* be the attaining of a truly virtuous moral character from which duty will flow "as a matter of course". And we see one reason here why Schiller thinks that the two go together, a reason expressed by his version of psychic mechanics. If, to be reliable, the Will must be free and hence dominated by a character that is given over neither to sense nor to reason, it must flow out of a character in which they are in equilibrium, and that is precisely the character that was supposed to derive from our metaphysical essence as the ideal that reason bids us strive to achieve. Since beauty is necessarily what makes for the realization of the ideal, it necessarily makes for the moral character on which virtuous and socially desirable action is presumed to be consequent. By the mechanical model, the two are idealized and identified; in their idealization they are necessarily connected.

It will be plain now that we cannot possibly be content with this, for the terms in which I have finally come to expound Schiller's thoughts about the Will entirely do away with the mechanics. Shorn of that his thought is simply that a man who is truly virtuous and can be relied on to make the right moral choices is one who acts well by reason of having a goodly disposition or character. But what is now left a mystery is the basis of the assumed connection between being possessed of goodly dispositions and having a character which pursues an 'ideal' life, one whose constitutive experience is optimally broad and deep. Once the a priori identity of sound moral character and the ideal of humanity is undone, as it is with the abandonment of the psychic mechanics, it appears that Schiller has nothing to put in its place. The very last jump is what unseats him. We know that beauty as what promotes the ideal of man is possible. We may perhaps accept that a reliable morality stemming from virtuous character is necessary for the achievement of our a priori liberal political ideals. But how are we now to get from engagement with beauty to the achievement of that same character and to its reputed political consequences?

V

In Letter XXVII, dressed up in rather fanciful terms, Schiller presents a story about man's development from the first, barely noticeable, (XXVII.5) stirrings of the play drive traced through to the fully-fledged aesthetic man. It turns out that the fully fledged aesthetic man is indeed benevolent; he has replaced lust by love, hatred by mercy, and self-interest by altruism (XXVII.7). He has moved from at first seeing moral demands as external to him, to recognizing them as his true self and to seeing self-interest as what is really alien to him (XXIV.8). Is there not something here, we may ask, that Schiller might use to meet the painfully apparent difficulty that now faces him? After all, the story does take us from one end point to the other, so it must presume to find room on its own account for the delicate crossing that in the formal argument has so suddenly broken down.

To stand any chance of success we have to be clear just what the connection needs to be between the aesthetic and the moral. For nothing that is offered here will make it an a priori one as it was presented as being between XIX and XXV. Fortunately that requirement was overstated anyway. It would surely be quite enough for his purposes if Schiller could show that there was a possible natural progression in the growth of aesthetic sensibility that could, by easy steps, regularly lead men in the pursuit of their ideal to form a suitably benevolent character; quite enough if he could show that in the absence of such a progression men will regularly feel that something important is missing in the formation of a satisfactory self under the guidance of the play drive. He does not need to claim that men are bound to develop in such a way; neither does he have to say that it is a necessary truth about what we take self-fulfilment to be. All he needs is to point it out as a truth we are liable to recognize and feel convinced by. I should like to think that the material of XXVII.4–8 can be taken in just this way.

In that passage Schiller remarks six stages on the way towards aesthetic equilibrium. They are described without reference to the artist, who may be brought in to lend body to the later moments of the sketch that is proposed, but whose efforts would not make any fundamental structural addition to the story that is told. (A) At first, a man in the state of nature will be entirely preoccupied with practical matters, hunting, keeping his dwelling together, keeping himself warm. Here there is no room for the play drive to function (cf XXVII.2). (B) With a moderately secure material base he may find himself taking satisfaction simply in the functionality of his weapons and the tools of his trade (XXVII.3). (C) Then, with further surplus of leisure and energy he may come to take pleasure in ornamenting these things, at first crudely (XXVII.2/4), but progressively with more and more refinement (XXVII.5). (D) The urge to find the surrounding world aesthetically pleasing takes in things in which he finds the clearest expression of himself, his home and his clothes (XXVII.6). (E) At last he seeks to please in himself and render himself agreeable to others (XXVII.5). (F) The extension of this last desire naturally leads him to temper his violence with gentleness, his initial selfishness with altruism, until in the end his character is fully benevolent (XXVII.7/8). The way is thus open for the fully moral state and with it the attainment of social person (XXVII.9–11).

The judgment to be made then is whether this purported progression is as smooth and natural as Schiller would have us believe. In particular we have to decide whether stage (E), which records the first response to the desires of others and initiates the altruistic strain of action, arises too abruptly or whether it can genuinely be seen as an extension of something already contained in germ in stages (A)–(D). The judgment is undoubtedly made more difficult by its needing to be made at one of those many points of the argument where "we are obliged to rely more on feeling than on principle" (I.1). However that is not to say that there are no considerations of generality we might look to for guidance. Two in particular combine to make me doubt whether the transition is quite as smooth as Schiller's purpose requires. One concerns the content of Schiller's thoughts; the other, its expression.

I suspect that development could be perceived as smooth only if there were one common non-question begging characterization of each stage of growth that identified it via some standing desire that gets satisfied in progressively richer and richer ways. While this may well be possible between stages (E) and (F), and between (B) and (C) or (C) and (D), it is not so between stages (D) and (E). For at (D) the object of desire is the subject's own pleasure, whereas at (E) it is the pleasure of others. True, at both stages men are described as having pleasure as their goal, but by no stretch of the imagination can the pleasure of others be represented as a richer case of pleasure for the subject himself.[21] Once this rift is noticed one starts to suspect that Schiller's "demonstration" comes to no more than an assertion that altruism may naturally grow out of egotism, or could naturally be brought to do so. But that is just what this passage is supposed to make convincing.

The wording of XXVII.5 in which the transition from (D) to (E) is made does much to gloss over the fact that a large and dubious step is being taken rather than a minimal, uncontroversial, one. Schiller puts it by saying:

> Soon man is no longer satisfied that things should please him: himself he wants to please, at first only through what is his, but in the end through what he himself is. (Bald ist er nicht mehr damit zufrieden, dass ihm die Dinge gefallen: er will selbst gefallen, anfangs zwar nur durch das, was sein ist, endlich durch das, was er ist.)

Now I do not wish to claim that the German for "himself he wants to please" viz "*er will selbst gefallen*" is ambiguous. It isn't. It cannot mean both that he himself wants to please others and that he wants to please himself. Expression of the latter thought would require the reflexive pronoun "sich" before "selbst", and that is absent. But the implicitly chiasmic structure of the sentence leads the reader to expect that man, starting out being satisfied that things should please him, goes on to desire some new thing to please him, to wit, himself. Although this is not the thought that the sentence expresses, the expectation of the continuation of that rhetorically conjured up developmental thought does something to cloak the quite different step that is here so swiftly taken, and taken with such apparent ease. Since we have looked to XXVII to make good the deficiency of the argument of XIX–XXV and now find nothing here that is of greater than mere promissory strength, it seems fair to say that the conduct of his argument to

---

[21] Even if one found that providing pleasure to others through what one was reinforced one's own sense of self that will not take one far along the path of altruism and benevolence. The break is radical and not half-hearted.

its desired conclusion in the end rather overstretches Schiller's dialectical powers.

VI

There does however remain the question whether among the various materials of which Schiller disposes he does not overlook an untried, but more hopeful, path to aesthetic equilibrium and the fulfilment of self as involving the acquisition of benevolence of character. We saw before that Schiller took the proper response to the truly beautiful to be that of love. That response marks a stability and depth of attachment to whatever it is we come to find beautiful, and it is a response that links us not only with the prized object, but also points beyond it to attitudes and dispositions that I come to have and which will manifest themselves in my behaviour towards and thought about it and other objects perceived to be relevantly like it. In particular, I have suggested, we should expect the subject to cherish, foster and protect what he loves wherever he comes across it in the absence of what he considers to be overriding claims upon him.

With this in mind, suppose we return to the transition from stage (D) of Schiller's model to stage (E), where what is at stake is the formation of a self that is benevolently disposed to others. Could it not be that as I start to form loving attachments to beautiful things of my making or my acquaintance that serve well to express myself at the supposedly unproblematic stage (D), I have latently *already* come to a point at which I am set to show a concern for the interests of others, at least initially when their interests and mine are shared and not in conflict with each other?

To take an example, suppose on the way to attaining my Schillerian ideal, I start to build a character that is in part structured around attachment to the natural world and in accordance with which I find myself happily expressed in my attitudes and behaviour towards it. Then I shall, as I love the natural world, be inclined to join with others in protecting and safeguarding it. More, I shall not be indifferent to their attempts to express themselves through attachment to the natural world even when my own cooperation is not called on and when the attainment of their satisfactions brings no direct or indirect benefit to me. Here we find a germ of benevolence as Schiller conceived of it, for the reason that thought and action are seen as stemming from love of an object that grows up in the course of structuring the self and not at all from considerations of what will benefit the agent and which both Kant and Schiller would want to write off as unsuitably "interested".

While this reflection makes some progress, it does not quite take us to the extensive benevolence that Schiller must primarily be concerned with, where the desires and needs of others do conflict with my own and yet in appropriate cases prompt a response on my part that favours them rather than me. Schiller is bound not to rest content unless and until he can arrive at this further point, because if his political ideal is to follow more or less straightforwardly from a sufficiently moralized character, the insight that the political ideal has to embrace the pursuit of conflicting interests and desires obliges Schiller to think that the properly virtuous character must be one that accepts self-denial and self-restraint. Failing that the resulting society will be ruled by forces (*Kräfte*) and not by reason (XXVII.8).

I see nothing in Schiller's writings that might prevent him from pursuing further the train of thought we have already started. The formation of aesthetic sensibility to the point just described has taken place in the service of a man's struggle to come by a satisfying view of himself, one enabling him to find rich meaning for his life (XIII.3). But it would be a mistake to think that everything that can strike him as attractive and lovable must engage an active place in the foreground of the life that he actually comes to lead. Indeed, we should find it exceedingly strange if it did, since we saw before that Schiller was clearly aware how little possible it is for us to attain everything that we desire, and how some things we are attached to can only be pursued at the expense of others. Since we have no reason to expect the choices that have to be made here are easy choices, we can acknowledge that much of the appeal for us of what we find little active room for in our life can endure even when we have given primacy to other goals and values, and can be found appealing in the person of others who have chosen to make central to their lives what I have relegated to the edge of mine.

Being open then in general to the appeal of goods that I have elected not to pursue actively, or that I have perhaps even got to the point of no longer being able to pursue, or which I have not even entertained, I can nonetheless find attachments to them generated (or strengthened) through engagement with the ways in which they are handled in the imagination and particularly in the imagination of the artist. The artist, we saw in Section II, is not dependent on my practical inclinations and actual predispositions to engage my love for what he presents as noble and excellent (IX.7), and in doing that he will bring it about just as before, that I am strongly drawn to foster, promote and cherish these goods. At this point Schiller can say these disinterestedly formed tastes and impulses can dominate in action even when my own more narrowly conceived interests may be opposed to their doing so. If I am fully responsive to the beauty that is offered me and my attachment to it is consequently a deep one, then I can be brought to a measure of self-denial and self-restraint in addition to the possession of a disposition to assist others in the attainment of ideals that coincide with my own.

It is particularly appropriate at this stage of the developmental story to appeal to the artist as Schiller at XXVII.5 quite extraordinarily does not, since it lies peculiarly within his power to work on our imagination and get us to form attachments to a whole range of things that can be presented in beautiful form and which we may not come to on the basis of our own resources alone. Drawing on the arts in this way, Schiller may be envisaged as saying, we will find no particular limits to the concern for others that will speak out of a nature that is thus liberally formed. Hence, there is an entirely plausible route through which character of the requisitely stable moral sort may be acquired, first through the interaction of values that are central to the subject's own life, but later of loving attachment to others' values, the ensuing protection and promotion of which forces onto the subject attitudes of just the kind that a harmonious social existence is supposed to require.

That Schiller could have taken this step at XXVII.5 should now be plain enough. That he did not explicitly take it is also plain. But that he would strongly sympathize with what I have here offered him may be conjectured from remarks that he makes in the course of the marvellous Footnote 2 to Letter XIII:

> If we are to become compassionate, helpful, effective human beings, feeling and character must unite, even as wide open senses must combine with wide open intellect if we are to acquire experience. How can we, however laudable our precepts, be just, kindly, human towards others if we lack the power of receiving into ourselves, faithfully and truly, natures unlike ours, of feeling our way into the situation of others, and of making other people's feeling our own?

As I have presented it, the ability to feel one's own way into the situation of others, into perspectives that are not one's own, is both (practically) necessary for stable moral character and scarcely something to be achieved on a wide scale without something akin to imaginative engagement with the arts. Given such engagement, we stand some chance of coming to acquire the character we need to if we are to institute the desired State of Reason, and be it noted by a natural and "aesthetic" route that progresses smoothly to the later stages as Schiller's own version failed to do. Hence we may be persuaded that there is a real possibility of achieving truly virtuous moral character along the aesthetic path, and that such is the course we need to pursue towards our ultimate, political, goal.

VII

Many queries arise at this point. But having strayed from Schiller's actual path, though I hope only to follow one that he would have been happy to take, I shall raise only two which do something to put that hope to the test.

The first is whether the moral character I have described and suggested to be attainable by a smooth stepwise progression in the development of aesthetic sensibility is really the moral character that Schiller is aiming for at his stage (E), when a man will act "to please others, at first through what is his and then through what he himself is". The crucial difference between my resting point and Schiller's is that in my story what prompts my benevolent action will be my having internalized values to which I respond in the person of others. On Schiller's view it is arguable that benevolent action is called for towards others regardless of the values they have, and regardless of whether I share them or not.

If that really were Schiller's view, it would be appropriate to ask whether it is one that he needs to hold in structuring a character well enough moralized to secure reliable cooperation in social contexts, and also to ask whether it is a kind of character that could possibly be generated along the aesthetic pathway he believes must lead to the sort of action that would fall in the scope of such a further extension of the model. My reaction to the first of these issues is that this is not needed. Of course there is ample room in what we have already for my acting on behalf of others to secure goals for which I have little sympathy, where I can simply take it on trust that there is something estimable about them that I am unable to appreciate. I assume that I may come to a sensitivity that I do not yet have and act on that faith. But the Schillerian position might be thought to go on further than this, and to oblige me to take consideration of others' desires, goals and preferences *no matter what I think of them*, simply on the grounds that they are goals that other people have and that as such they therefore have some claim on me. This sort of attitude one might think undesirable since it would lead to a general pseudo-"moral" requirement that we act for the sake of others even when what they are aiming at we find repulsive. A man has to make a judgment whether what is held out to him to be of value is so or not, and it would exceed the expectations of most of us that we should act in favour of purported values to which we are neither attached nor are prepared to take on trust pending the formation of attachment. If we rejected the thought that this sort of "benevolence" was morally required, then not to have it would not be to have a character of which it was false to say "duty flowed as if by instinct".

This is not of course to show that some such attitudes might not be required for reliable political cooperation. But it is highly implausible that they should be, since there is no reason to think that unless we are prepared to further people's aims at the extreme, to further and foster their quite idiosyncratic or socially way-out goals, political cooperation will not be possible over the more restricted, but nonetheless extensive, area over which we either share values with others or else are sympathetic with them or, if not, are at least prepared to take them on trust. As far as the limits of political cooperation are concerned, the only result of preferring my version of the developed moral character to that which I identify as Schiller's is that we expect a viable political society to be one in which there is a certain degree of mutual adjustment of goals between the society's members. They will expect cooperation and benevolence from others only to the extent that others can come to feel for the goals that are theirs. Beyond that point it is each man for himself, and social cooperation is not to be reckoned on. In *Kallias* Schiller offered an image of harmonious society organised like an English country dance.[22] The dancers each have their own figures to work out, but the whole functions smoothly without collision. What provides for that in society is of course no political equivalent of established choreography, but rather the feeling of each participant for what the others are about. Failing that we should expect order imposed by force, by guilt or by stern 'moral principle', or else expect disordered anarchy.

So I suggest Schiller does not need his aesthetic education to lead to limitless benevolence of character. And that is as well, because it could not do so anyway. For what guides aesthetic education is the play-drive, and that essentially finds pleasure only in what we can see as attaching. Limitless benevolence goes beyond what is attaching, hence could not be achieved by the aesthetic route. Since we have already seen that there is on Schiller's view no other way in which we might reliably get there, Schiller's view of the matter ought to be that limitless benevolence could not become a standardly required element

[22] Letter to Körner 23.2.1793 (Reclam p. 54). "I know of no fitter image of the ideal of beautiful behaviour than that of a well-danced English dance composed of many complicated figures. A spectator in the gallery sees countless movements which intertwine in the most colourful way and change their direction in a lively and capricious way, but which never collide. Everything is so ordered that one dancer has made way by the time another arrives, everything fits so deftly together, yet without artifice, that each lad seems to follow his own inclinations without ever getting in the way of his fellows. It is the aptest illustration of the assertion of a man's own freedom combined with the respect for that of others.'

in the fully-fledged virtuous character. In the light of this we might read his insistence at XIII fn 2 on the importance of feeling our way into the perspective of others to set a limit on the sort of thing he has in mind when he speaks at XXVII.5 of "pleasing others through what we are". Then the terminal point of his route to aesthetic equilibrium and that of the alternative I have been exploring will coincide.

The other worry it would be natural to feel is whether, in offering Schiller these moves, I have surreptitiously abandoned his conception of beauty and replaced it with one that takes within its extension more than he would allow. How is it that I encourage him to appeal to beauty in art to form moral character when he supposes beauty to be transcendentally identical with what promotes men's ideal of humanity, vulgarly, with what promotes breadth and depth in their experience? In talking of the artist as having a power to attach us to ways of seeing things that are not our own, am I not relying on a notion of beauty that extends far wider than that which (merely?) makes for the achievement of my ideal? If I have sinned here, then for all that I have said on Schiller's behalf, the passage from beauty to morality, and thence to the political state of reason, will be inadequately conducted, and the ultimate claim of aesthetic education have broken down.

As so often, it is difficult to do more than suggest a reply of a kind that Schiller ought to find congenial. The natural place to look is to the conception of the ideal of man in terms of which beauty is defined. We have seen that Schiller wants that to be derivable from metaphysical considerations about man and to embrace "power and depth of personality . . . fulness of being, maximal activity and receptiveness" (XIII.3) as well as freedom from the tyranny of sense and of reason. The way my comments have gone has led us to abandon the metaphysical underpinning in favour of a supposedly more self-evident regulative conception of the self that is concerned for experience of the world that is sufficiently broad and sufficiently deep. But it has to be allowed that that there is something rather flat about this description of such an ideal, and that a more realistic attempt to capture it adequately would multiply the parameters within which the ideal is developed. With the relaxation of the metaphysical underpinning there is no reason at all why this should not be done.

What makes for the flatness of the description of the ideal that I have offered in Schiller's name is that it leads to the expectation that the only place in which we can look to find "power and depth of personality and fullness of being" is in the experience that I actually acquire, and the actions that I myself perform. That is where the notions of breadth and depth have initially been located. But it would be a mistake to think that that is where we are restricted to look to find them. Any reasonably rich personality is one that is disposed to make something in imagination of experiences that do not come its way but are those that others have or which don't come anyone's way but might do so. To find sense in experience that isn't one's own or is thought of as merely a possibility must be part of the ideal itself, and part of what can be promoted through our commerce with the arts.[23] And this thought perhaps is just what Schiller needs to meet the present criticism. For if the artist promotes our ideal by getting us to form attachments, *inter alia*, to ways of viewing things that are not in fact our own, then on Schiller's own view of beauty what brings about this extension of our personality, what gives it complexity and depth will legitimately count as beautiful. Since I have been arguing that it is just this sort of work that we may turn to to explain how we can naturally extend the personality beyond selfishness to benevolence, as XXIV.8 insists we must, then Schiller can say it is the very same thing that enables us to achieve our ideal of man as brings about the fully moralized character that is the essential prerequisite of the achievement of our ultimate political ends: namely beauty. Education in that therefore may justly claim to pave the way to the acquisition of social character.

---

[23] In explaining what he takes an aesthetic education to be Schiller says "[It] adopts the aim of cultivating the totality of our sensible and spiritual powers in organising them as harmoniously as possible" (XX fn). If one takes a generous view of "totality" here and notices Schiller's concern with the merely associative imagination (cf XXVII.4) development of it my expansion of what Schiller says may be thought to be no more than that; not an expansion of what it is that he is talking about, but a fuller description of it than he ever offers.

Lessing: Index Locorum

Kant: Index Locorum

Schiller: Index Locorum

Index of Names